How Languages are Learned
Fourth edition

Also published in
Oxford Handbooks for Language Teachers

How Languages are Learned

Fourth edition

Patsy M. Lightbown and Nina Spada

OXFORD
UNIVERSITY PRESS

OXFORD
UNIVERSITY PRESS

Great Clarendon Street, Oxford, OX2 6DP,
United Kingdom

Oxford University Press is a department of the
University of Oxford. It furthers the University's
objective of excellence in research, scholarship,
and education by publishing worldwide. Oxford
is a registered trade mark of Oxford University
Press in the UK and in certain other countries

Photocopying

ISBN: 978 0 19 454126 8

Printed in China

This book is printed on paper from certified
and well-managed sources.

ACKNOWLEDGEMENTS

*The authors and publisher are grateful to those who have
given permission to reproduce the following extracts and
adaptations of copyright material:* p.17 Extract from
Language Development and Language Disorders by
Lois Bloom and Margaret Lahey (1978). Macmillan
Publishers; p.47 Figure from 'Some issues relating
to the Monitor Model' by Stephen Krashen, *On
TESOL* (1977). Reprinted by permission of TESOL
International Association; p.49 Extract from
'Constructing an acquisition-based procedure
for second language assessment' by Manfred
Pienemann, Malcolm Johnston, and Geoff Brindley
in *Studies in Second Language Acquisition*, Volume 10/2,
pp.217–43 (1988). Reproduced by permission of
Cambridge University Press; p.53 Extract from
'Speeding up acquisition of *his/her*: Explicit L1/L2
contracts help' in *Second Language Acquisition and
the Younger Learner: Child's Play?* by Joanna White
(2008) pp.193–228. With kind permission of John
Benjamins Publishing Company, Amsterdam/
Philadelphia; p.54 Extract from 'Second language
instruction does make a difference' by Catherine
Doughty in *Studies in Second Language Acquisition*,
Volume 13/4, pp.431–69 (1991). Reproduced by
permission of Cambridge University Press; p.136
Reprinted from *International Journal of Educational
Research*, Volume 37 by Merrill Swain and Sharon
Lapkin 'Talking it through: two French immersion
learners' response to reformulations' pp.285–304
(2002) with permission from Elsevier; p.139 Extract
from 'Corrective feedback and learner uptake'
by Roy Lyster and Leila Ranta in *Studies in Second
Language Acquisition*, Volume 19/1 pp.37–66 (1997).
Reproduced by permission of Cambridge
University Press.

Cartoons by: Sophie Grillet © Oxford University
Press 1993, 2005, and 2012.

To the teachers and students from whom
we have learned so much

CONTENTS

ACKNOWLEDGEMENTS

We wish first to thank the readers who responded so positively to the earlier editions of this book. With each edition, we have benefited from suggestions and feedback offered by colleagues and students. Our thanks to Ahlem Ammar, Alexander Ary, Philippa Bell, Luz Celaya, Laura Collins, Maria Fröhlich, Randall Halter, Zhaohong Han, Marlise Horst, Jim Hu, Phillip Hubbard, Youjin Kim, Roy Lyster, Alison Mackey, Kim McDonough, Shawn Loewen, Paul Meara, Imma Miralpeix, Vicki Murphy, Carmen Muñoz, Heike Neumann, Howard Nicholas, Paul Quinn, Katherine Rehner, Mela Sarkar, Raquel Serrano, Younghee Sheen, Wataru Suzuki, and Yasuyo Tomita. Leila Ranta, and Jude Rand made essential contributions to the first edition.

At Oxford University Press, we owe a debt to Henry Widdowson for his early encouragement and to Cristina Whitecross, who was our editor for the first three editions. We are grateful to Catherine Kneafsey, Julia Bell, Hazel Geatches, and Ann Hunter who have worked with us through the development of this new edition. We thank the English Speaking Union for conferring the 1993 Duke of Edinburgh book prize for Applied Linguistics on the book.

PREFACE TO THE FOURTH EDITION

How Languages Are Learned (HLAL) started out as a series of professional development workshops for teachers in Quebec, Canada, where we both worked for many years. Three editions of the book have now travelled far from those origins. When we were working on the first edition in the 1980s and 1990s we were still in the early days of remarkable growth of research in second language acquisition. In updating the research for each new edition, the decisions about what to include have grown more difficult. Keeping the book to a reasonable length has often meant choosing between classics in the field and important new studies, of which there are now so many. In this edition, we have annotated some 'Suggestions for further reading' at the end of each chapter. We encourage readers to follow these readings and the reference list to deepen their understanding of topics that we can only introduce here.

In this fourth edition of HLAL, we have added 'Questions for reflection' at the end of each chapter, and we have included some new 'Activities' that give readers opportunities to explore some of the topics. Another new feature of this edition is a companion website which contains additional activities, readings, and other web-based material and resources to enhance your reading and understanding of the contents of the book. It will also provide opportunities for readers to interact with others and to share their ideas for teaching and learning languages.

The website for *How Languages are Learned* can be accessed at www.oup.com/elt/teacher/hlal.

We are currently working on a new series of books for teachers, the *Oxford Key Concepts for the Language Classroom*. Each volume, written by a different author, will focus on a specific topic (such as assessment, content-based language teaching, literacy, and oral interaction), reviewing the relevant research and linking the findings to classroom practice. We hope that the books in this series will encourage teachers to continue learning about some of the topics that are introduced in HLAL.

We hope that both new readers and those who have read the previous editions of HLAL will find ideas and information that will challenge and inspire them to make their own contributions to second language learning, teaching, and research.

Patsy M. Lightbown, Harwich, MA, USA

Nina Spada, Toronto, ON, Canada

INTRODUCTION

When new methods and textbooks for second and foreign language teaching are introduced, they are often said to be based on the latest research in psychology, linguistics, or pedagogy. Teachers are told that they will be more effective than those that have gone before. In many cases, the new approaches are prescribed for immediate implementation in a school or region. Sometimes, the new materials come with opportunities for extensive training in their implementation. Sometimes, they are simply ordered and distributed to teachers who have to do their best to use them effectively.

Many approaches to language teaching have been proposed and implemented. One approach requires students to learn rules of grammar and lists of vocabulary to use in translating literary texts. Another emphasizes the value of having students imitate and practise a set of correct sentences and memorize entire dialogues. Yet another encourages 'natural' communication between students as they engage cooperatively in tasks or projects while using the new language. In some classrooms, the second language is used as the medium to teach subject matter, with the assumption that the language itself will be learned incidentally as students focus on the academic content.

How are teachers to evaluate the potential effectiveness of different instructional practices? To be sure, the most important influence on teachers' decisions is their own experience with previous successes or disappointments, as well as their understanding of the needs and abilities of their students. We believe that ideas drawn from research and theory in second language acquisition are also valuable in helping teachers to evaluate claims made by proponents of various language teaching methods. The goal of this book is to introduce teachers—both novice and experienced—to some of the language acquisition research that may help them not only to evaluate existing textbooks and materials but also to adapt them in ways that are more consistent with our understanding of how languages are learned.

The book begins with a chapter on language learning in early childhood. This background is important because both second language research and second language teaching have been influenced by our understanding of how children acquire their first language. Several theories about **first language** (L1) learning are presented in this chapter and they are revisited later in the book in relation to **second language** (L2) learning.

In Chapter 2 we look at second language learners' developing knowledge, their ability to use that knowledge, and how this compares with L1 learning. In Chapter 3, we turn our attention to how individual learner characteristics may affect success. In Chapter 4, several theories that have been advanced to explain second language learning are presented and discussed. Chapter 5 begins with a comparison of natural and instructional environments for second language learning. We then examine some different ways in which researchers have observed and described teaching and learning practices in second language classrooms.

In Chapter 6, we examine six proposals that have been made for second language teaching. Examples of research related to each of the proposals are presented, leading to a discussion of the evidence available for assessing their effectiveness. The chapter ends with a discussion of what research findings suggest about the most effective ways to teach and learn a second language in the classroom.

In Chapter 7, we will provide a general summary of the book by looking at how research can inform our response to some 'popular opinions' about language learning and teaching that are introduced below.

A Glossary provides a quick reference for a number of terms that may be new or have specific technical meanings in the context of language acquisition research. Glossary words are shown in bold letters where they first appear in the text. For readers who would like to find out more, an annotated list of suggestions for further reading is included at the end of each chapter. The Bibliography provides full reference information for the suggested readings and all the works that are referred to in the text.

We have tried to present the information in a way that does not assume that readers are already familiar with research methods or theoretical issues in second language learning. Examples and case studies are included throughout the book to illustrate the research ideas. Many of the examples are taken from second language classrooms. We have also included a number of activities for readers to practise some of the techniques of observation and analysis used in the research that we review in this book. At the end of each chapter are 'Questions for reflection' to help readers consolidate and expand their understanding of the material.

Before we begin …

It is probably true, as some have claimed, that most of us teach as we were taught or in a way that matches our ideas and preferences about how we learn. Take a moment to reflect on your views about how languages are learned and what you think this means about how they should be taught. The statements in the activity below summarize some popular opinions about language learning and teaching. Think about whether you agree or disagree with each opinion. Keep these statements and your reactions to them in mind as you read about current research and theory in second language learning.

ACTIVITY   **Give your opinion on these statements**

Indicate the extent to which you agree with each statement by marking an X in the box associated with your opinion:

SA–strongly agree
A–agree somewhat
D–disagree somewhat
SD–strongly disagree

	SA	A	D	SD
I Languages are learned mainly through imitation.				
2 Parents usually correct young children when they make grammatical errors.				
3 Highly intelligent people are good language learners.				
4 The most important predictor of success in second language acquisition is motivation.				
5 The earlier a second language is introduced in school programmes, the greater the likelihood of success in learning.				
6 Most of the mistakes that second language learners make are due to interference from their first language.				
7 The best way to learn new vocabulary is through reading.				
8 It is essential for learners to be able to pronounce all the individual sounds in the second language.				
9 Once learners know 1,000 words and the basic structure of a language, they can easily participate in conversations with native speakers.				
10 Teachers should present grammatical rules one at a time, and learners should practise examples of each one before going on to another.				
II Teachers should teach simple language structures before complex ones.				

12 Learners' errors should be corrected as soon as they are made in order to prevent the formation of bad habits.				
13 Teachers should use materials that expose students only to language structures they have already been taught.				
14 When learners are allowed to interact freely (for example, in group or pair activities), they copy each other's mistakes.				
15 Students learn what they are taught.				
16 Teachers should respond to students' errors by correctly rephrasing what they have said rather than by explicitly pointing out the error.				
17 Students can learn both language and academic content (for example, science and history) simultaneously in classes where the subject matter is taught in their second language.				
18 Classrooms are good places to learn about language but not for learning how to use language.				

1 LANGUAGE LEARNING IN EARLY CHILDHOOD

Preview

In this chapter, we will look briefly at the language development of young children. We will then consider several theories that have been offered as explanations for how language is learned. There is an immense amount of research on child language. Although much of this research has been done in middle-class North American and European families, there is a rich body of cross-linguistic and cross-cultural research as well. Our purpose in this chapter is to touch on a few main points in this research, primarily as a preparation for the discussion of second language acquisition (SLA), which is the focus of this book.

First language acquisition

Language acquisition is one of the most impressive and fascinating aspects of human development. We listen with pleasure to the sounds made by a three-month-old baby. We laugh and 'answer' the conversational 'ba-ba-ba' babbling of older babies, and we share in the pride and joy of parents whose one-year-old has uttered the first 'bye-bye'. Indeed, learning a language is an amazing feat—one that has attracted the attention of linguists and psychologists for generations. How do children accomplish this? What enables a child not only to learn words, but to put them together in meaningful sentences? What pushes children to go on developing complex grammatical language even though their early simple communication is successful for most purposes? Does child language develop similarly around the world? How do bilingual children acquire more than one language?

The first three years: Milestones and developmental sequences

One remarkable thing about first language acquisition is the high degree of similarity in the early language of children all over the world. Researchers have described **developmental sequences** for many aspects of first language acquisition. The earliest vocalizations are simply the involuntary crying that babies do when they are hungry or uncomfortable. Soon, however, we hear the cooing and gurgling sounds of contented babies, lying in their beds looking at fascinating shapes and movement around them. Even though they have little control over the sounds they make in these early weeks of life, infants are able to hear subtle differences between the sounds of human languages. Not only do they distinguish the voice of their mothers from those of other speakers, they also seem to recognize the language that was spoken around their mother before they were born. Furthermore, in cleverly designed experiments, researchers have demonstrated that tiny babies are capable of very fine **auditory discrimination**. For example, they can hear the difference between sounds as similar as 'pa' and 'ba'.

Janet Werker, Patricia Kuhl, and others have used new technologies that allow us to see how sensitive infants are to speech sounds. What may seem even more remarkable is that infants stop making distinctions between sounds that are not **phonemic** in the language that is spoken around them. For example, by the time they are a year old, babies who will become speakers of Arabic stop reacting to the difference between 'pa' and 'ba' which is not phonemic in Arabic. Babies who regularly hear more than one language in their environment continue to respond to these differences for a longer period (Werker, Weikum, and Yoshida 2006). One important finding is that it is not enough for babies to hear language sounds from electronic devices. In order to learn—or retain—the ability to distinguish between sounds, they need to interact with a human speaker (Conboy and Kuhl 2011). The Internet abounds with remarkable videos of infants reacting to language sounds.

Whether they are becoming monolingual or bilingual children, however, it will be many months before their own vocalizations begin to reflect the characteristics of the language or languages they hear and longer still before they connect language sounds with specific meaning. However, by the end of their first year, most babies understand quite a few frequently repeated words in the language or languages spoken around them. They wave when someone says 'bye-bye'; they clap when someone says 'pat-a-cake'; they eagerly hurry to the kitchen when 'juice and cookies' are mentioned.

At 12 months, most babies will have begun to produce a word or two that everyone recognizes. By the age of two, most children reliably produce at least 50 different words and some produce many more. About this time, they begin to combine words into simple sentences such as 'Mommy juice' and 'baby fall down'. These sentences are sometimes called 'telegraphic' because they leave out such things as articles, prepositions, and auxiliary verbs. We recognize them as sentences because, even though **function words** and **grammatical morphemes** are missing, the word order reflects the word order of the language they are hearing and the combined words have a meaningful relationship that makes them more than just a list of words. Thus, for an English-speaking child, 'kiss baby' does not mean the same thing as 'baby kiss'. Remarkably, we also see evidence, even in these early sentences that children are doing more than imperfectly imitating what they have heard. Their two- and three-word sentences show signs that they can creatively combine words. For example, 'more outside' may mean 'I want to go outside again.' Depending on the situation, 'Daddy uh-oh' might mean 'Daddy fell down' or 'Daddy dropped something' or even 'Daddy, please do that funny thing where you pretend to drop me off your lap.'

As children progress through the discovery of language in their first three years, there are predictable patterns in the emergence and development of many features of the language they are learning. For some language features, these patterns have been described in terms of developmental sequences or 'stages'. To some extent, these stages in language acquisition are related to children's cognitive development. For example, children do not use temporal adverbs such as 'tomorrow' or 'last week' until they develop some understanding of time. In other cases, the developmental sequences seem to reflect the gradual acquisition of the linguistic elements for expressing ideas that have been present in children's cognitive understanding for a long time. For example, children can distinguish between singular and plural long before they reliably add plural endings to nouns. Correct use of irregular plurals (such as 'feet') takes even more time and may not be completely under control until the school years.

Grammatical morphemes

In the 1960s, several researchers focused on how children acquire grammatical morphemes in English. One of the best-known studies was carried out by Roger Brown and his colleagues and students. In a **longitudinal study** of the language development of three children (called Adam, Eve, and Sarah) they found that 14 grammatical morphemes were acquired in a similar sequence. The list below (adapted from Brown's 1973 book) shows some of the morphemes they studied.

present progressive *-ing* (Mommy running)
plural *-s* (two books)
irregular past forms (Baby *went*)
possessive *-s* (Daddy's hat)
copula (Mommy *is* happy)
articles *the* and *a*

regular past -*ed* (she walk*ed*)
third person singular simple present -*s* (she runs)
auxiliary *be* (he *is* coming)

Brown and his colleagues found that a child who had mastered the grammatical morphemes at the bottom of the list had also mastered those at the top, but the reverse was not true. Thus, there was evidence for a 'developmental sequence' or **order of acquisition**. However, the children did not acquire the morphemes at the same age or rate. Eve had mastered nearly all the morphemes before she was two-and-a-half years old, while Sarah and Adam were still working on them when they were three-and-a-half or four.

Brown's longitudinal work was confirmed in a **cross-sectional study** of 21 children. Jill and Peter de Villiers (1973) found that children who correctly used the morphemes that Adam, Eve, and Sarah had acquired late were also able to use the ones that Adam, Eve, and Sarah had acquired earlier. The children mastered the morphemes at different ages, just as Adam, Eve, and Sarah had done, but the order of their acquisition was very similar.

Many **hypotheses** have been advanced to explain why these grammatical morphemes are acquired in the observed order. Researchers have studied the frequency with which the morphemes occur in parents' speech, the cognitive complexity of the meanings represented by each morpheme, and the difficulty of perceiving or pronouncing them. In the end, there has been no simple satisfactory explanation for the sequence, and most researchers agree that the order is determined by an interaction among a number of different factors.

To supplement the evidence we have from simply observing children, some carefully designed procedures have been developed to further explore children's knowledge of grammatical morphemes. One of the first and best known is the so-called 'wug test' developed by Jean Berko (1958). In this 'test', children are shown drawings of imaginary creatures with novel names or people performing mysterious actions. For example, they are told, 'Here is a wug. Now there are two of them. There are two ____' or 'Here is a man who knows how to bod. Yesterday he did the same thing. Yesterday, he ____'. By completing these sentences with 'wugs' and 'bodded', children demonstrate that they know the patterns for plural and simple past in English. By **generalizing** these patterns to words they have never heard before, they show that their language is more than just a list of memorized word pairs such as 'book/books' and 'nod/nodded'.

ACTIVITY   **Try out the 'wug' test**

A web search for 'wug test' will turn up many examples of the pictures and the text created for this landmark research. If you know some English-speaking children under the age of five years, try using the test with them.

1 What similarities and differences do you notice among the children at different ages?

2 Which grammatical morphemes do they find easy and which ones are more difficult?

The acquisition of other language features also shows how children's language develops systematically, and how they go beyond what they have heard to create new forms and structures.

Negation

Children learn the functions of negation very early. That is, they learn to comment on the disappearance of objects, to refuse a suggestion, or to reject an assertion, even at the single word stage. However, as Lois Bloom's (1991) longitudinal studies show, even though children understand these functions and express them with single words and gestures, it takes some time before they can express them in sentences, using the appropriate words and word order. The following stages in the development of negation have been observed in the acquisition of English. Similar stages have been observed in other languages as well (Wode 1981).

Stage 1
Negation is usually expressed by the word 'no', either all alone or as the first word in the utterance.

No. No cookie. No comb hair.

Stage 2
Utterances grow longer and the sentence subject may be included. The negative word appears just before the verb. Sentences expressing rejection or prohibition often use 'don't'.

Daddy no comb hair. Don't touch that!

Stage 3
The negative element is inserted into a more complex sentence. Children may add forms of the negative other than 'no', including words like 'can't' and 'don't'. These sentences appear to follow the correct English pattern of attaching the negative to the auxiliary or modal verb. However, children do not yet vary these forms for different persons or tenses.

I can't do it. He don't want it.

Stage 4
Children begin to attach the negative element to the correct form of auxiliary verbs such as 'do' and 'be'.

You didn't have supper. She doesn't want it.

Even though their language system is by now quite complex, they may still have difficulty with some other features related to negatives.

I don't have no more candies.

Questions

The challenge of learning complex language systems is also illustrated in the developmental stages through which children learn to ask questions.

There is a remarkable consistency in the way children learn to form questions in English. For one thing, there is a predictable order in which the '*wh-* words' emerge (Bloom 1991). 'What' is generally the first *wh-* question word to be used. It is often learned as part of a **chunk** ('Whassat?') and it is some time before the child learns that there are variations of the form, such as 'What is that?' and 'What are these?'.

'Where' and 'who' emerge very soon. Identifying and locating people and objects are within the child's understanding of the world. Furthermore, adults tend to ask children just these types of questions in the early days of **language learning**, for example, 'Where's Mommy?' or 'Who's that?'

'Why' emerges around the end of the second year and becomes a favourite for the next year or two. Children seem to ask an endless number of questions beginning with 'why', having discovered how effectively this little word gets adults to engage in conversation, for example, 'Why that lady has blue hair?'

Finally, when the child has a better understanding of manner and time, 'how' and 'when' emerge. In contrast to 'what', 'where', and 'who' questions, children sometimes ask the more cognitively difficult 'why', 'when', and 'how' questions without understanding the answers they get, as the following conversation with a four-year-old clearly shows.

CHILD   When can we go outside?
PARENT   In about five minutes.
CHILD   1-2-3-4-5! Can we go now?

The ability to use these question words is at least partly tied to children's cognitive development. It is also predicted in part by the questions children are asked and the linguistic complexity of questions with different *wh-* words. Thus it does not seem surprising that there is consistency in the sequence of their acquisition. Perhaps more surprising is the consistency in the acquisition of word order in questions. This development is not based on learning new meanings, but rather on learning different linguistic patterns to express meanings that are already understood.

Stage 1

Children's earliest questions are single words or simple two- or three-word sentences with rising intonation:

Cookie? Mommy book?

At the same time, they may produce some correct questions—correct because they have been learned as chunks:

Where's Daddy? What's that?

Stage 2

As they begin to ask more new questions, children use the word order of the declarative sentence, with rising intonation.

You like this? I have some?

They continue to produce the correct chunk-learned forms such as 'What's that?' alongside their own created questions.

Stage 3

Gradually, children notice that the structure of questions is different and begin to produce questions such as:

Can I go?
Are you happy?

Although some questions at this stage match the adult pattern, they may be right for the wrong reason. To describe this, we need to see the pattern from the child's perspective rather than from the perspective of the adult grammar. We call this stage 'fronting' because the child's rule seems to be that questions are formed by putting something (a verb or question word) at the 'front' of a sentence, leaving the rest of the sentence in its statement form.

Is the teddy is tired? Do I can have a cookie?
Why you don't have one? Why you catched it?

Stage 4

At Stage 4, some questions are formed by subject–auxiliary inversion. The questions resemble those of Stage 3, but there is more variety in the auxiliaries that appear before the subject.

Are you going to play with me?

At this stage, children can even add 'do' in questions in which there would be no auxiliary in the declarative version of the sentence.

Do dogs like ice cream?

Even at this stage, however, children seem able to use either inversion or a *wh-*word, but not both (for example, 'Is he crying?' but not 'Why is he crying?'

Therefore, we may find inversion in *yes/no* questions but not in *wh-* questions, unless they are **formulaic** units such as 'What's that?'

Stage 5

At Stage 5, both *wh-* and *yes/no* questions are formed correctly.

> Are these your boots?
> Why did you do that?
> Does Daddy have a box?

Negative questions may still be a bit too difficult.

> Why the teddy bear can't go outside?

And even though **performance** on most questions is correct, there is still one more hurdle. When *wh-* words appear in subordinate clauses or embedded questions, children **overgeneralize** the inverted form that would be correct for simple questions and produce sentences such as:

> Ask him why can't he go out.

Stage 6

At this stage, children are able to correctly form all question types, including negative and complex embedded questions.

Passage through developmental sequences does not always follow a steady uninterrupted path. Children appear to learn new things and then fall back on old patterns when there is added stress in a new situation or when they are using other new elements in their language. But the overall path takes them toward a closer and closer approximation of the language that is spoken around them.

The pre-school years

By the age of four, most children can ask questions, give commands, report real events, and create stories about imaginary ones, using correct word order and grammatical markers most of the time. In fact, it is generally accepted that by age four, children have acquired the basic structures of the language or languages spoken to them in these early years. Three- and four-year-olds continue to learn vocabulary at the rate of several words a day. They begin to acquire less frequent and more complex linguistic structures such as passives and relative clauses.

Much of children's language acquisition effort in the late pre-school years is spent in developing their ability to use language in a widening social environment. They use language in a greater variety of situations. They interact more often with unfamiliar adults. They begin to talk sensibly on the telephone to invisible grandparents (younger children do not understand that their telephone partner cannot see what they see). They acquire the aggressive or cajoling language that is needed to defend their toys in the playground. They show that they have learned the difference between how adults talk to babies and how they talk to each other, and they use this knowledge in elaborate pretend play in which they practise using these different 'voices'. In this way, they explore and begin to understand how and why language varies.

In the pre-school years, children also begin to develop **metalinguistic awareness**, the ability to treat language as an object separate from the meaning it conveys. Three-year-old children can tell you that it's 'silly' to say 'drink the chair', because it doesn't make sense. However, although they would never say 'cake the eat', they are less sure that there's anything wrong with it. They may show that they know it's a bit odd, but they will focus mainly on the fact that they can understand what it means. Five-year-olds, on the other hand, know that 'drink the chair' is wrong in a different way from 'cake the eat'. They can tell you that one is 'silly' but the other is 'the wrong way around'.

Language acquisition in the pre-school years is impressive. It is also noteworthy that children have spent thousands of hours interacting with language—participating in conversations, eavesdropping on others' conversations, being read to, watching television, etc. A quick mathematical exercise will show you just how many hours children spend in language-rich environments. If children are awake for ten or twelve hours a day, we may estimate that they are in contact with the language of their environment for 20,000 hours or more by the time they go to school.

Although pre-school children acquire complex knowledge and skills for language and language use, the school setting requires new ways of using language and brings new opportunities for language development.

The school years

Children develop the ability to use language to understand others and to express their own meanings in the pre-school years, and in the school years, this ability expands and grows. Learning to read gives a major boost to metalinguistic awareness. Seeing words represented by letters and other symbols on a page leads children to a new understanding that language has form as well as meaning. Reading reinforces the understanding that a 'word' is separate from the thing it represents. Unlike three-year-olds, children who can read understand that 'the' is a word, just as 'house' is. They understand that 'caterpillar' is a longer word than 'train', even though the object it represents is substantially shorter! Metalinguistic awareness also includes the discovery of such things as ambiguity. Knowing that words and sentences can have multiple meaning gives children access to word jokes, trick questions, and riddles, which they love to share with their friends and family.

One of the most impressive aspects of language development in the school years is the astonishing growth of vocabulary. Children enter school with the ability to understand and produce several thousand words, and thousands more will be learned at school. In both the spoken and written language at school, words such as 'homework' or 'ruler' appear frequently in situations where their meaning is either immediately or gradually revealed. Words like 'population' or 'latitude' occur less frequently, but they are made important by their significance in academic subject matter.

Vocabulary grows at a rate of between several hundred and more than a thousand words a year, depending mainly on how much and how widely children read (Nagy, Herman, and Anderson 1985). The kind of vocabulary growth required for school success is likely to come from both reading for assignments and reading for pleasure, whether narrative or non-fiction. Dee Gardner (2004) suggests that reading a variety of text types is an essential part of vocabulary growth. His research has shown how the range of vocabulary in narrative texts is different from that in non-fiction. There are words in non-fiction texts that are unlikely to occur in stories or novels. In addition, non-fiction tends to include more opportunities to see a word in its different forms (for example, 'mummy', 'mummies', 'mummified'). The importance of reading for vocabulary growth is seen when observant parents report a child using a new word but mispronouncing it in a way that reveals it has been encountered only in written form.

Another important development in the school years is the acquisition of different language **registers**. Children learn how written language differs from spoken language, how the language used to speak to the principal is different from the language of the playground, how the language of a science report is different from the language of a narrative. As Terry Piper (2006) and others have documented, some children will have even more to learn if they come to school speaking an ethnic or regional **variety** of the school language that is quite different from the one used by the teacher. They will have to learn that another variety, often referred to as the **standard variety**, is required for successful academic work. Other children arrive at school speaking a different language altogether. For these children, the work of language learning in the early school years presents additional opportunities and challenges. We will return to this topic when we discuss **bilingualism** in early childhood.

Explaining first language acquisition

These descriptions of language development from infancy through the early school years show that we have considerable knowledge of *what* children learn in their early language development. More controversial, however, are questions about *how* this development takes place. What abilities does the child bring to the task and what are the contributions of the environment?

Since the middle of the 20th century, three main theoretical positions have been advanced to explain language development: behaviourist, innatist, and interactional/developmental perspectives.

The behaviourist perspective

Behaviourism is a theory of learning that was influential in the 1940s and 1950s, especially in the United States. With regard to language learning, the best-known proponent of this psychological theory was B. F. Skinner (1957). Traditional behaviourists hypothesized that when children imitated the language produced by those around them, their attempts to reproduce what they heard received 'positive reinforcement'. This could take the form of praise or just successful communication. Thus encouraged by their environment, children would continue to imitate and practise these sounds and patterns until they formed 'habits' of correct language use. According to this view, the quality and quantity of the language the child hears, as well as the consistency of the reinforcement offered by others in the environment, would shape the child's language behaviour. This theory gives great importance to the environment as the source of everything the child needs to learn.

Analysing children's speech: Definitions and examples

The behaviourists viewed *imitation* and *practice* as the primary processes in language development. To clarify what is meant by these two terms, consider the following definitions and examples.

Imitation: word-for-word repetition of all or part of someone else's utterance.

MOTHER	Shall we play with the dolls?
LUCY	Play with dolls

Practice: repetitive manipulation of form.

CINDY	He eat carrots. The other one eat carrots. They both eat carrots.

Now examine the transcripts from Peter, Cindy, and Kathryn. They were all about 24 months old when they were recorded as they played with a visiting adult. Using the definitions above, notice how Peter imitates the adult in the following dialogue.

Peter (24 months) is playing with a dump truck while two adults, Patsy and Lois, look on.

PETER	Get more.
LOIS	You're gonna put more wheels in the dump truck?
PETER	Dump truck. Wheels. Dump truck.

(later)

PATSY	What happened to it (the truck)?

PETER   (looking under chair for it) Lose it. Dump truck! Dump
         truck! Fall! Fall!
LOIS   Yes, the dump truck fell down.
PETER   Dump truck fell down. Dump truck.

(Unpublished data from P. M. Lightbown)

If we analysed a larger sample of Peter's speech, we would see that 30–40 per cent of his sentences were imitations of what someone else had just said. We would also see that his imitations were not random. That is, he did not simply imitate 30–40 per cent of everything he heard. Detailed analyses of large samples of Peter's speech over about a year showed that he imitated words and sentence structures that were just beginning to appear in his spontaneous speech. Once these new elements became solidly grounded in his language system, he stopped imitating them and went on to imitate others.

Unlike a parrot who imitates the familiar and continues to repeat the same things again and again, children appear to imitate selectively. The choice of what to imitate seems to be based on something new that they have just begun to understand and use, not simply on what is available in the environment. For example, consider how Cindy imitates and practises language in the following conversations.

Cindy (24 months, 16 days) is looking at a picture of a carrot in a book and trying to get Patsy's attention.

CINDY   Kawo? kawo? kawo? kawo? kawo?
PATSY   What are the rabbits eating?
CINDY   They eating … kando?
PATSY   No, that's a carrot.
CINDY   Carrot. (pointing to each carrot on the page) The other …
         carrot. The other carrot. The other carrot.

(A few minutes later, Cindy brings Patsy a stuffed toy rabbit.)

PATSY   What does this rabbit like to eat?
CINDY   (incomprehensible) eat the carrots.

(Cindy gets another stuffed rabbit.)

CINDY   He (incomprehensible) eat carrots. The other one eat carrots.
         They both eat carrots.

(One week later, Cindy opens the book to the same page.)

CINDY   Here's the carrots. (pointing) Is that a carrot?
PATSY   Yes.

(Unpublished data from P. M. Lightbown)

Cindy appears to be working hard on her language acquisition. She practises new words and structures in a way that sounds like a student in some foreign language classes! Perhaps most interesting is that she remembers the 'language lesson' a week later and turns straight to the page in the book she had not seen since Patsy's last visit. What is most striking is that, like Peter, her imitation and practice appear to be focused on what she is currently 'working on'.

The samples of speech from Peter and Cindy seem to lend some support to the behaviourist explanation of language acquisition. Even so, as we saw, the choice of what to imitate and practise seemed determined by something inside the child rather than by the environment.

Not all children imitate and practise as much as Peter and Cindy did. The amount of imitation in the speech of other children, whose development proceeded at a rate comparable to that of Cindy and Peter, has been calculated at less than 10 per cent. Consider the examples of imitation and practice in the following conversation between Kathryn and Lois.

Kathryn (24 months)

LOIS   Did you see the toys I brought?
KATHRYN I bring toys? Choo choo? Lois brought the choo choo train?
LOIS   Yes, Lois brought the choo choo train.
KATHRYN (reaching for bag) I want play with choo choo train. I want play with choo choo train. (taking out slide) Want play. What's this?
LOIS   Oh you know what that is.
KATHRYN Put down on floor. This. I do this.

(Kathryn puts the slide on the floor.)

KATHRYN (taking out two cars of train) Do this. I want do this. (trying to put train together) I do this. I do this.
LOIS   OK. You can do it. You can do it. Look I'll show you how.

(Lois puts it together.)

KATHRYN (searching in box) I get more. Get a more. No more choo choo train. Get truck. (taking out truck) Kathryn truck. Where? Where a more choo choo train?
LOIS   Inside. It's in the box.
KATHRYN A choo choo? (taking out part of train) This is a choo choo train.

(from Bloom and Lahey 1978: 135)

Like Cindy, Kathryn sometimes repeats herself or produces a series of related practice sentences, but she rarely imitates the other speaker. Instead, she asks and answers questions and elaborates on the other speaker's questions or statements.

Thus, children vary in the amount of imitation they do. In addition, many of the things they say show that they are using language creatively, not just repeating what they have heard. This is evident in the following examples.

Patterns in language

The first example shows a child in the process of learning patterns in language, in this case the rules of word formation, and overgeneralizing them to new contexts.

Randall (36 months) had a sore on his hand.

MOTHER   Maybe we need to take you to the doctor.
RANDALL   Why? So he can doc my little bump?

Randall forms the verb 'doc' from the noun 'doctor', by analogy with farmers who farm, swimmers who swim, and actors who act.

Focus on meaning

Even older children have to work out some puzzles, for example, when familiar language is used in unfamiliar ways, as in the example below. When David (5 years, 1 month) was at his older sister's birthday party, toasts were proposed with grape juice in stemmed glasses:

FATHER   I'd like to propose a toast.

Several minutes later, David raised his glass:

DAVID   I'd like to propose a piece of bread.

Only when laughter sent David slinking from the table did the group realize that he wasn't intentionally making a play on words! He was concentrating so hard on performing the fascinating new gesture and the formulaic expression 'I'd like to propose …' that he failed to realize that the word he thought he knew—'toast'—was not the same toast and could not be replaced with its apparent near-synonym, 'a piece of bread'.

Question formation

Randall (2 years, 9 months) asked the following questions in various situations over the course of a day.

> Are dogs can wiggle their tails?
> Are those are my boots?
> Are this is hot?

Randall had concluded that the trick of asking questions was to put 'are' at the beginning of the sentence. His questions are good examples of Stage 3 in question development.

Order of events

Randall (3 years, 5 months) was looking for a towel.

> You took all the towels away because I can't dry my hands.

He meant 'I can't dry my hands because you took all the towels away', but he made a mistake about which clause comes first. Children at this stage of language development tend to mention events in the order of their occurrence. In this case, the towels disappeared before Randall attempted to dry his hands, so that's what he said first. He did not yet understand how a word like 'before' or 'because' changes the order of cause and effect.

These examples of children's speech provide us with a window on the process of language learning. Imitation and practice alone cannot explain some of the forms created by children. They are not merely repetitions of sentences that they have heard from adults. Rather, children appear to pick out patterns and generalize them to new contexts. They create new forms or new uses of words. Their new sentences are usually comprehensible and often correct.

Behaviourism seems to offer a reasonable way of understanding how children learn some of the regular and routine aspects of language, especially at the earliest stages. However, children who do little overt imitation acquire language as fully and rapidly as those who imitate a lot. And although behaviourism goes some way to explaining the sorts of overgeneralization that children make, classical behaviourism is not a satisfactory explanation for the acquisition of the more complex grammar that children acquire. These limitations led researchers to look for different explanations for language acquisition.

The innatist perspective

Noam Chomsky is one of the most influential figures in linguistics, and his ideas about how language is acquired and how it is stored in the mind sparked a revolution in many aspects of linguistics and psychology, including the study of language acquisition. The **innatist** perspective is related to Chomsky's hypothesis that all human languages are based on some innate universal principles.

In his 1959 review of B. F. Skinner's book *Verbal Behavior*, Chomsky challenged the behaviourist explanation for language acquisition. He argued that children are biologically programmed for language and that language develops in the child in just the same way that other biological functions develop. For example, every child will learn to walk as long as adequate nourishment and reasonable freedom of movement are provided. The child does not have to be taught. Most children learn to walk at about the same age, and walking is essentially the same in all normal human beings. For Chomsky, language acquisition is very similar. The environment makes only a basic contribution—in this case, the availability of people who speak to the child. The child, or rather, the child's biological endowment, will do the rest.

Chomsky argued that the behaviourist theory failed to account for 'the logical problem of language acquisition'—the fact that children come to know more about the structure of their language than they could reasonably be expected to learn on the basis of the samples of language they hear. The language children are exposed to includes false starts, incomplete sentences, and slips of the tongue, and yet they learn to distinguish between grammatical and ungrammatical sentences. He concluded that children's minds are not blank slates to be filled by imitating language they hear in the environment. Instead, he hypothesized, children are born with a specific innate ability to discover for themselves the underlying rules of a language system on the basis of the samples of a natural language they are exposed to. This innate endowment was seen as a sort of template, containing the principles that are universal to all human languages. This **universal grammar** (UG) would prevent the child from pursuing all sorts of wrong hypotheses about how language systems might work. If children are pre-equipped with UG, then what they have to learn is the ways in which the language they are acquiring makes use of these principles.

Consider the following sentences, from a book by Lydia White (1989). These English sentences contain the reflexive pronoun 'himself'. Both the pronoun and the noun it refers to (the antecedent) are printed in *italics*. (An asterisk at the beginning of a sentence indicates that the sentence is ungrammatical.)

a *John saw himself.*
b **Himself saw John.*

In (a) and (b), it looks as if the reflexive pronoun must follow the noun it refers to. But (c) disproves this:

c Looking after *himself* bores *John*.

If we consider sentences such as:

d John said that *Fred* liked *himself*.
e **John* said that Fred liked *himself*.
f John told *Bill* to wash *himself*.
g **John* told Bill to wash *himself*.

we might conclude that the noun closest to the reflexive pronoun is the antecedent. However, (h) shows that this rule won't work either:

h *John* promised Bill to wash *himself*.

And it's even more complicated than that. Usually the reflexive must be in the same clause as the antecedent as in (a) and (d), but not always, as in (h). Furthermore, the reflexive can be in the subject position in (i) but not in (j).

i *John* believes *himself* to be intelligent (non-finite clause).
j **John* believes that *himself* is intelligent (finite clause).

In some cases, more than one antecedent is possible, as in (k) where the reflexive could refer to either John or Bill:

k *John*? showed *Bill*? a picture of *himself*.

When we look at this kind of complexity, it seems it would be very hard to learn, and children do make errors along the way. Yet, most school-age children would be able to correctly interpret the grammatical sentences and recognize the ungrammaticality of the others. Researchers who study language acquisition from the innatist perspective argue that such complex grammar could never be learned purely on the basis of imitating and practising sentences available in the **input**. They hypothesize that since all children acquire the language of their environment, they must have some innate mechanism or knowledge that allows them to discover such complex syntax in spite of limitations of the input. They hypothesize furthermore that the innate mechanism is used exclusively for language acquisition.

The innatist perspective emphasizes the fact that almost all children successfully acquire their native language—or more than one language if they live in a multilingual community. Children who are profoundly deaf will learn sign language if they are exposed to it in infancy, and their progress in the acquisition of that language system is similar to hearing children's acquisition of spoken language. Even children with very limited cognitive ability develop quite complex language systems if they are brought up in environments in which people interact with them.

Children acquire the basic syntax and morphology of the language spoken to them in a variety of conditions, some of which would be expected to enhance language development (for example, caring, attentive parents who focus on the child's language), and some which might be expected to inhibit it (for example, abusive or rejecting parents). Children achieve different levels of vocabulary, creativity, social grace, and so on, but virtually all achieve the ability to use the patterns of the language or languages spoken to them. This is seen as support for the hypothesis that language is somehow separate from other aspects of cognitive development and may depend on a specific module of the brain.

The Critical Period Hypothesis

The innatist perspective is often linked to the **Critical Period Hypothesis** (CPH)—the hypothesis that animals, including humans, are genetically programmed to acquire certain kinds of knowledge and skill at specific times in life. Beyond those 'critical periods', it is either difficult or impossible to acquire those abilities. With regard to language, the CPH suggests that children who are not given access to language in infancy and early childhood (because of deafness or extreme isolation) will never acquire language if these deprivations go on for too long.

It is difficult to find evidence for or against the CPH, since nearly all children are exposed to language at an early age. However, history has documented a few 'natural experiments' where children have been deprived of contact with language. Two of the most famous cases are those of 'Victor' and 'Genie'.

In 1799, a boy who became known as Victor was found wandering naked in the woods in France. His story was dramatized in a 1970 film by François Truffaut called *L'enfant sauvage* (*The Wild Child*). When Victor was captured, he was about 12 years old and completely wild, apparently having had no contact with humans. Jean-Marc-Gaspard Itard, a young doctor accustomed to working with deaf children, devoted five years to socializing Victor and trying to teach him language. Although he succeeded to some extent in developing Victor's sociability, memory, and judgement, there was little progress in his language ability.

Nearly 200 years later, Genie, a 13-year-old girl who had been isolated, neglected, and abused, was discovered in California. Because of the irrational demands of a disturbed father and the submission and fear of an abused mother, Genie had spent more than 11 years tied to a chair or a crib in a small, darkened room. Her father had forbidden his wife and son to speak to Genie and had himself only growled and barked at her. She was beaten when she made any kind of noise, and she had long since resorted to complete silence. Genie was undeveloped physically, emotionally, and intellectually. She had no language.

After she was discovered, Genie was cared for and educated with the participation of many teachers and therapists, including Susan Curtiss (1977). After a brief period in a rehabilitation centre, she lived in a foster home and attended special schools. Genie made remarkable progress in becoming socialized and cognitively aware. She developed deep personal relationships and strong individual tastes and traits. Nevertheless, after five years of exposure to language, Genie's language was not like that of a typical five-year old. There was a larger than normal gap between comprehension and production. She used grammatical forms inconsistently and overused formulaic and routine speech.

Although Victor and Genie appear to provide evidence in support of the CPH, it is difficult to argue that the hypothesis is confirmed on the basis of evidence from such unusual cases. We cannot know what other factors besides biological maturity might have contributed to their inability to learn language. It is not possible to determine whether either of them suffered from brain damage, developmental delays, or a specific language impairment, even before they were separated from normal human interaction.

A more appropriate test of the CPH is the case of children who come from homes where they receive love and care from their parents, yet do not have access to language at the usual time. This is the case for some profoundly deaf children who have hearing parents. Only 5–10 per cent of the profoundly deaf are born to deaf parents, and only these children are likely to be exposed to ASL from birth. Hearing parents may not realize that their child cannot hear because the child uses other senses to interact in an apparently normal way. Thus, the early childhood period may be normal in most ways but devoid of language that is accessible to the child. These children's later experience in learning sign language has been the subject of some important research related to the CPH.

Like oral and written languages, **American Sign Language** (ASL) makes use of grammatical markers to indicate such things as time (for example, past tense) and number. These markers are expressed through specific hand or body movements.

Elissa Newport (1990) and her colleagues studied the ability of deaf users of ASL to produce and comprehend grammatical markers. They compared Native signers (who were exposed to ASL from birth), Early signers (who began using ASL between four and six years of age), and Late signers (who began learning ASL after age 12). They found no difference between the groups in some aspects of their use of ASL, for example in vocabulary knowledge. However, on tests focusing on grammatical markers, the Native group used the markers more consistently than the Early group who, in turn, used them more consistently than the Late group. The researchers concluded that their study supports the hypothesis that there is a critical period for first language acquisition, whether that language is oral or gestural.

Another line of research that has given new insight into the importance of early language experience comes from studies of 'international adoptees.' These are children who were adopted at an early age by families who did not speak the language the child had heard during infancy. In their review of studies of international adoptees, Johanne Paradis, Fred Genesee, and Martha Crago (2011) concluded that cognitive and linguistic outcomes were generally very positive. Some comparisons of their language with that of children the same age who had always heard the same language showed that subtle differences persist even after several years, but these are not the kinds of differences that most people would notice. Here again, of course, one cannot know whether something other than a late exposure to the language spoken in the adoptive environment also contributed to differences between these children and others who did not experience an abrupt change in their language environment. Nevertheless, with continuing research on children's linguistic behaviours and intuitions, as well as the neurological studies of infants' speech perception that we saw above, it is becoming clearer that language acquisition begins at birth, and possibly even before, as the child's brain is shaped by exposure to the language(s) in the environment.

The innatist perspective is thus partly based on evidence that there is a critical period for language acquisition. It is also seen as an explanation for 'the logical problem of language acquisition', that is, the question of how adult speakers come to know the complex structure of their first language on the basis of the limited samples of language to which they are exposed.

Interactionist/developmental perspectives

Developmental and cognitive psychologists have focused on the interplay between the innate learning ability of children and the environment in which they develop. They argue that the innatists place too much emphasis on the 'final state' (the **competence** of adult **native speakers**) and not enough on the developmental aspects of language acquisition. In their view, language acquisition is but one example of the human child's ability to learn from experience, and they see no need to assume that there are specific brain structures devoted to language acquisition. They hypothesize that what children need to know is essentially available in the language they are exposed to as they hear it used in thousands of hours of interactions with the people and objects around them.

Psychologists attribute considerably more importance to the environment than the innatists do even though they also recognize a powerful learning mechanism in the human brain. They see language acquisition as similar to and influenced by the acquisition of other kinds of skill and knowledge, rather than as something that is different from and largely independent of the child's experience and cognitive development. Indeed, researchers such as Dan Slobin (1973) have long emphasized the close relationship between children's cognitive development and their acquisition of language.

Piaget and Vygotsky

One of the earliest proponents of the view that children's language is built on their cognitive development was the Swiss psychologist/epistemologist, Jean Piaget (1951). In the early decades of the 20th century, Piaget observed infants and children in their play and in their interaction with objects and people. He was able to trace the development of their cognitive understanding of such things as object permanence (knowing that things hidden from sight are still there), the stability of quantities regardless of changes in their appearance (knowing that 10 pennies spread out to form a long line are not more numerous than 10 pennies in a tightly squeezed line), and logical inferencing (figuring out which properties of a set of rods (their size, weight, material, etc.) cause some rods to sink and others to float on water).

It is easy to see how children's cognitive development would partly determine how they acquire language. For example, the use of certain terms such as 'bigger' or 'more' depends on the children's understanding of the concepts they represent. The developing cognitive understanding is built on the interaction between the child and the things that can be observed or manipulated. For Piaget, language was one of a number of symbol systems that are developed in childhood. Language can be used to represent knowledge that children have acquired through physical interaction with the environment.

Another influential student of child development was the psychologist Lev Vygotsky (1978). He observed interactions among children and also between children and adults in schools in the Soviet Union in the 1920s and 1930s. He concluded that language develops primarily from social interaction. He argued that in a supportive interactive environment, children are able to advance to higher levels of knowledge and performance. Vygotsky referred to a metaphorical place in which children could do more than they would be capable of doing independently as the **zone of proximal development** (ZPD).

Vygotsky observed the importance of conversations that children have with adults and with other children and saw in these conversations the origins of both language and thought. The conversations provide the child with **scaffolding**, that is, a kind of supportive structure that helps them make the most of the knowledge they have and also to acquire new knowledge.

Vygotsky's view differs from Piaget's. Piaget saw language as a symbol system that could be used to express knowledge acquired through interaction with the physical world. For Vygotsky, thought was essentially internalized speech, and speech emerged in social interaction. Vygotsky's views have become increasingly central in research on second language development, as we will see in Chapter 4.

Cross-cultural research

Since the 1970s, researchers have studied children's language learning environments in a great many different cultural communities. The research has focused not only on the development of language itself, but also on the ways in which the environment provides what children need for language acquisition. Between 1985 and 1997, Dan Slobin edited five volumes devoted to research on the acquisition of 28 languages, providing examples and analyses of child language and the language-learning environment from communities around the world. One of the most remarkable resources for child language researchers is the Child Language Data Exchange System (CHILDES), where researchers have contributed child language data in dozens of languages in recorded and transcribed forms that are available as electronic files from the CHILDES website (MacWhinney 2000).

One feature of cross-cultural research is the description of child-rearing patterns. Catherine Snow (1995) and others have studied the apparent effects on language acquisition of the ways in which adults talk to and interact with young children. In middle-class North American homes, researchers observed that adults often modify the way they speak when talking to little children. This **child-directed speech** may be characterized by a slower rate of delivery, higher pitch, more varied intonation, shorter, simpler sentence patterns, stress on key words, frequent repetition, and paraphrase. Furthermore, topics of conversation emphasize the child's immediate environment, picture books, or experiences that the adult knows the child has had. Adults often repeat the content of a child's utterance, but they expand or **recast** it into a grammatically correct sentence. For example, when Peter says, 'Dump truck! Dump truck! Fall! Fall!', Lois responds, 'Yes, the dump truck fell down.'

Researchers working in a 'language socialization' framework have found that the kind of child-directed speech observed in middle-class American homes is by no means universal. In some societies, adults do not engage in conversation or verbal play with very young children. For example, Bambi Schieffelin (1990) found that Kaluli mothers in Papua New Guinea did not consider their children to be appropriate conversational partners. Martha Crago (1992) observed that in traditional Inuit society, children are expected to watch and listen to adults. They are not expected or encouraged to participate in conversations with adults until they are older and have more developed language skills.

Other researchers have observed that in some societies, young children interact primarily with older siblings who serve as their caregivers. Even within the United States, Shirley Brice Heath (1983) and others have documented substantial differences in the ways parents in different socioeconomic and ethnic groups interact with their children. Nevertheless, in every society, children are in situations in which they hear language that is meaningful to them in their environment. And they acquire the community language. Thus, it is difficult to judge the long-term effect of the modifications that some adults make in speech addressed to children.

The importance of interaction

The role of interaction between a language-learning child and an **interlocutor** who responds to the child is illuminated by cases where such interaction is missing. Jacqueline Sachs and her colleagues (1981) studied the language development of a child they called Jim. He was a hearing child of deaf parents, and his only contact with oral language was through television, which he watched frequently. The family was unusual in that the parents did not use sign language with Jim. Thus, although in other respects he was well cared for, Jim did not begin his linguistic development in a normal environment in which a parent communicated with him in either oral or sign language. A language assessment at three years and nine months indicated that he was well below age level in all aspects of language. Although he attempted to express ideas appropriate to his age, he used unusual, ungrammatical word order.

When Jim began conversational sessions with an adult, his expressive abilities began to improve. By the age of four years and two months most of the unusual speech patterns had disappeared, replaced by language more typical of his age. Jim's younger brother Glenn did not display the same type of language delay. Glenn's linguistic environment was different from Jim's: he had his older brother—not only as a model, but, more importantly as a conversational partner whose interaction allowed Glenn to develop language in a more typical way.

Jim showed very rapid acquisition of English once he began to interact with an adult on a one-to-one basis. The fact that he had failed to acquire language normally prior to this experience suggests that impersonal sources of language such as television or radio alone are not sufficient. One-to-one interaction gives children access to language that is adjusted to their level of comprehension. When a child does not understand, the adult may repeat or paraphrase. The response of the adult may also allow children to find out when their own utterances are understood. Television, for obvious reasons, does not provide such interaction. Even in children's programmes, where simpler language is used and topics are relevant to younger viewers, no immediate adjustment is made for the needs of an individual child. Once children have acquired some language, however, television can be a source of language and cultural information.

Usage-based learning

As more and more research has documented the ways in which children interact with the environment, developmental and cognitive psychologists find further evidence that language acquisition is 'usage-based'. In this view, language acquisition is possible because of children's general cognitive capacities and the vast number of opportunities they have to make connections between the language they hear and what they experience in their environment. Sophisticated electronic recording devices have been used to track and count words and phrases children hear in their daily lives. Deb Roy documented his son's acquisition of words, showing the frequency and the contexts for the occurrence of language. Most remarkable, perhaps, is the demonstration of the power of interaction between the child and the adults and how adults focus on the language the child has begun to use (Roy 2009).

The usage-based perspective on language acquisition differs from the behaviourist view in that the emphasis is more on the child's ability to create networks of associations rather than on processes of imitation and habit formation. Referred to by various names, including **cognitive** linguistics, this view also differs sharply from the innatists' because language acquisition is not seen as requiring a separate 'module of the mind' but rather depends on the child's general learning abilities and the contributions of the environment. As Elena Lieven and Michael Tomasello (2008) put it, 'Children learn language from their language experiences—there is no other way' (p.168). According to this view, what children need to know is essentially available to them in the language they are exposed to.

Some of the early research in this framework was done in the context of **connectionism** and involved computer simulations in which language samples were provided as input to a fairly simple program. The goal was to show that the computer could 'learn' certain things if exposed to enough examples. The program was found to be able to sort out the patterns from the input and even generalize beyond what it was actually exposed to. It even made the same kinds of creative 'mistakes' that children make, such as putting a regular *-ed* ending on an irregular verb, for example, *eated*.

In a usage-based model, language acquisition involves not only associating words with elements of external reality. It is also a process of associating words and phrases with the other words and phrases that occur with them, or words with grammatical morphemes that occur with them. For example, children learning languages in which nouns have grammatical gender learn to associate the appropriate article and adjective forms with nouns. So if children are learning French, they learn that *la* and *une* go with *chaise* (chair) and *le* and *un* go with *livre* (book). Similarly, they learn to associate pronouns with the verb forms that mark person and number—*il aime* (he likes) and *nous aimons* (we like). They also learn which temporal adverbs go with which verb tenses.

Of particular importance to this hypothesis is the fact that children are exposed to many thousands of opportunities to learn words and phrases. Learning takes place gradually, as the number of links between language and meaning and among language forms are built up. For usage-based theorists, acquisition of language, while impressive, is not the only remarkable feat accomplished by the child. They compare it to other cognitive and perceptual learning, including learning to 'see'. That is, the visual abilities that we take for granted, for example, focusing on and interpreting objects in our visual field, are actually learned through experience.

Language disorders and delays

Although most children progress through the stages of language development without significant difficulty or delay, there are some children for whom this is not the case. A discussion of the various types of disabilities (including deafness, articulatory problems, autism, dyslexia, and so on) that sometimes affect language development is outside the scope of this book. It is essential that parents and teachers be encouraged to seek professional advice if they feel that a child is not developing language normally, keeping in mind that the range for 'normal' is wide indeed.

While most children produce recognizable first words by 12 months, some may not speak before the age of three years. In very young children, one way to determine whether delayed language reflects a problem or simply an individual difference within the normal range is to determine whether the child responds to language and appears to understand even if he or she is not speaking.

For older children, delays in learning to read that seem out of keeping with a child's overall cognitive functioning may suggest that there is a specific problem in that domain. Some children seem to begin reading almost by magic, discovering the mysteries of print with little direct instruction. For most children, instruction that includes some systematic attention to sound–letter correspondences allows them to unlock the treasure chest of reading. Both groups fall within a normal range. For some children, however, reading presents such great challenges that they need expert help beyond what is available in a typical classroom.

Childhood bilingualism

The language development of children who learn multiple languages during childhood is of enormous importance throughout the world. Indeed, the majority of the world's children are exposed to more than one language. Some children learn multiple languages from earliest childhood; others acquire additional languages when they go to school. The acquisition and maintenance of more than one language can open doors to many personal, social, and economic opportunities.

Unfortunately, as Jim Cummins (2000) and others have pointed out, children who already know one or more languages and who arrive at their first day of school without an age-appropriate knowledge of the language of the school have often been misdiagnosed as having language delays or disorders. This includes immigrant and minority language children who do not speak the school language at home and children who speak a different variety of the school language. These children's knowledge of a different language or language variety is often incorrectly interpreted as a lack of normal language development and a lack of background knowledge for school subjects. They may be placed in remedial or special education classes because schools are not equipped to provide an adequate assessment of children's ability to use their home language or of their general cognitive abilities or their knowledge of school subjects, learned through another language. Researchers have recently made important progress in providing guidelines that can help educators distinguish between disability and diversity (Paradis, Genesee, and Crago 2011), but much practical work remains to be done so that children can make the most of their cognitive and linguistic abilities.

Children who learn more than one language from earliest childhood are referred to as 'simultaneous bilinguals', whereas those who learn another language later may be called 'sequential bilinguals'. We sometimes hear people express the opinion that it is too difficult for children to cope with two languages. They fear that the children will be confused or will not learn either language well. However, there is little support for the myth that learning more than one language in early childhood is a problem for children who have adequate opportunities to use each one. There is a considerable body of research on children's ability to learn more than one language in their earliest years. Although some studies show minor early delays in one or both languages for simultaneous bilinguals, there is no evidence that learning two languages substantially slows down their linguistic development or interferes with cognitive development.

Indeed, many children attain high levels of proficiency in both languages. Ellen Bialystok (2001) and other cognitive and developmental psychologists have found convincing evidence that achieving bilingual proficiency can have positive effects on abilities that are related to academic success, such as metalinguistic awareness. Limitations that may be observed in the language of bilingual individuals are more likely to be related to the circumstances in which each language is learned than to any limitation in the human capacity to learn more than one language. For example, if one language is heard much more often than the other or is more highly valued in the community, that language may eventually be used better than, or in preference to, the other.

One aspect of bilingual language use is referred to as code switching—the use of words or phrases from more than one language within a conversation. For example, a child who speaks both French and English might say, 'I'm playing with *le château*'. Such switching between languages may sometimes reflect the absence of a particular vocabulary word or expression, but it can just as often be the intentional use of a word from the other language for a variety of interactional purposes. Highly proficient adult bilinguals also code switch when they speak to others who also know both languages. The use of both languages within a bilingual context is not evidence of a lack of proficiency. It may have many different motivations, from expressing solidarity to making a joke. Psychologists have shown that speakers of more than one language are constantly making choices about how to express themselves and that code switching is patterned and often predictable. Indeed, this experience in making choices has been identified as contributing to cognitive flexibility throughout life (Bialystok 2009).

As children learn a second language at school, they need to learn both the variety of language that children use among themselves (and in informal settings with familiar adults) and the variety that is used in academic settings. In his early research on childhood bilingualism, Jim Cummins called these two varieties BICS (basic interpersonal communication skills) and CALP (cognitive academic language proficiency). Characteristics of the two varieties overlap to a certain extent, but there are important differences, not just in the range of vocabulary that each requires but also in the way information is expressed. Mary Schleppegrell (2004) and others have sought to discover what exactly it is that characterizes these varieties of language and the interaction patterns that tend to go with them, and some aspects of the distinction remain controversial. It is widely agreed, however, that the language needed for academic discourse is more difficult for children to acquire than the informal language of day-to-day interaction (Cummins 2000).

Children entering school with little or no knowledge of the language spoken there may acquire BICS within a relatively short time—as little as a year or two. They learn from watching and imitating interactions among their peers and between teachers and students. They make connections between frequently heard words and phrases and the routines and recurring events of the classroom, cafeteria, and playground. For this reason, students are sometimes perceived as 'fluent' in their second language. This can lead teachers to assume that any difficulties in academic tasks are not due to limited language skills but to other causes—from lack of motivation to learning disabilities. More careful observation shows that the students, while fluent in social settings, do not have the CALP skills needed for academic tasks such as understanding a problem in mathematics, defining a word, or writing a science report.

Virginia Collier (1989) found that, for most students, acquiring age-appropriate CALP takes several years. As the second language learner tries to catch up, the children who came to school already speaking the school language are continuing to learn hundreds of new words every year and to learn the concepts that these words represent. If second language learners have limited knowledge of the school language and do not have opportunities to continue learning academic content in a language they already know, it is not surprising that they fall behind in learning the academic subject matter that their peers have continued to develop.

Children need time to develop their second language skills. Many people assume that this means that the best approach is to start learning as early as possible and to avoid the use of the child's previously learned languages. Certainly, it is important for children to begin learning and using the school language as early as possible, but considerable research suggests that continued development of the child's home language actually contributes in the long term to more successful acquisition of the school language. Researchers and educators have expressed concern about situations where children are cut off from their family language when they are very young, spending long hours away from their families in settings where the home language is absent or even forbidden. Lily Wong Fillmore (2000) observed that when children are 'submerged' in a different language for long periods in pre-school or day care, their development of the family language may be slowed down or stalled before they have developed an age-appropriate proficiency in the new language. Eventually they may stop speaking the family language altogether, and this loss of a common language can lead to significant social and psychological problems.

Wallace Lambert (1987) called the loss of one language on the way to learning another **subtractive bilingualism**. It can have negative consequences for children's self-esteem, and their relationships with family members are also likely to be affected by such early loss of the family language. In these cases, children seem to continue to be caught between two languages: they have not yet mastered the school language, and they have not continued to develop the family language. During the transition period, they may fall behind in their academic learning. Unfortunately, the 'solution' educators sometimes propose to parents is that they should stop speaking the family language at home and concentrate instead on speaking the school language with their children.

The research evidence suggests that a better approach is to strive for **additive bilingualism**—the maintenance of the home language while the second language is being learned. This is especially true if the parents are also learners of the second language. If parents continue to use the language that they know best with their children, they are able to express their knowledge and ideas in ways that are richer and more elaborate than they can manage in a language they do not know as well. Using their own language in family settings is also a way for parents to maintain their own self-esteem, especially as they may have their own struggles with the new language outside the home, at work, or in the community. Maintaining the family language also allows children to retain family connections with grandparents or relatives who do not speak the new language. They benefit from the opportunity to continue both cognitive and affective development using a language they understand easily while they are still learning the second language.

Other positive effects of bilingual or multilingual development go beyond those that accrue to the children and their families. Knowledge of more than one language can also increase opportunities for cross-cultural communication and economic cooperation among people. As we have seen, developing a second language takes years. But teachers, parents, and students need to know that the many benefits of additive bilingualism will reward their patience and effort.

Summary

In this chapter we have focused on some of the research on children's early language development that has influenced research on second language acquisition. We have described three broad theoretical perspectives for explaining first language acquisition. In Chapter 2 we will look at some of the findings of research examining the developing language of second language learners.

Questions for reflection

1 Some research has found that the best predictor of children's vocabulary growth is the amount of language addressed to them by their parents and other caregivers. What have you seen in this chapter that is compatible with that finding?

2 Go to the children's section of a library or bookstore and look at the vocabulary used in books that are published for children between three

and six years old. Compare these to books for young readers, aged six to eight. What does this suggest about the importance of continuing to read to children after they have begun to learn to read at school? Finally, look at the language used in textbooks for children at age 10 or 11. What can you conclude about the challenge faced by English language learners entering school at this age?

3 If you are or may be teaching a second language to a group of school-aged learners with different first language backgrounds, can you think of pedagogical tasks/activities in which children can display and use their L1 knowledge to help them learn the second language?

Suggestions for further reading

Berko Gleason, J. and **N. Bernstein-Ratner** (eds.). 2009. *The Development of Language* 7th edn. New York: Allyn and Bacon.

Many of the chapters by leading experts in child language introduce readers to the best-known findings of the past 50 years of research on children's language development. In addition, there are chapters based on new research, using the kinds of technology that have only recently become available. Thus, the rich database created by researchers with notepads, tape recorders, and tools such as the 'wug test' is complemented by studies of the neurological bases of language learning and language use.

Paradis, J., F. Genesee, and **M. B. Crago.** 2011. *Dual Language Development and Disorders: A Handbook on Bilingualism and Second Language Learning* 2nd edn. Baltimore: Paul H. Brookes.

The authors describe language acquisition by children who learn more than one language simultaneously or sequentially, drawing on research from education, psychology, and linguistics. They make the research accessible by their writing style, the inclusion of a glossary of terms, and above all by relating the research to profiles of children who are acquiring their languages in a variety of home, school, and community situations. The authors provide insights into both normal and atypical multilingual development.

Pearson, B. Z. 2008. *Raising a Bilingual Child: A Step-by-Step Guide for Parents.* New York: Living Language (Random House).

Addressing herself mainly to parents, Barbara Zurer Pearson (2008) reviews research from many studies and shows how children become bilingual in many different environments. She also emphasizes the advantages of growing up with a knowledge of more than one language—from the evidence for cognitive flexibility to the benefits of cultural knowledge. Written in an approachable and humorous style, the text is supported by Zurer Pearson's thorough knowledge of the research literature that is included in the bibliography.

2 SECOND LANGUAGE LEARNING

Preview

In this chapter we focus on second language learners' developing knowledge and use of their new language. We begin by looking at the different contexts for first and second language learning as well as the different characteristics of learners in these contexts. We examine some of the errors that learners make and discuss what errors can tell us about their knowledge of the language and their ability to use that knowledge. We look at stages and sequences in the acquisition of some syntactic and morphological features in the second language. We also review some aspects of learners' development of vocabulary, **pragmatics**, and phonology.

ACTIVITY   **Explore contexts for second language learning**

A second language learner is different in many ways from a young child acquiring a first language or an older child learning a second language. This is true in terms of both the learners' characteristics and the environments in which the language acquisition typically occurs. Think about how the characteristics and learning conditions of the following learners may differ:

- a young child learning a first language
- a child learning a second language in day care or on the playground
- an adolescent studying a foreign language in their own country
- an adult immigrant with limited or disrupted education working in a second language environment and having no opportunity to go to language classes.

Now ask yourself the following questions about these different learners.

1 Do they already know at least one language?

2 Are they cognitively mature? Are they able to engage in problem solving, deduction, and complex memory tasks?

3 How well developed is their metalinguistic awareness? Can they define a word, say what sounds make up that word, or state a rule such as 'add an -*s* to form the plural'?

4 How extensive is their general knowledge of the world? Does this knowledge enable them to make good guesses about what a second language interlocutor is probably saying?

5 Are they likely to be anxious about making mistakes and concerned about sounding 'silly' when speaking the language?

6 Does the learning environment allow them to be silent in the early stages of learning, or are they expected to speak from the beginning?

7 Do they have plenty of time available for language learning and plenty of contact with proficient speakers of the language?

8 Do they frequently receive corrective feedback when they make errors in grammar or pronunciation, or do listeners usually overlook these errors and pay attention to the meaning?

9 Do they receive corrective feedback when their meaning is not clear, when they use the wrong word, or when they say something that seems inappropriate or impolite?

10 Is modified input available? That is, do interlocutors adapt their speech so that learners can understand (for example, in terms of speed of delivery, complexity of grammatical structure, or vocabulary)?

Then compare your views with the discussion of learner characteristics and learning conditions below.

Learner characteristics

By definition, all second language learners, regardless of age, have already acquired at least one language. This prior knowledge may be an advantage in the sense that they have an idea of how languages work. On the other hand, knowledge of other languages can lead learners to make incorrect guesses about how the second language works, and this may result in errors that first language learners would not make.

Very young language learners begin the task of first language acquisition without the **cognitive maturity** or metalinguistic awareness that older second language learners have. Although young second language learners have begun to develop these characteristics, they will still have far to go in these areas, as well as in the area of world knowledge, before they reach the levels already attained by adults and adolescents.

Using the chart in Table 2.1, give your opinion about the presence or absence of learner characteristics and learning conditions for the four different learners mentioned above. Use the following notation:

+ = usually present   − = usually absent

? = sometimes present, sometimes absent, or you're not sure

	First language	**Second language**		
	Young child (at home)	Young child (playground)	Adolescent (classroom)	Adult (on the job)
Learner characteristics				
Another language				
Cognitive maturity				
Metalinguistic awareness				
World knowledge				
Anxiety about speaking				
Learning conditions				
Freedom to be silent				
Ample time				
Corrective feedback (grammar and pronunciation)				
Corrective feedback (meaning, word choice, politeness)				
Modified input				

Photocopiable © Oxford University Press

Table 2.1 Contexts for language learning

On the one hand, cognitive maturity and metalinguistic awareness allow older learners to solve problems and engage in discussions about language. This is particularly important for those who are learning language in a classroom, with limited time in contact with the language. On the other hand, some theorists have suggested that the use of these cognitive skills—so valuable for many kinds of tasks—can actually interfere with language acquisition. They argue that successful language acquisition draws on different mental abilities, abilities that are specific to language learning. It has been suggested that older learners draw on their problem-solving and metalinguistic abilities precisely because they can no longer access the innate language acquisition ability they had as young children. We will have more to say about this in Chapter 3, when we discuss the role of age in second language acquisition.

In addition to possible cognitive differences, there are also attitudinal and cultural differences between children and adults. Most child learners are willing to try to use the language—even when their proficiency is quite limited. Many adults and adolescents find it stressful when they are unable to express themselves clearly and correctly. Nevertheless, even very young (pre-school) children differ in their willingness to speak a language they do not know well. Some children happily chatter away in their new language; others prefer to listen and participate silently in social interaction with their peers.

Learning conditions

Young second language learners are often allowed to be silent until they are ready to speak. They may also practise their second language in songs and games that allow them to blend their voices with those of other children. Older second language learners are often forced to speak from the earliest days of their learning, whether to meet the requirements of classroom instruction or to carry out everyday tasks such as shopping, medical visits, or job interviews.

Another way in which younger and older learners may differ is in the amount of time they can actually spend learning a second language. We know that first language learners spend thousands of hours in contact with the language or languages spoken around them. Young second language learners may also be exposed to their second language for many hours every day—in the classroom, on the playground, or in front of the television. Older learners, especially students in foreign language classrooms, receive far less exposure—perhaps only a few hours a week. Indeed, a typical foreign language student will have no more than a few hundred hours of exposure, spread out over a number of years. Adult learners who are immigrants or minority language speakers often continue to use the language they already know as they fulfil their daily responsibilities for work and family, and they may use the second language only in limited situations.

Classroom learners not only spend less time in contact with the new language, they also tend to be exposed to a far smaller range of discourse types. For example, classroom learners are often taught language that is somewhat formal in comparison to the language as it is used in most social settings. In many foreign language classes, teachers may even switch to their students' first language for discipline or classroom management, thus depriving learners of opportunities to experience uses of the language in real communication.

As we saw in Chapter 1, parents tend to respond to the meaning rather than to the grammatical accuracy of their children's language. Similarly, in second language learning outside classrooms, errors that do not interfere with meaning are usually overlooked. Most people would feel they were being impolite if they interrupted and corrected someone who was trying to have a conversation with them. Nevertheless, interlocutors may react to an error if they cannot understand what the speaker is trying to say. Thus, errors of grammar and pronunciation may not be remarked on, but the wrong word choice may receive comment from a puzzled interlocutor. In a situation where a second language speaker appears to use inappropriate language, interlocutors may feel uncomfortable, not knowing whether the speaker intends to be rude or simply does not know the polite way to say what is intended. In this case too, especially between adults, it is unlikely that the second language speaker would be told that something had gone wrong. The only place where feedback on error is typically present with high frequency is the language classroom. Even there, it is not always provided consistently. In Chapters 5 and 6, research on the role of feedback in the classroom will be reviewed.

One condition that appears to be common to learners of all ages—though not in equal quality or quantity—is exposure to modified or adapted input. This adjusted speech style, called child-directed speech in first language acquisition, has sometimes been called **foreigner talk** or **teacher talk** depending on the contexts of second language acquisition. Some people who interact regularly with language learners seem to have an intuitive sense of what adjustments they need to make to help learners understand. Of course, not everyone knows what adjustments will be most helpful. We have all witnessed those painful conversations in which people seem to think that they can make learners understand better if they simply talk louder! Some Canadian friends told us of an experience they had in China. They were visiting some historic temples and wanted to get more information about them than they could glean from a guidebook, so they asked their guide some questions. Unfortunately, their limited Chinese and his non-existent English made it difficult for them to exchange information. The guide kept speaking louder and louder, but our friends understood very little. Finally, in frustration, the guide concluded that it would help if they could see the information, so he took a stick and began writing in the sand—in Chinese characters!

This brief discussion places the emphasis on how both the characteristics of learners and the contexts in which they acquire a second language may be different. In the following pages, we will focus more on similarities in how their knowledge of the new language develops over time.

Studying the language of second language learners

We have seen that children's knowledge of the grammatical system of their first language is built up in predictable sequences. For example, grammatical morphemes such as the *-ing* of the present progressive or the *-ed* of the simple past are not acquired at the same time, but in a sequence. Are there developmental sequences for second language acquisition? How does the prior knowledge of the first language affect the acquisition of the second (or third) language? How does instruction affect second language acquisition? Are there differences in the development of learners whose only contact with the new language is in a classroom and those who use the language in daily life? These are some of the questions researchers have sought to answer, and we will address them in this chapter as well as in Chapters 5 and 6.

Knowing more about the development of learner language helps teachers to assess teaching procedures in the light of what they can reasonably expect to accomplish in the classroom. As we will see, some characteristics of learner language can be quite perplexing if one does not have an overall picture of the steps learners go through in acquiring the second language.

In presenting some of the findings of second language research, we have included a number of examples of learner language as well as some additional samples to give you an opportunity to practise analysing learner language. Of course, teachers analyse learner language all the time. They try to determine whether students have learned what has been taught and how closely their language matches the **target language**. But progress cannot always be measured in these terms. Sometimes language acquisition progress is reflected in a decrease in the use of a correct form that was based on rote memorization or chunk learning. New errors may be based on an emerging ability to generalize a particular grammatical form beyond the specific items with which it was first learned. In this sense, an increase in error may be an indication of progress. For example, like first language learners, second language learners usually learn the irregular past tense forms of certain common verbs before they learn to apply the regular simple past *-ed* marker. That means that a learner who says 'I buyed a bus ticket' may know more about English grammar than one who says 'I bought a bus ticket'. Without further information, we cannot conclude that the one who says 'bought' would use the regular past *-ed* marker where it is appropriate, but the learner who says 'buyed' has provided evidence of developing knowledge of a systematic aspect of English.

Teachers and researchers cannot read learners' minds, so they must infer what learners know by observing what they do. Like those who study first language acquisition, we observe learners' spontaneous language use, but we also design procedures that help to reveal more about the knowledge underlying their observable use of language. Without these procedures, it is often difficult to determine whether a particular behaviour is representative of something systematic in a learner's current language knowledge or simply an isolated item, learned as a chunk.

Like first language learners, second language learners do not learn language simply through imitation and practice. They produce sentences that are not exactly like those they have heard. These new sentences appear to be based on internal cognitive processes and prior knowledge that interact with the language they hear around them. Both first and second language acquisition are best described as developing systems with their own evolving rules and patterns, not simply as imperfect versions of the target language.

Contrastive analysis, error analysis, and interlanguage

Until the late 1960s, people tended to see second language learners' speech simply as an incorrect version of the target language. According to the **contrastive analysis hypothesis** (CAH), errors were assumed to be the result of **transfer** from learners' first language. Detailed analysis of learners' errors revealed, however, that not all errors made by second language learners can be explained in terms of first language transfer alone. A number of studies show that many errors can be explained better in terms of learners' developing knowledge of the structure of the target language rather than an attempt to transfer patterns of their first language (Richards 1974). Furthermore, some of the errors are remarkably similar to those made by young first language learners, for example, the use of a regular -*ed* past tense ending on an irregular verb.

A simplified version of the CAH would predict that, where differences exist, errors would be bi-directional, that is, for example, French speakers learning English and English speakers learning French would make errors on parallel linguistic features. Helmut Zobl (1980) observed that this is not always the case. For example, in simple English sentences, direct objects, whether nouns or pronouns, come after the verb ('The dog eats the cookie. The dog eats it.'). In French, direct objects that are nouns follow the verb (*Le chien mange le biscuit*—literally, 'The dog eats the cookie'). However, direct object pronouns precede the verb (*Le chien le mange*—literally, 'The dog it eats'). The CAH would predict that a native speaker of English might make the error of saying: '*Le chien mange le*' when learning French, and that a native speaker of French might say 'The dog it eats' when learning English. In fact, English speakers learning French are more likely to make the predicted error than French speakers learning English. This may be due to the fact that English speakers learning French hear many examples of sentences with subject–verb–object word order (for example, *Le chien mange le biscuit*) and make the incorrect generalization—based on both the word order of their first language and evidence from the second language—that all direct objects come after the verb. French-speaking learners of English, on the other hand, hearing and seeing no evidence that English direct object pronouns precede verbs, do not tend to use this pattern from their first language.

The finding that many aspects of learners' language could not be explained by the CAH led a number of researchers to take a different approach to analysing learners' errors. This approach, which developed during the 1970s, became known as 'error analysis' and involved detailed descriptions of the errors second language learners made. The goal of this research was to discover what learners really knew about the language. As Pit Corder observed in a famous article published in 1967, when learners produce correct sentences, they may simply be repeating something they have already heard; when they produce sentences that differ from the target language, we may assume that these sentences reflect the learners' current understanding of the rules and patterns of that language. We saw this in the example of a learner who says 'buyed' instead of 'bought.' Error analysis differed from contrastive analysis in that it did not set out to predict errors. Rather, it sought to discover and describe different kinds of errors in an effort to understand how learners process second language data. Error analysis was based on the hypothesis that, like child language, second language learner language is a system in its own right—one that is rule-governed and predictable.

Larry Selinker (1972) gave the name **interlanguage** to learners' developing second language knowledge. Analysis of a learner's interlanguage shows that it has some characteristics influenced by previously learned languages, some characteristics of the second language, and some characteristics, such as the omission of function words and grammatical morphemes, that seem to be general and to occur in all interlanguage systems. Interlanguages have been found to be systematic, but they are also dynamic, continually evolving as learners receive more input and revise their hypotheses about the second language. The path through language acquisition is not necessarily smooth and even. Learners have bursts of progress, then reach a plateau for a while before something stimulates further progress. Selinker also coined the term **fossilization** to refer to the fact that some features in a learner's language seem to stop changing. This may be especially true for learners whose exposure to the second language does not include instruction or the kind of feedback that would help them to recognize differences between their interlanguage and the target language.

ACTIVITY   **Analyse learner language**

The following texts were written by two learners of English, one a French-speaking secondary school student, the other a Chinese-speaking adult learner. Both learners were describing a cartoon film entitled *The Great Toy Robbery* (National Film Board of Canada). After viewing the film, they were asked to retell the story in writing, as if they were telling it to someone who had not seen the film.

Read the texts and answer the following questions:

1 Can you understand what each learner is trying to say?

2 Examine the errors made by each learner. What kinds of errors interfere most with your ability to understand?

3 Do both learners make the same kinds of errors?

4 In what ways do the two interlanguages differ?

Learner 1: French first language, secondary school student
During a sunny day, a cowboy go in the desert with his horse. he has a big hat. His horse eat a flour. In the same time, Santa Clause go in a city to give some surprises. He has a red costume and a red packet of surprises. You have three robbers in the mountain who sees Santa Clause with a king of glaces that it permitted us to see at a long distance. Every robbers have a horse. They go in

the way of Santa Clause, not Santa Clause but his pocket of surprises. After they will go in a city and they go in a saloon. [...]
(Unpublished data from P. M. Lightbown and B. Barkman)

Learner 2: Chinese first language, adult
This year Christmas comes soon! Santa Claus ride a one horse open sleigh to sent present for children. on the back of his body has big packet. it have a lot of toys. in the way he meet three robbers. They want to take his big packet. Santa Claus no way and no body help, so only a way give them, then three robbers ride their horse dashing through the town. There have saloon, they go to drink some beer and open the big packent. They plays toys in the Bar. They meet a cow boy in the saloon.

(Unpublished data provided by M. J. Martens)

Perhaps the most striking thing here is that many error types are common to both learners. Furthermore, both make errors of spelling and punctuation that we might find in the writing of a young first language speaker of English. Even though French uses grammatical morphemes to indicate person and number on verbs and Chinese does not, both these learners make errors of subject–verb agreement—both leaving off the third person *-s* marker and overusing it when the subject is plural ('a cowboy go' and 'three robbers in the mountain who sees' by Learner 1 and 'Santa Claus ride' and 'they plays' by Learner 2). Such errors reflect learners' understanding of the second language system itself rather than an attempt to transfer characteristics of their first language. They are sometimes referred to as 'developmental' errors because they are similar to those made by children acquiring English as their first language. Sometimes these are errors of overgeneralization, that is, errors caused by trying to use a rule in a context where it does not belong, for example, the *-s* ending on the verb in 'they plays'. Sometimes the errors are better described as simplification, where elements of a sentence are left out or where all verbs have the same form regardless of person, number, or tense.

One can also see, especially in Learner 2's text, the influence of classroom experience. An example is the use of formulaic expressions such as 'one horse open sleigh' which is taken verbatim from a well-known Christmas song that had been taught and sung in his English as a Second Language (ESL) class. The vivid 'dashing through the town' probably comes from the same source, with the substitution of 'town' for 'snow'.

For those who are familiar with the English spoken by native speakers of French, some of the errors (for example, preposition choice 'in the same time') made by the first learner will be seen as probably based on French. Similarly, those familiar with the English of Chinese speakers may recognize some word order patterns (for example, 'on the back of his body has big packet') as based on Chinese patterns. These may be called transfer or 'interference' errors. What is most clear, however, is that it is often difficult to determine the source of errors. Thus, while error analysis has the advantage of describing *what* learners actually do rather than what they might do, it does not always give us clear insights into *why* they do it. Furthermore, as Jacquelyn Schachter pointed out in a 1974 article, learners sometimes avoid using some features of language that they perceive to be difficult for them. This avoidance may lead to the absence of certain errors, leaving the analyst without information about some aspects of the learners' developing interlanguage. The absence of particular errors is difficult to interpret, and the phenomenon of 'avoidance' may itself be a part of the learner's systematic second language performance.

Developmental sequences

Second language learners, like first language learners, pass through sequences of development: what is learned early by one is learned early by others.

Among first language learners, the existence of developmental sequences may not seem surprising because their language learning is partly tied to their cognitive development and to their experiences in learning about relationships between people, events, and objects around them. But the cognitive development of adult or adolescent second language learners is much more stable, and their experiences with the language are likely to be quite different, not only from the experiences of a small child, but also different from each other. Furthermore, second language learners already know another language that has different patterns for creating sentences and word forms. In light of this, it is more remarkable that we find developmental sequences that are similar in the developing interlanguage of learners from different language backgrounds and also similar to those observed in first language acquisition of the same language. Moreover, the features of the language that are most frequent are not always learned first. For example, virtually every English sentence has one or more articles ('a' or 'the'), but even advanced learners have difficulty using these forms correctly in all contexts. Finally, although the learner's first language does have an influence, many aspects of these developmental stages are similar among learners from different first language backgrounds.

In Chapter 1 we saw some developmental sequences for English first language acquisition of grammatical morphemes, negation, and questions. Researchers in second language acquisition have also examined these, as well as other features. They have found patterns in the development of syntax and morphology that are similar among learners from different language backgrounds. Evidence for these developmental patterns first came from studies of learners whose primary learning environment was outside the classroom. For example, Jürgen Meisel, Harald Clahsen, and Manfred Pienemann

(1981) identified developmental sequences in the acquisition of German by speakers of several Romance languages who had little or no instruction.

Subsequent research has shown that learners who receive instruction exhibit similar developmental sequences and error patterns. In the interlanguage of English speakers whose only exposure to German was in university classes in Australia, Pienemann (1988) found patterns that were similar to those of the uninstructed learners. In Chapter 6, we will discuss other studies that have investigated the influence of instruction on developmental sequences.

Grammatical morphemes

Researchers have examined the development of grammatical morphemes by learners of English as a second language in a variety of environments, at different ages, and from different first language backgrounds. In analysing each learner's speech, researchers identify the **obligatory contexts** for each morpheme, that is, the places in a sentence where the morpheme is necessary to make the sentence grammatically correct. For example, in the sentence 'Yesterday I play baseball for two hours', the adverb 'yesterday' creates an obligatory context for a past tense, and 'for two hours' tells us that the required form is a simple past ('played') rather than a past progressive ('was playing'). Similarly, 'two' creates an obligatory context for a plural -*s* on 'hours'.

For the analysis, obligatory contexts for each grammatical morpheme are counted separately, that is, one count for simple past, one for plural, one for third person singular present tense, and so on. After counting the number of obligatory contexts, the researcher counts the correctly supplied morphemes. The next step is to divide the number of correctly supplied morphemes by the total number of obligatory contexts to answer the question 'what is the percentage accuracy for each morpheme?' An accuracy score is created for each morpheme, and these can then be ranked from highest to lowest, giving an **accuracy order** for the morphemes.

The overall results of the studies suggested an order that was similar but not identical to the developmental sequence found for first language learners. However, the order the researchers found was quite similar among second language learners from different first language backgrounds. For example, most studies showed a higher degree of accuracy for plural -*s* than for posses-sive -'*s*, and for -*ing* than for regular past (-*ed*). Stephen Krashen summarized the order as shown in Figure 2.1. The diagram should be interpreted as showing that learners will produce the morphemes in higher boxes with higher accuracy than those in lower boxes, but that within boxes, there is no clear pattern of difference.

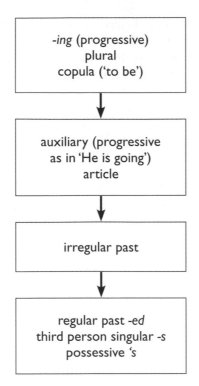

Figure 2.1 Krashen's (1982) summary of second language grammatical morpheme acquisition sequence

The similarity among learners suggests that the accuracy order cannot be described or explained in terms of transfer from the learners' first language, and some researchers saw this as strong evidence against the CAH. However, a thorough review of all the 'morpheme acquisition' studies shows that the learners' first language does have an influence on acquisition sequences. For example, learners whose first language has a possessive form that resembles the English *'s* (such as German and Danish) seem to acquire the English possessive earlier than those whose first language has a very different way of forming the possessive (such as French or Spanish). And even though articles appear early in the sequence, learners from many language backgrounds (including Slavic languages, Chinese, and Japanese) continue to struggle with this aspect of English, even at advanced levels. Learners may do well in supplying articles in certain obligatory contexts but not others. If the language sample that is analysed contains only the 'easier' obligatory contexts, the learner may have a misleadingly high accuracy score.

Another reason why something as difficult as English articles appears to be acquired early is that the order in the diagram is based on the analysis of correct use in obligatory contexts only. It does not take into account uses of grammatical morphemes in places where they do not belong, for example, when a learner says, 'The France is in Europe'. These issues led researchers to question the adequacy of obligatory context analyses as the sole basis for understanding developmental sequences. Teresa Pica (1983) argued that accuracy scores should take account of overuse and incorrect uses to determine a score for target-like use rather than reflect only use in obligatory contexts.

The morpheme acquisition literature raises other issues, not least of them the question of why there should be an order of acquisition for these language features. Some of the similarities observed in different studies seemed to be due to the use of particular tasks for collecting the data, and researchers found that different tasks tended to yield different results. Nevertheless, a number of studies have revealed similarities that cannot be explained by the data collection procedures alone. As with first language acquisition, researchers have not found a single simple explanation for the order. Jennifer Goldschneider and Robert DeKeyser (2001) reviewed this research and identified a number of **variables** that contribute to the order. Salience (how easy it is to notice the morpheme), linguistic complexity (for example, how many elements you have to keep track of), semantic transparency (how clear the meaning is), similarity to a first language form, and frequency in the input all seem to play a role.

Negation

The acquisition of negative sentences by second language learners follows a path that looks nearly identical to the stages we saw in Chapter 1 for first language acquisition. However, second language learners from different first language backgrounds behave somewhat differently within those stages. This was illustrated in John Schumann's (1979) research with Spanish speakers learning English and Henning Wode's (1978) work on German speakers learning English.

Stage 1
The negative element (usually 'no' or 'not') is typically placed before the verb or the element being negated. Often, it occurs as the first word in the sentence because the subject is not there.

> No bicycle.
> I no like it.
> Not my friend.

'No' is preferred by most learners in this early stage, perhaps because it is the negative form that is easiest to hear and recognize in the speech they are exposed to. Italian- and Spanish-speaking learners may prefer 'no' because it corresponds to the negative form in Italian and Spanish (*No tienen muchos libros*). They may continue to use Stage 1 negation longer than other learners because of the similarity to a pattern from their first language. Even at more advanced stages, they may also use Stage 1 negatives in longer sentences or when they are under pressure. Thus, similarity to a learner's first language may slow down a learner's progress through a particular developmental stage.

Stage 2

At this stage, 'no' and 'not' may alternate with 'don't'. However, 'don't' is not marked for person, number, or tense and it may even be used before modals like 'can' and 'should'.

> He don't like it.
> I don't can sing.

Stage 3

Learners begin to place the negative element after auxiliary verbs like 'are', 'is', and 'can'. But at this stage, the 'don't' form is still not fully analysed.

> You can not go there.
> He was not happy.
> She don't like rice.

At this stage, German speakers, whose first language has a structure that places the negative after the verb may generalize the auxiliary–negative pattern to verb–negative and produce sentences such as:

> They come not [to] home. (*Sie kommen nicht nach Hause.*)

Stage 4

In this stage, 'do' is marked for tense, person, and number, and most interlanguage sentences appear to be just like those of the target language.

> It doesn't work. We didn't have supper.

However, some learners continue to mark tense, person, and number on both the auxiliary and the verb.

> I didn't went there.

Questions

Manfred Pienemann, Malcolm Johnston, and Geoff Brindley (1988) described a sequence in the acquisition of questions by learners of English from a variety of first language backgrounds. An adapted version of the sequence is shown in Stages 1–6 below. The examples (except those in Stage 6) come from French speakers who were playing a game in which they had to ask questions in order to find out which picture the other player (the researcher) was holding. As we saw for negation, the overall sequence is similar to the one observed in first language acquisition. And again, there are some differences that are attributable to first language influence.

Stage 1

Single words, formulae, or sentence fragments.

> Dog?
> Four children?
> What's that?

Stage 2
Declarative word order, no inversion, no fronting.

> It's a monster in the right corner?
> The boys throw the shoes?

Declarative order with rising intonation is common in yes/no questions in informal spoken French. French speakers may hypothesize that in English, as in French, inversion is optional.

Stage 3
Fronting: *do*-fronting, *wh*-fronting without inversion, other fronting.

> Do you have a shoes on your picture?
> Where the children are playing?
> Does in this picture there is four astronauts?
> Is the picture has two planets on top?

French has an invariant form *est-ce que* (literally 'is it that') that can be placed before a declarative sentence to make a question. For example, *Jean aime le cinéma* becomes *Est-ce que Jean aime le cinéma*? ('is it that) John likes movies?' French speakers may think that 'do' or 'does' is such an invariant form and continue to produce Stage 3 questions for some time.

Stage 4
Inversion in *wh-* + copula; *yes/no* questions with other auxiliaries.

> Where is the sun?
> Is there a fish in the water?

At Stage 4, German speakers may infer that if English uses subject–auxiliary inversion, it may also permit inversion with full verbs, as German does, leading them to produce questions such as 'Like you baseball?' (*Magst du baseball?*)

Stage 5
Inversion in *wh-* questions with both an auxiliary and a main verb.

> How do you say 'proche'?
> What's the boy doing?

French-speaking learners may have difficulty using Stage 5 questions in which the subject is a noun rather than a pronoun. They may say (and accept as grammatical) 'Why do you like chocolate?' but not 'Why do children like chocolate?' In this, they are drawing on French, where it is often ungrammatical to use inversion with a noun subject (*Pourquoi aiment les enfants le chocolat?*).

Stage 6
Complex questions.

> question tag: It's better, isn't it?
> negative question: Why can't you go?
> embedded question: Can you tell me what the date is today?

Pienemann's developmental sequence for questions has been the basis for a number of studies, some of which will be discussed in Chapter 6. Alison Mackey and her colleagues have done a number of these studies, and she provided the data in Table 2.2. These examples come from three adult Japanese learners of English as a second language who were interacting with a native speaker in a 'spot the differences' task. In this task, learners have similar but not identical pictures and they have to ask questions until they work out how the picture they can see is different from the one their interlocutor has. Note that progress to a higher stage does not always mean that learners produce fewer errors.

ACTIVITY   **Analyse learners' questions**

Using the information about the developmental sequence for questions, circle the stage of second language question development that best corresponds to each question.

(Hint: Read all of each learner's questions before you begin.)

	Stage
Learner 1	
1 Where is he going and what is he saying?	1 2 3 4 5 6
2 Is the room his room?	1 2 3 4 5 6
3 Is he taking out his skate board?	1 2 3 4 5 6
4 What is he thinking?	1 2 3 4 5 6
5 The girl, what do you, what does she do, what is she doing?	1 2 3 4 5 6
Learner 2	
6 Are they buying some things?	1 2 3 4 5 6
7 Is they bought present?	1 2 3 4 5 6

8 Is they're retirement people?	1 2 3 4 5 6
9 Is this perfume or … I don't know.	1 2 3 4 5 6
10 And it is necktie?	1 2 3 4 5 6
Learner 3	
11 Are there any shuttle? Space shuttle?	1 2 3 4 5 6
12 Inside, is there any girl?	1 2 3 4 5 6
13 You don't see?	1 2 3 4 5 6
14 What are, what the people wearing?	1 2 3 4 5 6
15 And they are carrying pink box?	1 2 3 4 5 6

Answer key

Learner 1: Questions 1, 4, and 5 are Stage 5 questions. Question 5 is interesting because it shows the speaker self-correcting, suggesting that Stage 5 is still a level that requires some greater effort. Questions 2 and 3 are Stage 4 questions.

Learner 2: Questions 6 and 9 could be Stage 4 questions. However, the fact that questions 7 and 8 are Stage 3 questions suggests that this speaker has not actually progressed from 'fronting' to 'inversion', particularly since question 10 is a Stage 2 question.

Learner 3: Questions 11 and 12 are Stage 4 questions. Questions 13 and 15 are Stage 2 questions. Question 14 shows the speaker apparently on the verge of a Stage 5 question, then retreating to a Stage 3 question.

Photocopiable © Oxford University Press

Table 2.2 Questions by Japanese-speaking learners of English

Possessive determiners

A developmental sequence for the English possessive forms 'his' and 'her' has been observed in the interlanguage of French- and Spanish-speaking learners. In English, the choice of 'his' or 'her' (or 'its') is determined by the natural gender of the possessor. In French and Spanish (and many other languages), the correct form of the possessive determiner matches the grammatical gender of the object or person that is possessed. This can be illustrated with the following translation equivalents for French and English:

Sa mère = his mother or her mother
Son chien = his dog or her dog
Ses enfants = his children or her children

Note that when the object possessed is a body part, French typically uses a definite article rather than a possessive determiner.

Il s'est cassé le bras = He broke the [his] arm.

Joanna White (1998, 2008) studied the acquisition of possessive determiners by French-speaking students, adapting a developmental sequence that was first proposed by Helmut Zobl (1984). White found a total of eight stages in the sequence, but they can be grouped into three main stages. The examples shown below come from French-speaking students learning English. They are describing cartoon drawings of family events and interactions.

Stage 1: Pre-emergence
No use of 'his' and 'her'. Definite article or 'your' used for all persons, genders, and numbers.

> The little boy play with the bicycle.
> He have band-aid on the arm, the leg, the stomach.
> This boy cry in the arm of your mother.
> There is one girl talk with your dad.

Stage 2: Emergence
Emergence of 'his' and/or 'her', with a strong preference to use only one of the forms.

> The mother is dressing her little boy, and she put her clothes, her pant, her coat, and then she finish.
> The girl making hisself beautiful. She put the make-up on his hand, on his head, and his father is surprise.

Stage 3: Post-emergence
Differentiated use of 'his' and 'her' but not when the object possessed has natural gender.

> The girl fell on her bicycle. She look his father and cry.
> The dad put her little girl on his shoulder, and after, on his back.

At the end of the post-emergence stage, in what White (2008) calls Stage 8, learners finally achieve error-free use of 'his' and 'her' in all contexts including natural gender and body parts.

> The little girl with her dad play together. And the dad take his girl on his shoulder and he hurt his back.

When English speakers learn French, or other languages that use grammatical gender as the basis for choosing possessive determiners, they must also learn a new way of determining the gender of the possessive determiner. The need to learn the grammatical gender of each and every noun further adds to the challenge.

Relative clauses

Second language learners first acquire relative clauses that refer to nouns in the subject and direct object positions, and only later (and in some cases, never) learn to use them to modify nouns in other sentence roles (for example, indirect object and object of preposition). A summary of the observed pattern of acquisition for relative clauses is shown in Table 2.3. It is referred to as the **accessibility hierarchy**, and it reflects the apparent ease with which learners have access to certain structures in the target language.

Part of speech	Relative clause
Subject	The girl who was sick went home.
Direct object	The story that I read was long.
Indirect object	The man who[m] Susan gave the present to was happy.
Object of preposition	I found the book that John was talking about.
Possessive	I know the woman whose father is visiting.
Object of comparison	The person that Susan is taller than is Mary.

Photocopiable © Oxford University Press

Table 2.3 Accessibility hierarchy for relative clauses in English (adapted from Doughty 1991)

Unlike the study of grammatical morphemes, negation, and questions, the study of relative clauses was not inspired by research on child language. Rather, it came from patterns that Edward Keenan and Bernard Comrie (1977) observed in a large number of languages. They found that those languages that included the structures at the bottom of the list in Table 2.3 would also have those at the top, but the opposite was not necessarily true. Subsequently, Susan Gass (1982) and others found that if a second language learner could use one of the structures at the bottom of the list, he or she would probably be able to use any that precede it. On the other hand, a learner who could produce sentences with relative clauses in the subject or direct object positions (at the top of the list) would not necessarily be able to use them in any of the clause types further down the list.

Despite the similarity of the general pattern, several types of first language influence have also been observed in the acquisition of relative clauses. First, it has been observed that for learners whose first language does not have a particular clause type (for example, object of comparison), it is more difficult to learn to use that type in English. Second, where learners have a first language with a substantially different way of forming relative clauses (for example, Chinese and Japanese, where the relative clause precedes the noun it modifies), they may avoid using relative clauses even when their interlanguage is fairly advanced. Third, first language influence is seen in the errors learners make. For example, Arabic speakers often produce both the relative marker and the pronoun it replaces (for example, 'The man who I saw him was very angry') as they would in Arabic.

Reference to past

A number of researchers, including Jürgen Meisel (1987), have observed the developing ability to use language to locate events in time. The research has shown that learners from different first language backgrounds and acquiring a variety of second languages, acquire the language for referring to past events in a similar pattern.

Like young children, learners with limited language may simply refer to events in the order in which they occurred or mention a time or place to show that the event occurred in the past.

> Viet Nam. We work too hard.
> My son come. He work in restaurant.

Later, learners start to attach a grammatical morpheme marking the verb for past, although it may not be the one that the target language uses for that meaning.

> Me working long time. Now stop.

Past tense forms of irregular verbs may be used before the regular past is used reliably.

> We went to school every day. We spoke Spanish.

After they begin marking past tense on regular verbs, learners may overgeneralize the regular *-ed* ending or the use of the wrong past tense form (for example, the present perfect rather than the simple past).

> My sister catched a big fish.
> She has lived here since fifteen years.

Kathleen Bardovi-Harlig (2000) and others have found that learners are more likely to mark past tense in sentences such as 'I broke the vase' and 'My sister fixed it with glue' than in sentences such as 'She seemed happy last week' or 'My father swam in that lake'. These differences appear to be due to the 'lexical aspect', that is, the kinds of meanings expressed by the different verbs. Learners seem to find it easier to mark past tense on verbs that refer to something whose end point can easily be determined. These are referred to as 'accomplishments' and 'achievements' ('I ran three miles.' 'My brother took an aspirin and went to bed'). For 'activities' that may continue for some period ('I swam all afternoon') or 'states' that may be perceived as constants ('He seemed happy to sit by the lake'), learners use simple past markers less frequently.

First language can have an influence here too. Laura Collins (2002) investigated the different English verb forms used by French speakers. The past tense that is most commonly used in spoken French and that is usually a translation of a simple past form in English is a form that resembles the present perfect in English. Thus, the equivalent of 'Yesterday he ate an apple' is *Hier il a mangé une pomme*—literally, 'Yesterday he has eaten an apple'. Teachers often comment on French speakers' tendency to overuse the present perfect. In Collins' study, learners completed passages by filling in blanks with the appropriate form of a verb. As expected, in places where English speakers would use the simple past, French speakers did sometimes use the perfect (either present perfect or past perfect) forms. Furthermore, they used them more frequently than a comparison group of Japanese speakers. However, the French speakers were more likely to use perfect forms for achievement and accomplishment verbs than for the states and activities. Collins observes, 'The [first language] influence does not appear to override the effect of lexical aspect; rather it occurs within it' (p. 85).

Movement through developmental sequences

We have seen in this section that, as in first language acquisition, there are systematic and predictable developmental sequences in second language acquisition. However, it is important to emphasize that developmental stages are not like closed rooms. Learners do not leave one behind when they enter another. In examining a language sample from an individual learner, one should not expect to find behaviours from only one stage. On the contrary, at a given point in time, learners may use sentences typical of several different stages. It is perhaps better to think of a stage as being characterized by the emergence and increasing frequency of new forms rather than by the complete disappearance of earlier ones. Even when a more advanced stage comes to dominate in a learner's speech, conditions of stress or complexity in a communicative interaction can cause the learner to slip back to an earlier stage.

In addition, as we have already noted, progress to a higher stage does not always mean fewer errors. For example, a learner may produce correct questions at Stage 1 or Stage 3, but those correct forms are not necessarily based on underlying knowledge of subject–verb inversion. That is, correct questions at Stage 1 are formulaic chunks, not sentences that have been constructed from the words that make them up. At Stage 2, learners have advanced, in the sense that they are forming original questions, but the word order of those questions is not grammatical in the target language. At Stage 3, questions are formed by placing a question form (most often a *wh-* word or a form of the verb 'do') at the beginning of a sentence with declarative word order. This may result in questions such as 'Do you want to go?' that conform to English patterns. However, when the learner asks a question such as 'Do you can help me?' we can see that the learner's interlanguage rule really is something like 'Put a question word at the beginning of the sentence.'

Another important observation about developmental sequences is the way they interact with first language influence. Learners do not appear to assume that they can simply transfer the structures of their first language into the second. Rather, as Henning Wode (1978) and Helmut Zobl (1980) observed, when they reach a developmental stage at which they perceive a 'crucial similarity' between their first language and their interlanguage, they may generalize their first language pattern and end up making errors that speakers of other languages are less likely to make. They may also have difficulty moving beyond that stage if their errors do not interfere with communication.

More about first language influence

One reason that some researchers rejected the hypothesis that 'transfer' or 'interference' would best explain a learner's difficulties with the target language was the fact that contrastive analysis was closely associated with behaviourist views of language acquisition. In rejecting behaviourism, some researchers also discarded contrastive analysis. In doing so, they potentially lost an essential source of information about language acquisition.

Researchers at the European Science Foundation carried out a study that created some valuable opportunities to examine the influence of the first language on second language learning. Adult language learners, most of whom had little or no second language instruction, were followed as they learned another European language. For each target language, learners from two different first language backgrounds were compared. Also, for each first language background, the progress of learners in their acquisition of the two target languages was studied. As Wolfgang Klein and Clive Perdue (1993) report, there were substantial similarities in the interlanguage patterns of the learners, in spite of the great variety in the first and second language combinations. The similarities were greatest in the earliest stages of second language acquisition, when learners produced similar simple sentences.

There is no doubt that learners draw on the patterns of other languages they know as they try to discover the complexities of the new language they are learning. The patterns of those earlier languages are firmly established, and as learners have experience with the new language, there is an interplay between the new and old patterns. As Nick Ellis (2009: 153) put it, 'The language calculator has no "clear" button.' In learning something new, we build on what we already know.

We have seen some ways in which the first language interacts with developmental sequences. When learners reach a certain stage and perceive a similarity to their first language, they may linger longer at that stage (for example, the extended use of preverbal 'no' by Spanish speakers) or add a sub-stage (for example, the German speaker's inversion of subject and lexical verbs in questions) to the sequence which, overall, is similar across learners, regardless of their first language. They may learn a second language rule but restrict its application (for example, the French speaker's rejection of subject–auxiliary inversion with noun subjects that we saw in Stage 5 questions on page 50).

The first language may influence learners' interlanguage in other ways as well. As we saw earlier, the phenomenon of avoidance that Jacquelyn Schachter (1974) described appeared to be caused at least in part by learners' perception that a feature in the target language was so distant and different from their first language that they preferred not to try it.

Other researchers have also found evidence of learners' sensitivity to degrees of distance or difference and a reluctance to attempt a transfer when they perceive the languages as too different. In one revealing study, Håkan Ringbom (1986) found that the interference errors made in English by both Finnish–Swedish and Swedish–Finnish bilinguals were most often traceable to Swedish, not Finnish. The fact that Swedish and English are closely related languages that actually do share many characteristics seems to have led learners to take a chance that a word or a sentence structure that worked in Swedish would have an English equivalent. Finnish, on the other hand, belongs to a completely different language family, and whether their own first language was Swedish or Finnish, learners appeared reluctant to draw on Finnish in learning English.

The risk-taking associated with this perception of similarity has its limits, however. For example, Eric Kellerman (1986) observed that learners often believe that idiomatic or metaphorical uses of words are unique to a particular language. Kellerman found that Dutch learners of English were reluctant to accept that certain idiomatic expressions or unusual uses of words were also possible in English. For example, they rejected 'The wave broke on the shore' but accepted 'He broke the cup' even though both are straightforward translations of sentences with the Dutch verb *breken*.

Another way in which learners' first languages can affect second language acquisition is by making it difficult for them to notice that something they are saying is not a feature of the language as it is used by more proficient speakers. Lydia White (1991) gave the example of adverb placement in French and English. Both languages allow adverbs in several positions in simple sentences. However, as the examples in Table 2.4 show, there are some differences. English, but not French, allows SAVO order; French, but not English, allows SVAO.

S = Subject V = Verb O = Object A = Adverb
ASVO Often, Mary drinks tea. *Souvent, Marie boit du thé.*
SVOA Mary drinks tea often. *Marie boit du thé souvent.*
SAVO Mary often drinks tea. **Marie souvent boit du thé.*
SVAO *Mary drinks often tea. *Marie boit souvent du thé.*
Note: The asterisk (*) means that the sentence is not grammatical.

Table 2.4 Adverb placement in French and English

It seems fairly easy for French-speaking learners of English to add SAVO to their repertoire and for English-speaking learners of French to add SVAO, but both groups have difficulty getting rid of a pattern that does not occur in the target language if it is similar to one in their first language. English-speaking learners of French continue to accept SAVO as grammatical, and French-speaking learners of English accept SVAO. As White points out, it is difficult to notice that something is not present in the input, especially when its translation equivalent sounds perfectly all right and communication is not disrupted. This may be even more challenging when learners interact with others from the same first language background. Their own errors are not likely to cause misunderstanding and, in fact, they may hear others make the same errors. We will return to this when we look at the role of instruction and feedback on errors in Chapters 5 and 6.

Our understanding of the relationship between first- and later-learned languages has been refined in recent decades. The term **cross-linguistic influence** is now often used, in part to reflect the fact that the relationship is by no means unidirectional. That is, as we acquire a second or third language, the patterns that we learn can also have an impact on the way we use and understand the language(s) we learned earlier. Current views of second language development emphasize the interaction between the first language (or other previously learned languages), cognitive processes, and the samples of the target language that learners encounter in the input. As extensive reviews by Terence Odlin (2003) and Scott Jarvis and Aneta Pavlenko (2008) show, the complexity of this relationship has inspired scores of investigations.

So far this chapter has focused on the acquisition of morphology and syntax in the second language. We now turn to the learning of some other important components of **communicative competence**: vocabulary, pragmatics, and pronunciation.

Vocabulary

In 1980, Paul Meara characterized vocabulary learning as a 'neglected aspect of language learning'. Researchers in the 1970s and early 1980s were drawn to syntax and morphology because of the way error patterns and developmental sequences of these features might reveal something about universals in languages and language acquisition. How different things are now! Just as Meara was commenting on the state of neglect, an explosion of research on vocabulary learning was beginning, and the acquisition of vocabulary has become one of the most active areas in second language acquisition research.

For most people, the importance of vocabulary seems very clear. As it has often been remarked, we can communicate by using words that are not placed in the proper order, pronounced perfectly, or marked with the proper grammatical morphemes, but communication often breaks down if we do not use the correct word. Although circumlocution and gestures can sometimes compensate, the importance of vocabulary can hardly be overestimated.

The challenge of acquiring a large enough vocabulary for successful communication in a variety of settings has been the focus of much recent research. Every language has an astonishingly large number of words. English, which has built its vocabulary from a great variety of source languages, is variously estimated to have anywhere from 100,000 to one million words, depending in part on how words are counted. For example, some would treat 'teach, teacher, teaching, and taught' as separate words while others would count all of them as part of one 'word'—a single root from which the others are derived.

An educated adult speaker of English is believed to know at least 20,000 words; some estimates suggest a number that is more than twice that. But most everyday conversation requires a far smaller number, something more like 2,000 words. Similarly, although Chinese and Japanese have tens of thousands of characters, most are rare, and non-technical material can usually be read with a knowledge of about 2,000 characters. Even so, acquiring a basic vocabulary is a significant accomplishment for a second language learner.

As we saw in Chapter 1, children learn thousands of words in their first language with little observable effort. The task of acquiring a large vocabulary is quite different for second language learners. For one thing, they are likely to be exposed to far smaller samples of the language to be learned. Also, the contexts in which second language learners encounter new vocabulary may not be as helpful as those in which children learn the first one or two thousand words of their first language. If they are older children or adults, the words they are exposed to may be more difficult, referring to meanings that are not easily guessed from context. Marcella Hu and Paul Nation (2000) showed that, in order to understand a text without frequent stops to consult a dictionary, one needs to know more than 95 per cent of the words—a rare case for second language learners at most stages of acquisition. Although the two or three thousand most frequent words in English make up as much as 80–90 per cent of most non-technical texts, less frequent words are crucial to the meaning of many things we hear and read. For example, the meaning of a newspaper article about a court case may be lost without the knowledge of words such as 'testimony', 'alleged', or 'accomplice'.

The first step in knowing a word is simply to recognize that it is a word. Paul Meara and his colleagues (2005) have developed tests that take advantage of this fact. Some of these tests take the form of word lists, and learners are instructed to check 'yes' or 'no' according to whether or not they know the word. Each list also includes some items that look like English words but are not. The number of real words that the learner identifies is adjusted for guessing by a factor that takes account of the number of non-words that are also chosen. Such a procedure is more effective than it might sound. A carefully constructed list can be used to estimate the vocabulary size of even advanced learners. For example, if shown the following list: 'frolip, laggy, scrule, and 'albeit', a proficient speaker of English would know that only one of these words is a real English word, albeit a rare and somewhat odd one. On the other hand, even proficient speakers might recognize none of the following items: 'goniometer, micelle, laminitis, throstle'. Even our computer's spell-checker rejected two out of four, but all are real English words, according to the *New Oxford Dictionary of American English*.

Among the factors that make new vocabulary more easily learnable by second language learners is the frequency with which the word is seen, heard, and understood. Paul Nation (2001) reviews a number of studies suggesting that a learner needs to have many meaningful encounters with a new word before it becomes firmly established in memory. The estimates range as high as 16 times in some studies. Even more encounters may be needed before a learner can retrieve the word in fluent speech or automatically understand the meaning of the word when it occurs in a new context. The ability to understand the meaning of most words without focused attention is essential for fluent reading as well as for fluent speaking.

Frequency is not the only factor that determines how easily words are learned, however, as illustrated by the words in the three lists shown in Table 2.5.

List 1	List 2	List 3
friend	hamburger	government
more	Coke	responsibility
town	T-shirt	dictionary
book	Facebook	elementary
hunt	taxi	remarkable
sing	pizza	description
box	hotel	expression
smile	dollar	international
eye	Internet	dénouement
night	disco	entente

Photocopiable © Oxford University Press

Table 2.5 English words that may be 'easy' or 'difficult' for second language learners

All of the words in List 1 look easy because they are simple one-syllable words that refer to easily illustrated actions or objects. They are also quite common words in English, appearing among the 1,000 most frequent words. And yet, they are not likely to be known to students who have not had previous instruc-tion in English or exposure to the language outside school. Furthermore, there is nothing in the written form or the pronunciation of the words them-selves that gives a clue to their meaning. If students are to learn them, they must see or hear the words in contexts that reveal their meaning, and, as a rule, they must do this many times before the link between a word and its meaning is well established.

On the other hand, some students who have never studied English might already know words in List 2, because they are part of an international vocabulary. With increasing internationalization of communications, many languages have 'borrowed' and adapted words from other languages. Students throughout the world may be surprised to learn how many words they already know in the language they are trying to learn.

The words in List 3 look difficult. They are rather long, not easily illustrated, and most are fairly infrequent in the language. However, many students would either 'know' them on sight or learn them after a single exposure because they look like their translation equivalent in other languages that they already know. Some, such as 'nation' and 'dictionary', are **cognates** (words that have come from the same original root); others, such as 'dénoue-ment' and 'entente', are borrowed words (words that have been adopted from other languages). These words that look alike and have shared meaning can help learners expand their vocabulary.

Teachers should not assume that students will always recognize borrowed words or cognates in their second language. Some cognates are identical in form and meaning, while others may require some knowledge of how spell-ing patterns are related in the two languages (for example, 'water' and *Wasser* in English and German respectively or 'music' and *musique* in English and French). Even with different spellings, words are likely to be easier to recog-nize in their written form than they are in the spoken language. Learners may need guidance in recognizing them, as illustrated in the following question, asked by an eight-year-old in a Quebec hockey arena: '*Hé coach, comment on dit 'coach' en anglais?*' ('Hey, coach. How do you say '*coach*' in English?'). And after a moment's reflection, English speakers may realize that they know both speciality items in a Japanese restaurant that calls itself 'Sushi and Bisuteki.'

On the other hand, students may have particular difficulty with words that look similar in the two languages but have different meanings. These 'false cognates' may come from different origins or they may have evolved differ-ently from the same origin. For example, the English verb 'demand' has a different meaning from its French cousin *demander*, which means 'request' or 'ask a question', even though they came from the same Latin verb.

Some theorists have argued that second language learners, like children learning their first language, can learn a great deal of vocabulary with little intentional effort. Stephen Krashen (1989) has asserted that the best source of vocabulary growth is reading for pleasure. There is no doubt that reading is an important potential source of vocabulary development for second language learners as it is for first language learners. However, there are some problems with the notion that vocabulary growth through reading requires little effort. As noted above, it is difficult to infer the meaning of a new word from reading unless one already knows 95 per cent or more of the other words, and learners usually need to have many meaningful encounters with a word before they recognize it in new contexts or produce it in their own speaking and writing. As we saw in Chapter 1, Dee Gardner's (2004) research demonstrates that certain types of words are rare in narratives. Thus, students who read mainly fiction may have little chance of learning words that are essential for their academic pursuits. Conversely, reading mainly science texts will not provide many opportunities to learn the vocabulary of social interaction.

Research on vocabulary learning through reading without focused instruction confirms that some vocabulary can be learned without explicit instruction (see Chapter 6, Study 17). On the other hand, Jan Hulstijn and Batia Laufer (2001) and others provide evidence that vocabulary development is more successful when learners are fully engaged in activities that require them to attend carefully to the new words and even to use them in productive tasks. Izabella Kojic-Sabo and Patsy Lightbown (1999) found that effort and the use of good learning strategies, such as keeping a notebook, looking words up in a dictionary, and reviewing what has been learned were associated with better vocabulary development. Cheryl Boyd Zimmerman (2009) provides many practical suggestions for teaching vocabulary and also for helping learners to continue learning outside the classroom.

Even with instruction and good strategies, the task of acquiring an adequate vocabulary is daunting. What does it mean to 'know' a word:

- Grasp the general meaning in a familiar context?
- Provide a definition or a translation equivalent?
- Provide appropriate word associations?
- Identify its component parts or etymology?
- Use the word to complete a sentence or to create a new sentence?
- Use it metaphorically?
- Understand a joke that uses homonyms (words that sound alike but mean different things, such as 'cents', 'sense', 'scents')?

Second language learners whose goal is to use the language for both social and academic purposes must learn to do all these things.

Pragmatics

Pragmatics is the study of how language is used in context to express such things as directness, politeness, and deference. Even if learners acquire a vocabulary of 5,000 words and a good knowledge of the syntax and morphology of the target language, they can still encounter difficulty in using language. They also need to acquire skills for interpreting requests, responding politely to compliments or apologies, recognizing humour, and managing conversations. They need to learn to recognize the many meanings that the same sentence can have in different situations. Think of the many ways one might interpret an apparently simple question such as 'Is that your dog?' It might precede an expression of admiration for an attractive pet, or it might be an urgent request to get the dog out of the speaker's flowerbed. Similarly, the same basic meaning is altered when it is expressed in different ways. For example, we would probably assume that the relationship between speaker and listener is very different if we hear 'Give me that book' or 'I wonder if you'd mind letting me have that book when you've finished with it'.

The study of how second language learners acquire this aspect of language is referred to as 'interlanguage pragmatics' (Bardovi-Harlig 1999). Some of this research has focused on the ways in which learners express speech acts such as inviting and apologizing in relation to differences in their proficiency level or their first language background. Other studies have examined learners' ability to perceive and comprehend pragmatic features in the second language and to judge whether a particular request is appropriate or inappropriate in a specific context.

Since the early 1990s more research has directly investigated the acquisition of second language pragmatic ability. This includes longitudinal and cross-sectional studies describing the acquisition of several different speech acts. One that has been the focus of considerable attention is 'requesting'. Requests are an interesting pragmatic feature to examine because there are identifiable ways in which requests are made within particular languages as well as differences in how they are expressed across different languages and cultures.

In a review of longitudinal and cross-sectional studies on the acquisition of requests in English, Gabriele Kasper and Kenneth Rose (2002) outline a series of five stages of development. Stage 1 consists of minimal language that is often incomplete and highly context-dependent. Stage 2 includes primarily memorized routines and frequent use of imperatives. Stage 3 is marked by less use of formulas, more productive speech, and some **mitigation** of requests. Stage 4 involves more complex language and increased use of mitigation, especially supportive statements. Stage 5 is marked by more refinement of the force of requests. The five stages, their characteristics and examples are given below.

Stage 1: Pre-basic
Highly context-dependent, no syntax, no relational goals.

> Me no blue.
> Sir.

Stage 2: Formulaic
Reliance on unanalysed formulas and imperatives.

> Let's play the game.
> Let's eat breakfast.
> Don't look.

Stage 3: Unpacking
Formulas incorporated into productive language use, shift to conventional indirectness.

> Can you pass the pencil please?
> Can you do another one for me?

Stage 4: Pragmatic expansion
Addition of new forms to repertoire, increased use of mitigation, more complex syntax.

> Could I have another chocolate because my children—I have five children.
> Can I see it so I can copy it?

Stage 5: Fine tuning
Fine tuning of requestive force to participants, goals, and contexts.

You could put some Blu Tack down there.
Is there any more white?

Learning how to make and reject suggestions has also been extensively investigated. Kathleen Bardovi-Harlig and Beverly Hartford (1993) observed
differences between the way in which native and non-native speakers of
English communicated with their professors as they discussed their course
selections in academic advising sessions. These differences contributed
to their greater or lesser success in negotiating their academic plans. For
example, the non-native speakers did not initiate suggestions whereas native
speakers initiated a great deal. There was also a tendency on the part of the
non-native speakers to reject suggestions made by the advisor in ways that the
advisors might find rude or inappropriate. For example, they would reject
an advisor's suggestion to take a particular course by saying 'I think I am not
interested in that course', instead of saying 'My schedule conflicts with that
course', or 'I think this other course would better meet my needs', which was
more typical of native-speaker rejection responses. The non-native speakers
were also much less adept than the native speakers at using mitigation. For
example, native speakers were observed to say 'I think I would like to take this
course', whereas the non-native speakers said 'I will take that course'.

Over a period of four and a half months, the researchers observed progress in
some aspects of the non-native speakers' pragmatic ability. For example, they
learned to take a more active role in the advising interaction and to provide
reasons for rejecting suggestions that the advisors were likely to perceive as
more credible or acceptable. Even so, they continued to have some difficulty
in mitigating their suggestions and rejections.

For a long time, it was assumed that second language classrooms could
not provide appropriate opportunities for students to learn many different
speech acts. This was especially true in teacher-fronted classrooms where
the dominant interaction pattern was 'teacher initiation—learner response—
teacher feedback' and where the emphasis was almost always on producing
full sentences that were grammatically correct (see further discussion of
this in Chapter 5). In **communicative**, **content-based**, and **task-based language teaching**, there are more opportunities not only for a greater variety
of input but also for learners to engage in different roles and participant
organization structures (for example, pair and group work). This enables
learners to produce and respond to a wider range of communicative functions. Furthermore, research on the teaching of pragmatics has demonstrated
that pragmatic features can be successfully learned in classroom settings and
that explicit rather than implicit instruction is most effective (Kasper and
Rose 2002). This is good news for foreign language learners who do not have

extensive exposure to conversational interaction outside the classroom. The question is no longer whether second language pragmatics should be taught but rather how it can be integrated into classroom instruction.

Phonology

As noted earlier, grammar has been the focus for second language teachers and researchers for a long time. Vocabulary and pragmatics have also received more attention in recent years. However, we know less about pronunciation and how it is learned and taught. Pronunciation was a central component in language teaching when the **audiolingual approach** was dominant. Several techniques for teaching pronunciation were developed at that time, and most of them focused on the pronunciation of **segmentals**, getting learners to perceive and to produce distinctions between single sounds in minimal pair drills (for example, 'ship' and 'sheep').

When the audiolingual approach was replaced by other ways of teaching, attention to pronunciation was minimized if not totally discarded. Furthermore, evidence for the critical period hypothesis, suggesting that **native-like** pronunciation was an unrealistic goal for older second language learners (see Chapter 3), led to the argument that instructional time would be better spent on teaching something that learners could learn more successfully. When communicative language teaching (CLT) was first introduced in the late 1970s, little attention was given to the teaching of pronunciation. If it was taught, the emphasis was on **suprasegmentals** (rhythm, stress, and intonation)—aspects of pronunciation that were considered more likely to affect communication (Celce-Murcia, Brinton, and Goodwin 1996).

Although research on the teaching and learning of pronunciation is not as extensive as that in other language domains, there is theoretical and empirical work to help us understand the processes involved in phonological development in a second language and the factors that contribute to it. For example, contrastive analysis helps to explain some aspects of first language influence on second language learners' pronunciation. We can all think of examples from our own experiences or those of our students. Japanese and Korean learners of English often have problems hearing and producing *l* and *r* because these sounds are not distinct in their language. Spanish speakers will often say 'I e-speak e-Spanish' because Spanish words do not have consonant clusters beginning with *s* at the beginning of a word. French speakers may place stress on the last syllable of a word because French usually stresses the last syllable. Few languages have the *th* sounds that are frequent in English, and learners may substitute similar sounds from their first language (for example, *t* or *d*, *s* or *z*). Sometimes, however, learners overcompensate for sounds that they know are difficult. Thus, learners may pronounce a *th* (as in 'thin' or 'this') where a *t* or a *d* sound belongs (saying 'thin' when they mean 'tin' for example). Such errors are similar to the overgeneralization errors that we saw for grammatical morphemes. If they replace earlier correct pronunciation of *t* or *d* sounds, this may represent progress in learners' ability to notice and produce the *th* sound.

The relationship between perception and production of sounds is complex. Evelyn Altenberg (2005) developed a series of tasks to explore Spanish speakers' perceptions and production of English consonant clusters at the beginning of a word. In one task, they had to say whether certain invented words were possible 'new English words'. The Spanish speakers were quite good at recognizing what English words are supposed to sound like. They accepted pseudowords like 'spus' and rejected those like 'zban', even though both words would be unacceptable as 'new Spanish words'. She found that they could usually write (from dictation) pseudowords with initial clusters such as *sp* and *sm*. However, in their own production, these same learners might still insert a vowel at the beginning of words such as 'spoon' and 'smile'.

As we have seen with regard to grammar and vocabulary, it is hypothesized that a greater difference between the learner's native language and the target language can lead to greater difficulty. The evidence supporting the hypothesis comes partly from the observation that it takes learners longer to reach a high level of fluency in a particular second or foreign language if that language is substantially different from the languages they already know. For example, a speaker of Chinese faces a greater challenge in learning English than does a speaker of German or Dutch. Language distance affects pronunciation as well as other language systems. Theo Bongaerts (1999) collected speech samples from highly proficient speakers who had learned Dutch in their adulthood and who came from a wide variety of first language backgrounds. When native speakers of Dutch were asked to judge the speech samples, only those learners who spoke a language that was closely related to Dutch (for example, English or German) were judged to have native-like accents. None of the speakers whose first languages were more distant from Dutch (for example, Vietnamese) were judged to have native-like pronunciation.

There has been little research to document the developmental sequences of individual sounds in second language phonological acquisition. Nonetheless, there is evidence for similarity in the acquisition of some features of stress and rhythm and it also clear that the learner's first language plays an important role. Other factors such as the amount and type of exposure to the target language and the degree of use of the first language have been identified as influential contributors to pronunciation. Thorsten Piske, Ian MacKay, and James Flege (2001) have reported that longer periods of exposure to the second language can lead to improved pronunciation. It has also been observed that adults who continue to make greater use of their first language may have stronger accents in the second language (Piske 2007).

Learners' ethnic affiliation and their sense of identity are also related to how they produce the sounds and rhythms of a second language. Elizabeth Gatbonton, Pavel Trofimovich, and Michael Magid (2005) found a complex relationship between feelings of ethnic affiliation and second language learners' acquisition of pronunciation. Among other things, they found that learners who had achieved a high degree of accuracy in pronouncing the second language were sometimes perceived as being less loyal to their ethnic group than those whose second language speech retained a strong 'foreign accent'. Such perceptions can affect learners' desire to achieve high levels of proficiency in the second language, especially in contexts where there are conflicts between groups or where power relationships imply a threat to one group's identity.

Pavel Trofimovich (2005) has looked at learning pronunciation from a somewhat unusual perspective. His research raises questions about how well learners perceive the specific sounds of the new language while their focus is on meaning. Second language learners of Spanish were asked to listen to a list of familiar Spanish words. For the purpose of comparison, they also heard a list of words in English, their native language. One group of participants were told to 'just listen' to the words; the second group were asked to pay attention to how good the recording quality was; the third group were asked to rate the 'pleasantness' of the things the words referred to. Then they heard another list, which included both the original words and some new words, and they were asked to repeat each word as they heard it. Trofimovich then compared how quickly each learner started to pronounce the words they had already heard and the new words. The difference in the time it took them to react to 'old' and 'new' words is a measure of how easily words could be retrieved from memory.

As expected, the participants were always faster at retrieving the old words in their native language, and two groups of learners also showed this pattern for their second language. But the third group, who had been told to focus on the 'pleasantness' of the meanings, did not retrieve the old words faster. Trofimovich suggests that when learners focus primarily on meaning, they may not be able to also pay attention to the sounds that make up the words. In Chapter 6, we will review other research showing that learners sometimes fail to notice certain language forms—grammatical morphemes, vocabulary words, syntactic patterns, pragmatic features—when their focus is on understanding meaning.

Few studies have investigated the effectiveness of pronunciation instruction, but the results of recent research suggest that it can make a difference, particularly if the instruction focuses on suprasegmental rather than segmental aspects of pronunciation (Hahn 2004). Tracey Derwing and her colleagues (2003) carried out a series of studies to determine how intelligible learners were judged to be. They found that learners who were given pronunciation lessons emphasizing stress and rhythm were judged to be easier to understand than learners who received lessons focused on individual sounds. Even though the learners who were given instruction on individual sounds were more accurate in their use of those sounds, this did not seem to increase listeners' perception of the intelligibility of their speech to others. Findings like these support the current emphasis on suprasegmentals in pronunciation classes.

One of the controversial issues in pronunciation is related to the question of whether the goal of second language acquisition is to sound like a 'native speaker.' One obvious problem with the question is that it suggests that there exists a single correct variety of English, and this is far from true. Not only are there many different pronunciations of English by American, Australian, British, Canadian 'native speakers', there are also many other varieties of English that have come to be used as a *lingua franca* around the world. Jane Setter and Jennifer Jenkins (2005) and Barbara Seidlhofer (2011) are among the many scholars who stress the role of English as a *lingua franca* (ELF). Indeed, there are now far more speakers of ELF than of English as a first language.

A related question is whether intelligibility rather than native-like pronunciation is the standard that learners should strive toward. Studies of relationships between English native speakers' perceptions of foreign accent, their perceptions of comprehensibility, and their actual ability to understand what speakers are saying show that the three are related. However, research by Murray Munro and Tracey Derwing (2011) shows that the presence of a strong foreign accent does not necessarily result in reduced intelligibility or comprehensibility.

Unfortunately, research evidence does not change the fact that some listeners respond negatively to second language speakers' pronunciation. In some situations, accent still serves as a marker of group membership and is used as the basis for discrimination. Thus, some second language learners, particularly those who have achieved a high level of knowledge and performance in other aspects of the target language, may be motivated to approximate a more 'native-like' accent for personal and professional reasons. Other second language learners view this as irrelevant to their goals and objectives as users of the second language (Derwing and Munro 2009).

Research related to teaching pronunciation is gaining more attention. It is already clear that decontextualized pronunciation instruction is not enough and that a combination of instruction, exposure, experience, and motivation is required if learners are to change their way of speaking. Robin Walker (2010) provides guidance for teaching pronunciation in a way that recognizes the importance of preparing students for interacting with other speakers of English as a lingua franca.

Sampling learners' language

One of the challenges of studying learners' language is the difficulty of collecting samples of their speech or writing that are large enough to ensure that analyses and their findings are based on more than just a few learners or from just a few examples from a larger number of learners. Researchers often find it difficult to recruit learners, to obtain their consent to participate in a study, and to persuade them to remain available over the time periods that are necessary to show development. It can also be challenging to schedule sessions for recording speech or collecting writing samples, and to transcribe or digitize the speech samples for analysis.

Computer-based tools are making it possible for researchers to ask and answer new questions and to revisit some of the tentative answers to questions that have been around for a long time. For example, **corpus linguistics** has provided us with large collections of naturally occurring data that can be used to discover information about the frequency of different language features (words, phrases, grammatical patterns) in a variety of language contexts and registers. Some of these corpora contain language samples that have been collected from newspapers and conversations, whereas others are more specific to particular types of language. In addition, there are learner corpora and pedagogic corpora. More and more researchers are making their learner language data available to others so that each **corpus** of learner language data can be used for a number of different studies. Some of these corpora are available in CD or DVD format or online (Tarone and Swierzbin, 2009). The links between corpus research and second language teaching are also becoming increasingly apparent (Bennet, 2010; Sinclair, 2004). For example, if a corpus of classroom language reveals that certain features occur frequently in classroom input, teachers might decide to focus on features that occur less frequently. Similarly if corpus research reveals that specific grammatical features are rarely used by native speakers in conversational interaction, teachers (and textbooks) may devote less time to the oral practice of these features.

Summary

The language that second language learners produce and understand changes as they have more exposure to the language and as they use it in a greater variety of situations. Describing those changes has been the focus of this chapter. We have seen that there are strong patterns of similarity across learners of different ages, learning in different contexts, and starting from different first language backgrounds. The focus of this chapter has been mainly on these similarities. In Chapter 3, we will turn our attention to some of the ways in which learners differ from each other and how those individual differences affect how quickly and how well they succeed in second language acquisition.

Questions for reflection

1 What are the general rules or patterns of negative sentences in English? Looking at the developmental sequence that has been described for English negation, think about what learners seem to notice first. Is it word order? Special words? What features seem hardest for them to acquire?

2 How would you collect samples of learner language for a study of the acquisition of grammatical morphemes? What kind of speaking or writing task would be most effective in leading learners to create obligatory contexts for each of the morphemes listed in Figure 2.1? Do you think some morphemes would be relatively easy to create contexts for? Which ones do you think would be difficult? Do you think the 'wug test' would be a useful tool?

3 What aspects of learners' interlanguage are most likely to affect their ability to use language effectively outside the classroom? Word order? Grammatical morphemes? Vocabulary? Phonology? Pragmatics? Do you think priorities for classroom interaction and instruction reflect the importance of these different language features?

Suggestions for further reading

Ellis, R. and **G. Barkhuizen.** 2005. *Analysing Learner Language.* Oxford: Oxford University Press.

Analysing Learner Language introduces readers to different approaches to investigating learner language. It also serves as an extensive review of published research using a range of methods and techniques for gathering and analysing data. Each chapter is devoted to a particular analytic approach, including error analysis, frequency analysis, and sociocultural analysis, as well as a chapter by Michael Barlow on how computer tools can be used. The book will be of special interest to students who are embarking on second language acquisition research at the post-graduate level.

Nation, I. S. P. 2001. *Learning Vocabulary in Another Language.* Cambridge: Cambridge University Press.

This comprehensive book covers research and theory and their implications for teaching and testing vocabulary development in a second or foreign language. Although many books on vocabulary teaching and learning have been published since this one, it remains an essential and accessible text for teachers and post-graduate students who wish to understand both the challenges of vocabulary learning and those involved in teaching and assessing vocabulary knowledge.

Tarone, E. and **B. Swierzbin.** 2009. *Exploring Learner Language.* Oxford: Oxford University Press.

The authors collected speech and writing samples from a group of English language learners from different L1 backgrounds participating in the same tasks. This created a data base showing how each learner tried to achieve the same communication goals. The text is supplemented by a DVD of the learners engaged in the oral tasks. Exercises focus on different approaches to understanding the learners' emerging language systems, including error analysis, developmental sequences, learners' response to feedback, and communication strategies. Many of the ideas that are introduced in this chapter of *How Languages Are Learned* are illustrated in the examples of learners' language that are presented in this book.

3 INDIVIDUAL DIFFERENCES IN SECOND LANGUAGE LEARNING

Preview

As we saw in Chapter 1, children are almost always successful in acquiring the language or languages that are spoken (or signed) to them in early childhood, provided that they have adequate opportunities to use the language over time. This contrasts with our experience of second language learners, whose success varies greatly. Both educators and researchers have an interest in understanding how the characteristics of individuals are related to their ability to succeed in learning a second language.

Many of us believe that individual differences that are inherent in the learner can predict success or failure in language learning. Such beliefs may be based on our own experience or that of people we have known. For example, many teachers are convinced that extroverted students who interact without inhibition in the second language and seek opportunities to practise language skills will be the most successful learners. In addition to an outgoing personality, other characteristics often believed to predict success in language learning are intelligence, motivation, and the age at which learning begins.

To what extent can we predict differences in the success of second language acquisition if we have information about learners' personalities, their general and specific intellectual abilities, their motivation, or their age? In this chapter, we will review some of the studies that have sought to understand the relationships between individual differences and learning outcomes.

ACTIVITY   **Reflect on language learning experience**

Before you read this chapter, use the questionnaire in Table 3.1 to reflect on your own experience as a language learner. Using additional copies of the questionnaire, interview several friends, colleagues, or family members about their experiences of learning a second or foreign language. Keep the responses to the questionnaire and refer to them as you read this chapter about individual differences in second language learning.

1a What language do you speak best? Do you speak more than one language equally well? **1b** When did you begin to learn this language (these languages)?		
2 Which second or foreign language(s) have you learned with the *most* success?		
3 Which second or foreign language(s) have you learned with the *least* success?		
4 For the languages you mentioned in response to questions 2 and 3, answer the following questions in the appropriate columns:		

	Languages learned successfully	**Languages not learned successfully**
How old were you when you first tried to learn the language?		
Did you have a choice about learning this language or were you required to learn it?		
Do you currently speak this language regularly?		
Do you regularly read this language for information or enjoyment?		
How much of your learning experience with this language was in a foreign language classroom?		
If you no longer use this language on a daily basis, can you estimate how many years you spent learning or using it?		
Estimate how many hours of classroom instruction you had for this language.		

How much time have you spent living in a place where the language is spoken?		
Have you used the language to learn other subjects at school? At what level (elementary, secondary, university)?		
Do you have personal or emotional attachments to this language? For example, do you have peers or family members who speak this language?		
Do/did you enjoy studying the grammar of this language?		
Do/did you enjoy studying vocabulary in this language?		
Are/were you a successful student in other school subjects?		
Do you think of yourself as a person who likes to socialize?		
Do you think of yourself as a person who learns a new language easily?		

Photocopiable © Oxford University Press

Table 3.1 Individual differences in language learning experience

---

Research on learner characteristics

Perhaps the best way to begin our discussion is to describe how research on the influence of individual differences on second language learning is usually done. When researchers are interested in finding out how a variable such as motivation is related to second language learning outcomes, they usually select a group of learners and give them a questionnaire to measure the type and degree of their motivation. Then some kind of test is used to assess their second language proficiency. The test and the questionnaire are both scored, and the researcher uses a statistical procedure called a **correlation**. The correlation is an indication of how likely it is that learners with high scores on the motivation questionnaire will also have high scores on the language test. If the two variables (motivation and language proficiency) are found to be correlated, the researcher will try to discover just what the relationship between them is. Note that correlations may be positive or negative. That is, one may find a pattern suggesting that learners with higher motivation scores have higher language proficiency scores (a *positive* correlation), or one might, in some circumstances, find that learners with lower motivation scores do better on proficiency measures (a *negative* correlation).

Although the correlation procedure seems straightforward, it requires careful interpretation. One problem is that, unlike variables such as height or age, it is not possible to directly observe and measure motivation, extroversion, or even intelligence. These are just labels for an entire range of behaviours and characteristics. Furthermore, characteristics such as these are not independent of each other, and researchers have sometimes used the same label to describe different sets of behavioural traits. For example, in motivation questionnaires, learners may be asked how often they use their second language outside a classroom context. The assumption behind the question is that those who report that they frequently do so are highly motivated to learn. This seems reasonable, but it is not so simple. If a learner responds that he or she frequently interacts with speakers of the second language, it may not be because he or she is more motivated to learn than one who reports less interaction. Rather, it might be that this individual lives where there are more opportunities—or a greater necessity—for language practice than those who report a low frequency of interaction. Because it is usually impossible to separate these two variables (i.e. motivation or *desire* to interact and opportunities or the *need* to interact), we cannot conclude whether it is motivation, necessity, or opportunity that is being measured by this question.

Perhaps the most serious error in interpreting correlations is the conclusion that one of the variables causes the other. The fact that two things tend to occur together or increase and decrease in a similar pattern does not necessarily mean that one causes the other. While it may be that one variable influences the other, it may also be that both are influenced by something else entirely. Research on motivation is perhaps the best context in which to illustrate this. Learners who are successful may indeed be highly motivated. But can we conclude that they became successful because of their motivation? It is also plausible that early success heightened their motivation, or that both success and motivation are due to their special aptitude for language learning or the favourable context in which they were learning.

Another difficulty in assessing the relationship between individual learner characteristics and second language learning is how language proficiency is defined and measured. In the L2 learning literature, some studies report that learners with a higher intelligence quotient (IQ) are more successful language learners than those with a lower IQ, while other studies report no such correlation. One explanation for these conflicting findings is that the language proficiency tests used in different studies do not measure the same kind of knowledge. For example, IQ may be less closely correlated to measures of conversational fluency than to tests that measure metalinguistic knowledge.

Research on individual differences must also take into account the social and educational settings in which learners find themselves. Bonny Norton and Kelleen Toohey (2001) argue that, even when individuals possess some of the characteristics that have been associated with successful language learning, their language acquisition may not be successful if they are not able to gain access to social relationships in situations where they are perceived as valued partners in communication. Members of some immigrant and minority groups are too often marginalized by social and educational practices that limit their opportunities to engage in communication with peers, colleagues, and even teachers. In these social conditions, individuals who approach a new language with the cognitive and motivational characteristics typical of successful language learners may not achieve the proficiency that these characteristics would predict.

Understanding the relationship between individual characteristics, social situations, and success in second language learning is a challenge. Nevertheless, research in this area is of great importance to both researchers and educators. Researchers seek to know how different cognitive and personality variables are related and how they interact with learners' experiences, so that they can gain a better understanding of human learning. Educators hope to find ways of helping learners with different characteristics to achieve success in second language learning. The larger community is also concerned because of the enormous impact second language learning has on shaping opportunities for education, employment, mobility, and other societal benefits.

Let's look at some of the individual characteristics that have been investigated in the effort to discover explanations for differences in learning outcomes.

Intelligence

The term 'intelligence' has traditionally been used to refer to performance on certain kinds of tests. These tests are often associated with success in school, and a link between intelligence and second language learning has sometimes been reported. Over the years, some research has shown that IQ scores were a good means of predicting success in second language learning. However, as suggested above, IQ tests may be more strongly related to metalinguistic knowledge than to communicative ability. For example, in a study with students in French **immersion programmes** in Canada, Fred Genesee (1976) found that, while intelligence was related to the development of French second language reading, grammar, and vocabulary, it was unrelated to oral production skills. This suggests that the kind of ability measured by traditional IQ tests may be a strong predictor when it comes to learning that involves language analysis and rule learning but may play a less important role outside the classroom or in classrooms where the instruction focuses more on communication and interaction. Indeed, many students whose general academic performance is weak experience considerable success in second language learning if they are given the right opportunities.

Many educators have been influenced by Howard Gardner's (1993) proposal that individuals have 'multiple intelligences' and that traditional IQ tests have assessed only a limited range of abilities. Among the 'multiple intelligences' Gardner includes abilities in the areas of music, interpersonal relations, and athletics, as well as the verbal intelligence that is most often associated with success in school.

Language learning aptitude

Specific abilities thought to predict success in language learning have been studied under the title of language learning 'aptitude'. One of the pioneers in this area, John Carroll (1991), has characterized aptitude in terms of the ability to learn quickly. Thus, we may hypothesize that a learner with high aptitude may learn with greater ease and speed but that other learners may also be successful if they persevere.

Over several decades, the most widely used aptitude measures have been the Modern Language Aptitude Test (MLAT) (Carroll and Sapon 1959) and the Pimsleur Language Aptitude Battery (PLAB) (Pimsleur 1966). All the tests are based on the view that aptitude has several components, for example, the ability to identify and memorize new sounds, understand the function of particular words in sentences, figure out grammatical rules from language samples, and remember new words. While early research revealed a substantial relationship between performance on the MLAT or PLAB and performance in **foreign language learning**, these studies were conducted at a time when language teaching was based on **grammar translation** or audiolingual methods.

With the adoption of a more communicative approach to teaching, many teachers and researchers came to believe that the abilities targeted by these tests were irrelevant to the process of language acquisition. However, others suggest that some of the abilities measured by aptitude tests are predictive of success even in settings where the emphasis is on communicative interaction. For example, Leila Ranta (2002) found that children who were good at analysing language (one component of aptitude that is targeted by the tests) were the most successful learners in an English second language programme in which activities almost never involved direct attention to grammar.

Nick Ellis (2001) and others have hypothesized that **working memory** (WM) capacity may be the most important variable in predicting success for learners in many language learning situations. Working memory, also called 'short-term memory' refers to the active processing of information. Although long-term memory capacity is very large indeed, working memory capacity is limited. That means that only a certain amount of information can be processed at a given time, and individuals differ in the amount of information they can process in working memory. Peter Skehan (1989) suggests that successful language learners need not be strong in all of the components of aptitude. For example, some may have strong memories but only average abilities in language analysis.

Learners' strengths and weaknesses in these different aptitude components may account for their ability to succeed in different types of instructional programmes. In a Canadian language programme for adult learners of French, Marjorie Wesche (1981) studied the progress of students who were placed in instructional programmes that were either compatible or incompatible with their aptitude profile. In the compatible groupings, students with high analytic ability but average memory were assigned to teaching that focused on grammatical structures; learners with good memory but average analytic skills were placed in a class organized around the functional use of the second language. In the incompatible groupings, students were placed in classes that did not correspond to their aptitude profiles. Wesche reported a high level of student and teacher satisfaction when students were matched with compatible teaching environments. In addition, some evidence indicated that matched students were able to attain significantly higher levels of achievement than those who were mismatched. While few schools could offer such choices to their students, teachers may be able to ensure that their teaching activities are sufficiently varied to accommodate learners with different aptitude profiles.

Further support for the claim that a particular type of instruction cannot benefit all learners in the same way comes from a study with secondary students of French as a foreign language in New Zealand. Rosemary Erlam (2005) explored whether there was a relationship between aptitude and the effectiveness of three different types of instruction, which she called *deductive*, *inductive*, and *structured* input. Students were assessed on three measures of language aptitude: language analytic ability, phonemic coding ability, and working memory. They were then divided into three groups and given different types of instruction on direct object pronouns in French.

Learners in the deductive instruction group received explicit rule-based grammar instruction followed by the opportunity to practise the rules they had learned. Learners in the inductive group received no grammar instruction; instead they participated in activities that encouraged them to figure out the different meanings conveyed by direct object pronouns and then to produce them. Learners in the structured input instruction group received explicit rule-based grammar instruction but did not produce the target forms. Instead they participated in activities that exposed them to spoken and written examples of direct object pronouns.

Erlam found that all learners benefited from the deductive instruction regardless of differences in aptitude. This was interpreted as support for Peter Skehan's (1989) hypothesis that more structured teaching may even out individual differences compared with less structured teaching. Erlam's findings also showed that learners with greater language analytic ability and memory capacity were able to benefit more from the inductive and structured input instruction on written (but not oral) tests. This supports the hypothesis that learners with greater aptitude can figure out the rules of language based on input, and that they are able to consolidate this knowledge without the need to produce language—at least in terms of their written ability.

Before we leave the topic of language learning aptitude, it is perhaps appropriate to look at two extremes of the aptitude continuum. Some people whose academic performance is usually very good find themselves frustrated in their attempts to learn a foreign language. Lenore Ganschow and Richard Sparks (2001) and their colleagues have studied many cases of young adults who find foreign language learning exceedingly difficult. They identified several ways in which these students differ from successful learners. Most perform poorly on at least some of the measures that make up aptitude tests. Some have problems with certain kinds of verbal skills, even in their own language. What is perhaps most important about this research is that, with great effort and instructional support, some of these students are able to succeed in spite of their difficulties. The challenge is to find instructional approaches that meet the needs of learners with a variety of aptitude profiles.

At the other end of the aptitude continuum we find individuals whose achievements seem to defy every prediction about what is possible in second language learning. Lorraine Obler (1989) reported on the case of one American man who seemed able to acquire oral fluency in a new language in 'a matter of weeks'. Neil Smith and Ianthi-Maria Tsimpli (1995) followed a polyglot savant who learned many languages with apparent ease. This achievement was particularly astonishing in light of the fact that his overall cognitive functioning and social skills were quite limited.

Such exceptional learners suggest that an aptitude for language learning is at least partly independent of cognitive, social, and personality characteristics that are often associated with successful learning. Nevertheless, Michael Erard's (2012) review of the cases of some of history's most successful learners of multiple languages shows that their unusual talent was also associated with a willingness to work hard at tasks that many would consider too boring or difficult, such as using word cards to study vocabulary.

Learning styles

Some researchers have investigated individual differences in terms of 'learning style', defined as an individual's 'natural, habitual, and preferred way(s) of absorbing, processing, and retaining new information and skills' (Reid 1995: viii). We have all heard people say that they cannot learn something until they have seen it. They would fall into the group called 'visual' learners. Others, who may be called 'auditory' learners, seem to learn best 'by ear'. For others, referred to as 'kinaesthetic' learners, physical action such as miming or role-play seems to help the learning process. These are referred to as perceptually-based learning styles. Considerable research has also focused on distinctions between different cognitive learning styles. Individuals have been described as **field independent** or **field dependent**, according to whether they tend to separate details from the general background or to see things more holistically. A typical measure of this cognitive style is the *embedded figures test*, in which participants are asked to find a simple geometric shape embedded in a more complex one. For a number of years, it was widely reported that there was a strong relationship between field independence and success in second language learning. However, a review of the research led Zoltán Dörnyei and Peter Skehan (2003) to conclude that more research will be needed to identify the nature of the relationship.

There are many questions about how learning styles interact with success in language learning. For one thing, it is difficult to determine whether they reflect immutable differences or whether they develop (and thus can be changed) through experience. There is a need for considerably more research. Nevertheless, when learners express a preference for seeing something written or spending more time in a language laboratory, we should not assume that their ways of working are wrong, even if they seem to be in conflict with the pedagogical approach we have adopted. Instead, we should encourage learners to use all means available to them. At a minimum, research on learning styles should make us sceptical of claims that a single teaching method or textbook will suit the needs of all learners.

Personality

A number of personality characteristics have been proposed as likely to affect second language learning, but it has not been easy to confirm in empirical studies. As with other research investigating the effects of individual characteristics on second language learning, studies of a similar personality trait produce different results. For example, it is often argued that an extroverted person is well suited to language learning but research does not always support this conclusion. Although some studies have found that success in language learning is correlated with learners' scores on questionnaires measuring characteristics associated with extroversion such as assertiveness and adventurousness, others have found that many successful language learners would not get high scores on measures of extroversion. Lily Wong Fillmore (1979) observed that, in certain learning situations, the quiet observant learner may have greater success.

Another aspect of personality that has been studied is inhibition. It has been suggested that inhibition discourages risk-taking, which is necessary for progress in language learning. This is often considered to be a particular problem for adolescents, who are more self-conscious than younger learners. In a series of studies in the 1970s, Alexander Guiora and his colleagues (1972) found support for the claim that inhibition is a negative force, at least for second language pronunciation performance. One study involved an analysis of the effects of small doses of alcohol, known for its ability to reduce inhibition, on pronunciation. Study participants who drank small amounts of alcohol did better on pronunciation tests than those who did not drink any. While results such as these are interesting, they may have more to do with performance than with learning. We may also note, in passing, that when larger doses of alcohol were administered, pronunciation rapidly deteriorated!

Learner anxiety—feelings of worry, nervousness, and stress that many students experience when learning a second language—has been extensively investigated. For a long time, researchers thought of anxiety as a permanent feature of a learner's personality. In fact, the majority of language anxiety scales like the Foreign Language Classroom Anxiety Scale (Horwitz, Horwitz, and Cope 1986) measure anxiety in this way. So, for example, students are assumed to be 'anxious' if they 'strongly agree' with statements such as 'I become nervous when I have to speak in the second language classroom'. However, such questionnaire responses do not take account of the possibility that anxiety can be temporary and context-specific.

Other researchers investigating learner anxiety in second language classrooms see anxiety as dynamic and dependent on particular situations and circumstances. This permits distinctions to be made between for example, feeling anxious when giving an oral presentation in front of the whole class but not when interacting with peers in group work. Whatever the context, anxiety can interfere with the learning process. Peter MacIntyre (1995) argues that 'because nervous students are focused on both the task at hand and their reactions to it ... [they] will not learn as quickly as relaxed students' (p. 96).

Of course, it has also been argued that not all anxiety is bad and that a certain amount of tension can have a positive effect and even facilitate learning. Experiencing anxiety before a test or an oral presentation can provide the right combination of motivation and focus to succeed. Because anxiety is often considered to be a negative term, some researchers have chosen to use other terms they consider to be more neutral. In a study of young adults learning French in an intensive summer programme, Guy Spielmann and Mary Radnofsky (2001) used the term 'tension'. They found that tension, as experienced by the learners in their study, was perceived as both beneficial and detrimental and that it was also related to the learners' social interactions inside and outside the classroom.

A learner's **willingness to communicate** (WTC) has also been related to anxiety. We have all experienced occasions when we tried to avoid communicating in a second language. WTC may change with the number of people present, the topic of conversation, the formality of the circumstances, and even with whether we feel tired or energetic at a given moment. A colleague in Canada, who works in the area of second language learning and speaks several languages, recently confessed that he avoided the corner store in his neighbourhood because the proprietor always spoke French to him. He recognized the proprietor's efforts to help him improve his skills in this new language, and was grateful for it, but, as he told us with embarrassment, it was just easier to go to the store where he could use English.

This is consistent with research carried out by Richard Clément, Peter MacIntyre, and their colleagues, who argue that learners who willingly communicate in a wide range of conversational interactions are able to do so because of their communicative confidence. In a series of studies they have shown that communicative confidence is shaped by two variables: how relaxed L2 learners are and how competent (or incompetent) they feel about their L2 ability. These factors are directly influenced by previous contacts with L2 speakers and are considered to be the main contributors to communicative confidence (Clément, Baker, and MacIntyre 2003).

Several other personality characteristics such as self-esteem, empathy, dominance, talkativeness, and responsiveness have also been studied. The research does not show a clearly-defined relationship between one personality trait and second language acquisition. And, as indicated earlier, the major difficulty in investigating personality characteristics is that of identification and measurement. Another explanation has been offered for the mixed findings. Personality variables seem to be more consistently related to conversational skills than to the acquisition of grammatical accuracy or academic language. Finally, most of the research on personality variables has been carried out within a **quantitative research** paradigm, that is, an approach that relies heavily on relating learners' scores on personality questionnaires to their language test performance. Some researchers have argued that a more **qualitative** approach to understanding and investigating personality variables is needed to adequately capture their depth and complexity, especially as they emerge and evolve over time.

Despite the contradictory results and the problems involved in carrying out research in the area of personality characteristics, many researchers believe that personality will be shown to have an important influence on success in language learning. This relationship is an intricate one, however, in that it is probably not personality alone, but the way in which it combines with other factors, that influences second language learning.

Attitudes and motivation

Robert Gardner and his colleagues have carried out a programme of research on the relationship between a learner's attitudes toward the second or foreign language and its community, and success in second language learning (Masgoret and Gardner 2003). As is the case with other variables, it is not easy to determine whether positive attitudes produce successful learning or successful learning engenders positive attitudes, or whether both are affected by other factors. Although the research cannot prove that positive attitudes cause success in learning, there is ample evidence that positive attitudes are associated with a willingness to keep learning.

Motivation in second language learning is a complex phenomenon. It has been defined in terms of two factors: on the one hand, learners' communicative needs, and on the other, their attitudes towards the second language community. If learners need to speak the second language in a wide range of social situations or to fulfil professional ambitions, they will perceive the communicative value of the second language and are therefore likely to be motivated to acquire proficiency in it. Similarly, if learners have favourable attitudes towards the speakers of the language, they will desire more contact with them. Robert Gardner and Wallace Lambert (1972) coined the terms **instrumental motivation** (language learning for immediate or practical goals) and **integrative motivation** (language learning for personal growth and cultural enrichment through contact with speakers of the other language). For a long time integrative motivation was considered to be the stronger predictor of successful learning. In some contexts, however, instrumental motivation was found to be a better predictor. Thus, both types of motivation have been found to be related to success in second language learning. However, in some learning environments, it is difficult to distinguish between these two types of orientation to the target language and its community. Furthermore, early research tended to conceptualize motivation as a stable characteristic of the learner. More recent work emphasizes the dynamic nature of motivation and tries to account for the changes that take place over time.

Zoltán Dörnyei (2001a) developed a process-oriented model of motivation that consists of three phases. The first phase, 'choice motivation' refers to getting started and to setting goals, the second phase, 'executive motivation', is about carrying out the necessary tasks to maintain motivation, and the third phase, 'motivation retrospection', refers to students' appraisal of and reaction to their performance. An example of how one might cycle through these phases would be: a secondary school learner in Poland is excited about an upcoming trip to Spain and decides to take a Spanish course (choice motivation). After a few months of grammar lessons he becomes frustrated with the course, stops going to classes (executive motivation) and finally decides to drop the course. A week later a friend tells him about a great Spanish conversation course she is taking, and his 'choice motivation' is activated again. He decides to register in the conversation course and in just a few weeks he develops some basic Spanish conversational skills and a feeling of accomplishment. His satisfaction level is so positive (motivation retrospection) that he decides to enrol in a more advanced Spanish course when he returns from his trip to Spain.

In a book devoted to helping second language teachers generate and maintain learners' motivation, Dörnyei (2001b) proposes and describes concrete and innovative methods and techniques that can help teachers motivate learners throughout these three phases.

Motivation in the classroom

In a teacher's mind, motivated students are usually those who participate actively in class, express interest in the subject matter, and study a great deal. Teachers also have more influence on these behaviours and the motivation they represent than on students' reasons for studying the second language or their attitudes toward the language and its speakers. Teachers can make a positive contribution to students' motivation to learn if classrooms are places that students enjoy coming to because the content is interesting and relevant to their age and level of ability, the learning goals are challenging yet manageable and clear, and the atmosphere is supportive. Teachers must also keep in mind that cultural and age differences will determine the most appropriate ways for them to motivate students.

Little research has investigated how pedagogy interacts directly with motivation in second/foreign language classrooms. One exception is a study by Marie Guilloteaux and Zoltán Dörnyei (2008) who explored the links between teachers' motivational practice and students' motivation for L2 learning. It was a large-scale study with 27 teachers and over 1,300 learners in English as a Foreign Language (EFL) classrooms in Korea. The teachers' motivational strategies were described using a **classroom observation scheme**—the Motivation Orientation of Language Teaching (MOLT). MOLT identified 25 motivational practices used by the teachers that were relatively easy to define and to observe. They were divided into four categories that are described below along with examples of the motivational behaviours included within each.

1 Teacher discourse: arousing curiosity or attention, promoting autonomy, stating communicative purpose/utility of activity
2 Participation structure: group work/pair work
3 Activity design: individual competition, team competition, intellectual challenge, tangible task product
4 Encouraging positive retrospective self-evaluation and activity design: effective praise, elicitation of self/peer correction session, class applause.

In each lesson, the learners' motivation was measured in terms of their level of engagement. The proportion of students who paid attention, who actively participated, and who eagerly volunteered during activities was calculated. A three-level scale was used to measure engagement in each observed lesson: very low (a few students), low (one third to two thirds of the students) and high (more than two thirds of the students). Learners also completed a questionnaire about their motivation levels specifically related to their EFL class.

The researchers found significant positive correlations between the teachers' motivational practices, the learners' engagement behaviours, and the learners' self-reports on the questionnaire. The researchers acknowledge that correlation results do not indicate cause–effect relationships. Nevertheless, the findings are important because this is the first study to provide 'any empirical evidence concerning the concrete, classroom-specific impact of language teachers' motivational strategies' (Guilloteaux and Dörnyei 2008: 72).

Identity and ethnic group affiliation

Social factors in the wider community can also affect motivation, attitudes, and language learning success. One such factor is the social dynamic or power relationship between languages. For example, members of a minority group learning the language of a majority group may have different attitudes and motivation from those of majority group members learning a minority language. Even though it is impossible to predict the exact effect of such societal factors on second language learning, the fact that languages exist in social contexts cannot be overlooked when we seek to understand the variables that affect success in learning. Children as well as adults are sensitive to social dynamics and power relationships.

A good example of how relations of power in the social world affect interaction between second language learners and target language speakers comes from the work of Bonny Norton Peirce. Drawing from data collected in a longitudinal case study of the language learning experiences of immigrant women in Canada, she argues that concepts such as instrumental and integrative motivation do not adequately capture the complex relations of power, identity, and language learning. Instead, she uses the term 'investment' to 'capture the relationship of the language learner [and his/her identity] to the changing social world.' (Norton Peirce 1995: 10). All the participants in her study were highly motivated to learn English. However, there were social situations in which they were reluctant to speak and these were typically ones in which there was a power imbalance. Their experiences in those situations limited the opportunities they had to practise and to continue to develop the second language outside the classroom.

Working with immigrant children in English-medium kindergarten classes, Kelleen Toohey (2000) observed that they were quickly assigned identities such as successful/unsuccessful, big/small, talkative/quiet, etc. in their first year of school. Of course, they also had the identity of 'being ESL'. Because learners' identities impact on what they can do and how they can participate in classrooms, this naturally affects how much they can learn. For example, one of the 'ESL' children was consistently excluded from imaginative interactive activities with her peers; another learner was perceived as someone who never listened or did the 'right thing'. Toohey argues that these identities could eventually lead to their isolation and to restricted or less powerful participation in their classroom community. While Toohey is careful to point out that identities are not static and can change over time, it is equally important to keep in mind that 'classrooms are organized to provide occasions upon which some children look more and some less able, and judgements are made which become social facts about individual children' (Toohey 2000: 77).

The two studies above describe how issues of identity and investment play important roles for both children and adults when learning a second language. Research has also documented how these factors contribute in complex and sometimes contradictory ways when learning a foreign language. For example, it has been observed that Japanese students are often reluctant to speak English in communicative lessons despite high levels of motivation to learn the language. Furthermore, when students with high levels of English language proficiency do communicate they often speak with a strong Japanese accent and intentionally produce grammatical errors for fear that they might be perceived as considering themselves to be superior (Greer 2000).

In a study with secondary school Japanese learners of English as a foreign language, Yasuyo Tomita (2011) observed that the students were more willing to communicate during activities that combined a focus on form and meaning than in exclusively meaning-based activities. In observations and interviews with the students, she concluded that learners were not willing to invest in English communication with each other unless they were able to establish their identities as 'learners' by discussing language form and raising questions about grammar. In exclusively communicative activities learners were reluctant to use English to communicate their ideas or opinions for fear that they would be identified as 'show offs' and pretending to be someone other than Japanese.

Learner beliefs

Second language learners are not always aware of their individual cognitive or perceptual learning styles, but virtually all learners, particularly older learners, have strong beliefs and opinions about how their instruction should be delivered. These beliefs are usually based on previous learning experiences and the assumption (right or wrong) that a particular type of instruction is the best way for them to learn.

Research on learner beliefs about the role of grammar and corrective feedback in second language learning confirms that there is often a mismatch between students' and teachers' views. In two large-scale studies Renate Schulz (2001) found that virtually all students expressed a desire to have their errors corrected while very few teachers felt this was desirable. In addition, while most students believed that 'formal study of the language is essential to the eventual mastery of the language', just over half of the teachers shared this view.

Shawn Loewen and his colleagues (2009) asked 745 learners of different languages to express their beliefs about grammar instruction and corrective feedback. They found that some but not all learners valued grammar instruction. For example, learners of English as a second language did not value it as much as did learners of foreign languages. This might have been related to the fact that the ESL learners had more years of previous grammar instruction compared to the foreign language learners and thus they were less enthusiastic about it and ready for more focus on communication. Overall, learners did not value corrective feedback as much as grammar instruction except for those learning Chinese and Arabic who valued both. The researchers suggested that this might be because the two languages are non Indo-European and thus more difficult for English speakers to learn than, for example, Spanish, German, and French.

Nina Spada and her research team (2009) have examined not *whether* learners perceive grammar instruction as useful but rather if they have preferences for *when* it should be taught. In a series of studies with learners (and teachers) of English as a second language and English as a foreign language, questionnaires were administered to 450 learners, asking them whether they preferred to focus on grammar separately from or embedded within communicative practice. The overall results indicated that both groups of learners preferred integrating attention to grammar within communicative practice. However, the ESL learners also reported that they valued separating grammar from communicative interaction much more than the EFL learners. This makes intuitive sense given that in the ESL context where there are more opportunities for communication outside the classroom, learners appreciate the opportunity to focus on grammar separately from communication when they are in the classroom. In the EFL context, however, where few opportunities for exposure to the L2 are available, the classroom is seen as the only place for communication—thus a preference for integrating grammar with communicative practice. The results from the ESL and EFL teachers who also participated in the studies showed that they tended to share their students' views (Spada and Santos Lima 2010 (in preparation)).

Individual differences and classroom instruction

There are many questions about how the existence of individual differences should influence instruction. On a simple practical level, it is not possible for a teacher with 50 students—or even one with 10 students—to customize instruction to suit the abilities or preferences of each one. Nevertheless, there can be little doubt that an instructional approach that rigidly adheres to a single way of teaching all students and an expectation that all students can learn in the same way will deprive some students of learning opportunities. Zoltán Dörnyei (2005) has reviewed the research on individual differences and proposes a number of ways for educators to help learners make the most of their individual abilities and learning preferences.

Learners' instructional preferences, whether due to inherent differences in their approach to learning or to their beliefs about how languages are learned, will influence the kinds of strategies they use in trying to learn new material. Teachers can help learners expand their repertoire of learning strategies and thus develop greater flexibility in their ways of approaching language learning.

Age and second language learning

We now turn to a learner characteristic of a different type: the age at which learning begins. Age is easier to define and measure than personality, aptitude, or motivation, but the relationship between age and success in second language acquisition is hardly less complex or controversial.

It is frequently observed that most children from immigrant families eventually speak the language of their new community with native-like fluency, while their parents often fall short of such high levels of proficiency, especially in the spoken language. To be sure, many adult second language learners achieve excellent language skills. One often sees reference to Joseph Conrad, a native speaker of Polish who became a major writer in the English language, and it is not uncommon to find adult second language learners with a rich vocabulary, sophisticated syntax, and effective pragmatic skills, even though there may be subtle differences between their language use and that of those who began learning the language while very young.

As we saw in Chapter 1, the Critical Period Hypothesis is that there is a time in human development when the brain is predisposed for success in language learning. It has been hypothesized that there is a critical period for second language acquisition just as there is for first language acquisition. Developmental changes in the brain, it is argued, affect the nature of language acquisition, and language learning that occurs after the end of the critical period may not be based on the innate biological structures believed to contribute to first language acquisition or second language acquisition in early childhood. Rather, older learners may depend on more general learning abilities—the same ones they might use to acquire other kinds of skills or information. It is argued that these general learning abilities are not as effective for language learning as the more specific, innate capacities that are available to the young child. It is most often claimed that the critical period ends somewhere around puberty, but some researchers suggest it could be even earlier. Others find evidence that there may be multiple critical periods, related to different aspects of language learning. For example, the ability to acquire the pronunciation patterns of a new language may end earlier than the ability to acquire vocabulary.

Of course, as we saw in Chapter 2, it is difficult to compare children and adults as second language learners. In addition to possible biological differences suggested by the Critical Period Hypothesis, the conditions for language learning are often very different. Younger learners in informal language learning environments usually have more time to devote to learning language. They often have more opportunities to hear and use the language in environments where they do not experience strong pressure to speak fluently and accurately from the very beginning. Furthermore, their early imperfect efforts are often praised, or at least accepted. Older learners are more likely to find themselves in situations that demand more complex language and the expression of more complicated ideas. Adults are often embarrassed by their lack of mastery of the language and they may develop a sense of inadequacy after experiences of frustration in trying to say exactly what they mean. Such negative feelings may affect their motivation and willingness to place themselves in situations where they will need to use the new language.

Research based on the CPH in addition to personal experience or informal observation of adult learners' difficulties has led some educators and policy makers as well as many parents to conclude that second language instruction is most likely to succeed if it begins when learners are very young. However, some studies of the second language development of older and younger learners learning in similar circumstances have shown that older learners are more efficient than younger learners. By using their metalinguistic knowledge, memory strategies, and problem-solving skills, they make the most of second or foreign language instruction. In educational settings, learners who begin learning a second language at primary school level do not always achieve greater proficiency in the long run than those who begin in adolescence. Furthermore, there are countless anecdotes about older learners (adolescents and adults) who achieve excellence in the second language. Does this mean that there is no critical period for second language acquisition?

The critical period: More than just pronunciation?

Most studies of the relationship between age of acquisition and second language development have concluded that older learners typically have a noticeable 'foreign accent' in the spoken language. But what about other linguistic features? Is syntax (word order, overall sentence structure) as dependent on age of acquisition as phonological development? What about morphology?

Mark Patkowski (1980) studied the relationship between age and the acquisition of features of a second language other than pronunciation. He hypothesized that, even if accent were ignored, only those who had begun learning their second language before the age of 15 could achieve full, native-like mastery of that language. Patkowski studied 67 highly educated immigrants to the United States. They had started to learn English at various ages, but all had lived in the United States for more than five years. He compared them to 15 native-born Americans with a similarly high level of education, whose variety of English could be considered the second language speakers' target language.

The main question in Patkowski's research was: 'Will there be a difference between learners who began to learn English before puberty and those who began learning English later?' However, he also compared learners on the basis of other characteristics and experiences that some people have suggested might be as good as age in predicting or explaining a person's success in mastering a second language. For example, he looked at the total amount of time a speaker had been in the United States as well as the amount of formal ESL instruction each speaker had had.

A lengthy interview with each person was tape-recorded. Because Patkowski wanted to remove the possibility that the results would be affected by accent, he transcribed five-minute samples from the interviews and asked trained native-speaker judges to place each transcript on a scale from 0 (no knowledge of English) to 5 (a level of English expected from an educated native speaker).

The findings were quite dramatic. The transcripts of all native speakers and 32 out of 33 second language speakers who had begun learning English before the age of 15 were rated 4+ or 5. The homogeneity of the pre-puberty learners suggests that, for this group, success in learning a second language was almost inevitable. In contrast, 27 of the 32 post-puberty learners were rated between 3 and 4, but a few learners were rated higher (4+ or 5) and one was rated at 2+. The performance of this group looked like the sort of range one would expect if one were measuring success in learning almost any kind of skill or knowledge: some people did extremely well; some did poorly; most were in the middle.

When Patkowski examined the other factors that might be thought to affect success in second language acquisition, the picture was much less clear. There was, naturally, some relationship between those factors and learning success, but it often turned out that age was so closely related to the other factors that it was not really possible to separate them completely. For example, length of residence in the United States sometimes seemed to be a fairly good predictor. However, it was often the case that those with longer residence had also arrived at an earlier age. Similarly, amount of instruction, when separated from age, did not predict success as well as age of immigration did. Thus, Patkowski found that for learners who acquire a second language primarily in the 'natural' environment, age of acquisition is an important factor in setting limits on the development of native-like mastery of a second language and that this limitation does not apply only to pronunciation.

Intuitions of grammaticality

Jacqueline Johnson and Elissa Newport (1989) conducted a study of 46 Chinese and Korean speakers who had begun to learn English at different ages. All were students or faculty members at an American university and all had been in the United States for at least three years. The study also included a comparison group of 23 native speakers of English. The participants were asked to make grammaticality judgements of a large number of sentences that tested 12 rules of English morphology and syntax. They heard recorded sentences and had to indicate whether each sentence was correct. Half of the sentences were grammatical, half were not.

Johnson and Newport found that age of arrival in the United States was a significant predictor of success on the test. Learners who began earliest achieved the highest scores on the judgement task. Those who began later were less likely to judge the sentences correctly and their performance on the test varied more widely.

Robert DeKeyser (2000) carried out a replication of the Johnson and Newport study, working with Hungarian immigrants to the United States. He also found a strong relationship between age of immigration and performance on the judgement task. In addition, he asked participants to take language aptitude tests and found that, for participants who began learning English as adults, aptitude scores were correlated with success. However, there was no such correlation for those who learned English in childhood. These findings appear to confirm the hypothesis that adult learners may learn language in a way that is different from the way young children learn.

Rate of learning

Some research suggests that older learners may have an advantage in terms of the **rate of learning**. They appear to learn faster in the early stages of second language development. In 1978, Catherine Snow and Marian Hoefnagel-Höhle published a study on a group of English speakers who were learning Dutch as a second language while living in the Netherlands. The learners included children as young as three years old as well as older children, adolescents, and adults. On tests administered when learners had been in the country for less than a year, adolescents were by far the most successful learners. They were ahead of everyone on nearly all of the tests. Furthermore, it was the adults, not the children, whose scores were second best. In other words, adolescents and adults learned faster than children in the first few months of exposure to Dutch.

By the end of the year, the children were catching up, or had surpassed, the adults on several measures. Nevertheless, the adolescents retained the highest levels of performance overall. The fact that the young children were catching up, together with evidence from other studies, suggests that they would probably surpass the older learners if they continued to have adequate opportunity to use the language. However, this study shows that adults and adolescents can make considerable and rapid progress in their proficiency in a second language in contexts where they use the language in social, personal, professional, or academic interaction.

One view of critical period research that has had an important impact on the way we look at studies of language acquisition has been expressed in the work of Vivian Cook (2008). He makes a strong case for the inappropriateness of using the criterion of 'indistinguishable from a native speaker' as the basis for success in second language acquisition. Indeed, Cook argues that a second language speaker or bilingual person should not be compared to monolingual native speakers because the real goal is 'multicompetence', that is, knowledge of multiple languages that inform and enrich one another.

Research on the long-term outcomes of second language learning as well as the rate of learning at different ages brings us to a question that is probably of greatest interest to most readers of this book: What can we conclude about the role of age when learning takes place primarily in an educational setting?

Age and second language instruction

Many people who have never heard of the critical period hypothesis believe that, in school programmes for second or foreign language teaching, 'younger is better'. However, both experience and research show that starting early is no guarantee of success and that older learners can attain high levels of proficiency in their second language. In considering the best age at which to begin second language instruction, it is essential to think carefully about the goals of an instructional programme and the context in which it occurs before we jump to conclusions about the necessity—or even the desirability—of the earliest possible start (Lightbown 2008a).

As we have seen, there is strong evidence that differences in learning outcomes are associated with age of learning. We have also seen that, especially for older learners, reaching high levels of second language proficiency involves aptitude, motivation, and the appropriate social conditions for learning. Thus, decisions about the age at which instruction should begin cannot be based solely on research on the critical period hypothesis, which focuses only on age and on the attainment of native-like proficiency.

In educational settings, it is particularly important to assess the goals and the resources available for second language development. In these settings, research has shown that older children and adolescents progress more rapidly than younger children particularly in the early stages of learning. The knowledge and skills that older learners are able to acquire in a relatively short period of time will satisfy the needs of many learners whose goal is to use the language for everyday communication, to succeed on foreign language examinations, or to read texts for an academic course rather than to speak with native-like pronunciation.

When the objective of second language learning is native-like proficiency in the target language, it may indeed be desirable for the learner to be completely surrounded by the language as early as possible. However, as we saw in Chapter 1, early intensive exposure to the second language may entail the loss or incomplete development of the child's first language. When the goal is basic communicative ability for all students in an educational system, and when it is assumed that the child's native language will continue to be an important part of their lives, it may be more efficient to begin second or foreign language teaching later.

In most second- and foreign-language classrooms, learners receive only a few hours of instruction per week. Those who start later (for example, at age 10, 11, or 12) often catch up with those who begin earlier. In Clare Burstall's (1975) landmark study, students who had made progress in early-start programmes, sometimes found themselves placed in secondary school classes with students who had had no previous instruction. Teachers who had both the more advanced early-start students and the students who had had fewer total hours of instruction tended to teach to a lower common denominator, and differences between the two groups of students essentially disappeared. This situation is not at all uncommon. Furthermore, in many educational settings, starting instruction earlier may not actually entail many more total hours of instruction. For example, in Quebec, responding to pressure from parents, the age at which instruction in English as a second language began was lowered in recent years from about age 9 or 10 to age 6, but the total number of hours of instruction was not increased. Rather, the number of minutes of instruction per week was spread over more years (Lightbown, 2012). Thus, after years of classes, learners who have had an early start may feel frustrated by the lack of progress, and their motivation to continue may be diminished. Clearly the age at which instruction begins is not the only variable that determines success in the second language classroom.

For many years, it was difficult to compare early-start and later-start learners because of all the variations in their educational contexts. Since the 1990s, many more studies have allowed us to investigate this question more effectively. Some large-scale research projects have been particularly useful in separating the effect of age and other factors in school-based foreign language learning. For example, in Spain, the Barcelona Age Factor (BAF) project studied the effects of changing the age of beginning to teach English to Catalan/Spanish bilingual students.

When the starting age for teaching English was lowered, Carmen Muñoz and her colleagues took advantage of the opportunity to compare the learning outcomes for students who had started learning at different ages. They were able to look at students' progress after 100, 416, and 726 hours of instruction. Those who had begun to learn later (aged 11, 14, or 18+) performed better on nearly every measure than those who had begun earlier (aged 8). This was particularly true of measures based on metalinguistic awareness or analytic ability. On listening comprehension, younger starters showed some advantages. Muñoz suggests that this may be based on younger learners' use of a more implicit approach to learning while older learners' advantages may reflect their ability to use more explicit approaches, based on their greater cognitive maturity. She points out that, in foreign language instruction, where time is usually limited, 'younger learners may not have enough time and exposure to benefit fully from the alleged advantages of implicit learning' (Muñoz 2006: 33).

One of the advantages of the BAF project is that the researchers were able to follow the same learners' language development over several years. This enabled them to examine whether the early learners would eventually surpass the older learners as has been observed in the 'natural' setting. This did not happen—although the younger learners caught up, the older learners maintained their advantage over time.

Decisions about when to start second language instruction in schools should be based on realistic goals and on realistic estimates of how long it takes to achieve them. One or two hours a week will not produce advanced second language speakers, no matter how young they were when they began. Older learners may be able to make better use of the limited time they have for second language instruction.

Age is only one of the characteristics that determine the way in which an individual approaches second language learning and the eventual success of that learning. The opportunities for learning (both inside and outside the classroom), the motivation to learn, and individual differences in aptitude for language learning are also important factors that affect both rate of learning and eventual success in learning. It is important to remind ourselves that some older learners do achieve the highest level of success and that many more are able to use their languages in a variety of personal, social, and workplace activities.

ACTIVITY   **Reflect on individual differences and language learning success**

Look back at the notes you made in Table 3.1 about your language learning experience and that of your colleagues and friends.

1 Which cases confirm your expectations about the variables that are associated with success—or the lack of it—in second language learning?

2 Which ones seem to challenge those expectations?

3 To what extent do you think that the contexts in which the learning took place are responsible for the outcomes?

4 To what extent do you think the differences in outcome are due to differences inherent in the individuals?

5 Do you think that the individuals might have experienced different outcomes in different situations?

Summary

In this chapter, we have learned that the results of research on individual differences are not always easy to interpret. This is partly due to the difficulty of defining and measuring individual characteristics and to the fact that the characteristics are not independent of one another. In addition, relationships between individual characteristics and learning environments are complex, and different learners will react differently to the same learning conditions. Indeed, the same learner will react differently to the same conditions at different times. Researchers are beginning to explore the nature of these complex interactions, but it remains difficult to predict how a particular individual's characteristics will influence his or her success as a language learner. Nonetheless, in a classroom, the goal of the sensitive teacher is to create a learning environment with a wide variety of instructional activities so that learners with different abilities and learning preferences can be successful in learning a second language.

Questions for reflection

I   Think of an example of a member of a majority group learning the language of a minority group and one of a member of a minority group learning a majority group's language. How might the power relationships between groups of speakers affect the attitudes of language learners? How might the status of the languages affect opportunities for learning?

2   As a second/foreign language teacher or learner, what are your views about teaching grammar? Do you have any specific preferences for how it should be taught or when? Do you know what your students' preferences might be for grammar teaching. If not, do you think it would be useful to find out?

3   If you were teaching English as a foreign language in a country with limited opportunities for secondary and post-secondary education in English, what recommendations would you make regarding the age at which English instruction would begin? What research would you draw on in supporting your recommendations?

Suggestions for further reading

Dörnyei, Z. 2005. *The Psychology of the Language Learner: Individual Differences in Second Language Acquisition.* Mahwah, NJ: Lawrence Erlbaum and Associates.

Dörnyei reviews decades of research on how individual differences affect second language learning. The book covers personality variables, aptitude, motivation, learning styles, learning strategies, and other individual characteristics such as anxiety and willingness to communicate that may vary according to the learning environment. Both thorough and accessible, this review concludes by emphasizing the evidence that individual differences are strongly affected by the situation in which learning takes place rather than being 'context-independent and absolute.'

Muñoz, C. (ed.). 2006. *Age and the Rate of Foreign Language Learning.* Clevedon: Multilingual Matters.

The Barcelona Age Factor study is the basis of this edited volume. Ten chapters report on various aspects of students' learning of English, comparing the outcomes for students whose foreign language instruction began at different ages. In addition to the specific research reports on, for example, the students' oral fluency, vocabulary, and rate of learning, there is an overview chapter in which Carmen Muñoz, the project director and editor of the volume, discusses the project in terms of broader issues of age and language learning at school.

Robinson, P. (ed). 2002. *Individual Differences and Instructed Language Learning.* Amsterdam: John Benjamins.

The contributors to this edited collection focus on interactions between individual learner characteristics and learning contexts. The chapters in the first section focus on theoretical work related to aptitude, motivation, anxiety, and emotion. Each chapter in the second section describes research investigating how individual learner variables interact with a particular learning context to affect L2 learning. This includes classroom and laboratory studies examining learner variables in relation to different types of instruction and studies of natural versus instructed L2 learning.

4 EXPLAINING SECOND LANGUAGE LEARNING

Preview

A general theory of second language acquisition needs to account for language acquisition by learners with a variety of characteristics in a variety of contexts. In this chapter we examine some of the theories that have been offered to account for second language developmental progress and final learning outcomes. We will look at how the behaviourist and innatist explanations for first language acquisition that we saw in Chapter 1 have been extended to account for second language acquisition. We will also look at some theories from cognitive psychology that have increasingly informed second language research in recent years. These theories emphasize the way the mind perceives, retains, organizes, and retrieves information. Finally, we will look at **sociocultural theory**, a perspective that places second language acquisition in a larger social context.

The behaviourist perspective

As we saw in Chapter 1, behaviourist theory explained learning in terms of imitation, practice, reinforcement (or feedback on success), and habit formation. Much of the early research within behaviourist theory was done with laboratory animals, but the learning process was hypothesized to be the same for humans.

Second language applications: Mimicry and memorization

Behaviourism had a powerful influence on second and foreign language teaching, especially in North America, from the 1940s to the 1970s. Nelson Brooks (1960) and Robert Lado (1964) were two proponents of this perspective. Their influence was felt directly in the development of widely used audiolingual teaching materials and in teacher training. Classroom activities emphasized mimicry and memorization, and students learned dialogues and sentence patterns by heart. Because language development was viewed as the formation of habits, it was assumed that a person learning a second language would start off with the habits formed in the first language and that these habits would interfere with the new ones needed for the second language. Thus, behaviourism was often linked to the contrastive analysis hypothesis. However, as we saw in Chapter 2, researchers found that many of the errors learners make are not predictable on the basis of their first language, nor do they always make the errors that would be predicted by a simple comparison of their first and second languages. This discovery led to the rejection of both the contrastive analysis hypothesis and behaviourism, leading to a period during which both the role of the first language and the role of practice in learning a second language received limited attention in both research and pedagogy.

In Chapter 2, we saw ample evidence that second language learners draw on what they already know—including previously learned languages. However, we also saw that they are sometimes reluctant to transfer certain first language patterns, even when the translation equivalent would be correct. And we saw that first language influence may become more apparent as more is learned about the second language, leading learners to see similarities that they had not perceived at an earlier stage. All this suggests that the influence of the learner's first language may not simply be a matter of habits, but a more subtle and complex process of identifying points of similarity, weighing the evidence in support of some particular feature, and even reflecting (though not necessarily consciously) about whether a certain feature seems to 'belong' in the target language.

By the 1970s, many researchers were convinced that behaviourism and the contrastive analysis hypothesis were inadequate explanations for second language acquisition. As we shall see, however, as research on second language acquisition has evolved, the explanations offered by behaviourism and the contrastive analysis hypothesis have been revisited and understood in terms of new learning theories.

The innatist perspective

As we saw in Chapter 1, the rejection of behaviourism as an explanation for first language acquisition was partly triggered by Chomsky's critique of it. Chomsky argued that innate knowledge of the principles of Universal Grammar permits all children to acquire the language of their environment during a critical period of their development. While Chomsky did not make specific claims about the implications of his theory for second language learning, Lydia White (2003) and other linguists have argued that Universal

Grammar offers the best perspective from which to understand second language acquisition. Others, for example Robert Bley-Vroman (1990) and Jacquelyn Schachter (1990) have suggested that, although UG may be an appropriate framework for understanding first language acquisition, it does not offer a good explanation for the acquisition of a second language, especially by learners who have passed the critical period. In their view, this means that second language acquisition has to be explained by some other theory, perhaps one of the more general psychological theories described below.

Vivian Cook (2003) and others point out that there is still 'the logical problem' of second language acquisition. That is, we need an explanation for the fact that learners eventually know more about the language than they could reasonably have learned if they had to depend entirely on the input they are exposed to. The implication is that knowledge of UG must be available to second language learners as well as to first language learners. Some of the theorists who hold this view claim that the nature and availability of UG are the same in first and second language acquisition. Others argue that UG may be present and available to second language learners, but that its exact nature has been altered by the acquisition of other languages.

Researchers working within the UG framework also differ in their hypotheses about how formal instruction or the availability of feedback will affect learners' knowledge of the second language. Bonnie Schwartz (1993), for example, concludes that instruction and feedback change only superficial aspects of language performance and do not affect the underlying systematic knowledge of the new language. She argues that language acquisition is based on the availability of natural language in the learner's environment. Interaction with speakers of that language is sufficient to trigger the acquisition of the underlying structure of the language. Lydia White (1991) and others agree that acquisition of many grammatical features of the new language takes place naturally when learners are engaged in meaningful use of the language. However, they also suggest that, because the nature of UG is altered by the acquisition of the first language, second language learners may sometimes need explicit information about what is not grammatical in the second language. Otherwise, they may assume that some structures of the first language have equivalents in the second language when, in fact, they do not. In Chapter 2, we saw a good example of this in White's study of the placement of English adverbs in sentences produced by French speakers. In Chapter 6 (Studies 18 and 33), we will see some research on the effect of instruction and feedback on such language features.

Researchers who study second language acquisition from a UG perspective are usually interested in the language competence of advanced learners—their knowledge of complex grammar—rather than in the simple language of beginning learners. They are interested in whether the competence that underlies the use of the second language resembles the competence underlying the language performance of native speakers. Thus, their investigations often involve **grammaticality judgement** or other methods to probe what learners know about the language rather than observations of natural language use.

Second language applications: Krashen's 'Monitor Model'

Perhaps the best known model of second language acquisition influenced by Chomsky's theory of first language acquisition is Stephen Krashen's (1982) Monitor Model, first described in the early 1970s, at a time when there was growing dissatisfaction with language teaching methods based on behaviourism. Krashen described his model in terms of five hypotheses.

In the *acquisition/learning* hypothesis, Krashen suggests that we 'acquire' language as we are exposed to samples of language that we understand in much the same way that children pick up their first language—with no conscious attention to language form. We 'learn' on the other hand through conscious attention to form and rule learning. In Krashen's view, far more language is acquired than learned.

Next, according to the *monitor* hypothesis, second language users draw on what they have *acquired* when they engage in spontaneous communication. They may use rules and patterns that have been *learned* as an editor or 'monitor', allowing them to make minor changes and polish what the acquired system has produced. Such monitoring takes place only when the speaker/writer has plenty of time, is concerned about producing correct language, and has learned the relevant rules.

The *natural order* hypothesis was based on the finding that, as in first language acquisition, second language acquisition unfolds in predictable sequences, as we saw in Chapter 2. The language rules that are easiest to state (and thus to *learn*) are not necessarily the first to be *acquired*.

The **comprehensible input** hypothesis is that acquisition occurs when one is exposed to language that is comprehensible and contains $i + 1$. The 'i' represents the level of language already acquired, and the '$+1$' is a metaphor for language (words, grammatical forms, aspects of pronunciation) that is just a step beyond that level.

Krashen's *affective filter* hypothesis is proposed to account for the fact that some people who are exposed to large quantities of comprehensible input do not necessarily acquire language successfully. The 'affective filter' is a metaphorical barrier that prevents learners from acquiring language even when appropriate input is available. *Affect* refers to feelings of anxiety or negative attitudes that, as we saw in Chapter 3, may be associated with poor learning outcomes. A learner who is tense, anxious, or bored may *filter out* input, making it unavailable for acquisition.

The Monitor Model been challenged by other researchers and theorists, some of whom have argued that it is not possible to test Krashen's hypotheses in empirical research (McLaughlin 1987) or that he has drawn the wrong conclusions from research (White 1987). Nevertheless, his ideas about second language development were influential during a period when second language teaching was in transition from structure-based approaches that emphasized learning rules or memorizing dialogues, to approaches that emphasized using language with a focus on meaning. Since then, as we will see in Chapter 6, communicative language teaching, including immersion, content-based, and task-based language teaching, has been widely implemented. Krashen's hypotheses, especially the comprehensible input hypothesis, have been a source of ideas for research in second language acquisition. Classroom research has confirmed that students can make a great deal of progress through exposure to comprehensible input without direct instruction. Studies have also shown, however, that students may reach a point from which they fail to make further progress on some features of the second language unless they also have access to guided instruction. Some insights from learning theories developed in cognitive psychology help to explain why this may be so.

ACTIVITY   Examine the Monitor Model

A number of writers have questioned the validity of Krashen's Monitor Model, partly on the basis that it is difficult to test the five hypotheses in empirical studies. Nevertheless, Krashen's views have remained influential in second language teaching.

1 Can you think of some reasons why this might be so?

2 Which of the hypotheses do you find intuitively convincing?

3 Which ones leave you sceptical? Why?

The cognitive perspective

Since the 1990s, research and theories from cognitive psychology have become increasingly central to our understanding of second language development. Some of these theories use the computer as a metaphor for the mind, comparing language acquisition to the capacities of computers for storing, integrating, and retrieving information. Some draw on neurobiology, seeking to relate observed behaviour as directly as possible to brain activity.

As in first language acquisition, cognitive and developmental psychologists argue that there is no need to hypothesize that humans have a language-specific module in the brain or that *acquisition* and *learning* are distinct mental processes. In their view, general theories of learning can account for the gradual development of complex syntax and for learners' inability to spontaneously use everything they know about a language at a given time. As noted above, some linguists have also concluded that, while the innatist perspective provides a plausible explanation for first language acquisition, something else is required for second language acquisition, since it so often falls short of full success. From the cognitive psychology perspective, however, first and second language acquisition are seen as drawing on the same processes of perception, memory, categorization, and generalization. The difference lies in the circumstances of learning as well as in what the learners already know about language and how that prior knowledge shapes their perception of the new language.

Information processing

Cognitive psychologists working in an **information-processing** model of human learning and performance see second language acquisition as the building up of knowledge that can eventually be called on automatically for speaking and understanding. Robert DeKeyser (1998), Richard Schmidt (2001) and others have suggested that learners must pay attention at first to any aspect of the language that they are trying to learn or produce. 'Pay attention' in this context is accepted to mean 'using cognitive resources to process information' but there is a limit to how much information a learner can pay attention to. Thus, learners at the earliest stages will tend to use most of their resources to understand the main words in a message. In that situation, they may not notice the grammatical morphemes attached to some of the words, especially those that do not substantially affect meaning. Gradually, through experience and practice, information that was new becomes easier to process, and learners become able to access it quickly and even automatically. This frees up cognitive processing resources to notice other aspects of the language that, in turn, gradually become automatic.

For proficient speakers, choosing words, pronouncing them, and stringing them together with the appropriate grammatical markers is essentially automatic. Furthermore, much of what these speakers say is drawn from predictable patterns of language that are at least partly formulaic. That is, fluent speakers do not create new sentences by choosing one word at a time but rather by using strings of words that typically occur together. This use of patterns applies not only to idiomatic expressions, but also to much conversational language and written language in a specific genre (Ellis, Simpson-Vlach, and Maynard 2008).

Another aspect of automaticity in language processing is the retrieval of word meanings. When proficient listeners hear a familiar word, even for a split second, they cannot help but understand it. Such automatic responses do not use up the kind of resources needed for processing new information. Thus, proficient language users can give their full attention to the overall meaning of a text or conversation, whereas less proficient learners use more of their attention on processing the meaning of individual words and the relationships between them. The lack of automatic access to meaning helps to explain why second language readers need more time to understand a text, even if they eventually do fully comprehend it. The information processing model suggests that there is a limit to the amount of focused mental activity we can engage in at one time.

Information processing approaches to second language acquisition have been explored by many researchers. Drawing on J. R. Anderson's (1995) work, Robert DeKeyser (1998, 2001, 2007) and others have investigated second language acquisition as 'skill learning'. They suggest that most learning, including language learning, starts with **declarative knowledge**, that is, knowledge that we are aware of having, for example, a grammar rule. The hypothesis is that, through practice, declarative knowledge may become **procedural knowledge**, or the ability to use the knowledge. With continued practice, the procedural knowledge can become automatized and the learner may forget having learned it first as declarative knowledge.

According to this perspective, once skills become automatized, thinking about the declarative knowledge while trying to perform the skill actually disrupts the smooth performance of it. Think, for example, of trying to drive a car or skate while intentionally thinking about and preparing every move. With enough practice, procedural knowledge eclipses the declarative knowledge, which, in time, may be forgotten. For this reason, fluent speakers may not even realize that they once possessed the declarative knowledge that set the process in motion.

Sometimes changes in language behaviour do not seem to be explainable in terms of a gradual build-up of fluency through practice. These changes have been described in terms of **restructuring** (McLaughlin 1990). They seem to be based on some qualitative change in the learner's knowledge. Restructuring may account for what appear to be bursts of progress, when learners suddenly seem to 'put it all together', even though they have not had any new instruction or apparently relevant exposure to the language. It may also explain apparent backsliding, when a systematic aspect of a learner's language incorporates too much or incorporates the wrong things. For example, as we saw in Chapter 2, when a learner finally masters the use of the regular *-ed* ending to show past tense, irregular verbs that had previously been used correctly may be affected. Thus, after months of saying 'I saw a film', the learner may say 'I seed' or even 'I sawed'. Such overgeneralization errors are not based on practice of those specific items but rather on their integration into a general pattern.

Another concept from psychology offers insight into how learners store and retrieve language. According to **transfer-appropriate processing** (TAP), information is best retrieved in situations that are similar to those in which it was acquired (Lightbown 2008b). This is because when we learn something our memories also record aspects of the context in which it was learned and even the cognitive processes involved in the way we learned it, for example, by reading or hearing it. To date, most of the research on transfer-appropriate processing has been done in laboratory experiments, for example, comparing the learning of word lists under different conditions. However, the hypothesis seems to offer a plausible way of explaining a widely observed phenomenon in second language learning: knowledge that is acquired mainly in rule learning or drill activities may be easier to access on tests that resemble the learning activities than in communicative situations. On the other hand, if learners' attention is drawn to grammatical forms during communicative activities in which their cognitive resources are occupied with a focus on meaning, the retrieval of those forms on a grammar test may be more difficult. In Chapter 6, a classroom investigation of L2 learning influenced by transfer-appropriate processing is described in Study 40.

Usage-based learning

As seen in the discussion of first language acquisition in Chapter 1, cognitive psychologists, unlike innatists, see no need to hypothesize the existence of a neurological module dedicated exclusively to language acquisition. They argue that what is innate is simply the ability to learn, rather than any specific *linguistic* principles. Some usage-based theories also attribute less importance to the kind of declarative knowledge that characterizes skill learning and traditional structure-based approaches to second language instruction. As Nick Ellis (2002) explains, the emphasis is on the frequency with which learners encounter specific linguistic features in the input and the frequency with which language features occur together. According to this view, learners develop a stronger and stronger network of associations or connections between these features as well as between language features and the contexts in which they occur. Eventually, the presence of one situational or linguistic feature will activate the other(s) in the learner's mind. For example, learners might get subject–verb agreement correct, not because they know a rule but because they have heard examples such as 'I say' and 'he says' so often that each subject pronoun activates the correct verb form.

Connections may be strong because the language features have occurred together frequently or they may be relatively weaker because there have been fewer opportunities to experience them together. Some of the evidence for usage-based views comes from the observation mentioned above that much of the language we use in ordinary conversation or in particular genres is predictable, and to a considerable extent based on formulaic units or chunks. As suggested by Nick Ellis (2003, 2005) and others, language is at least partly learned in units larger than single words, and sentences or phrases are not usually put together one word at a time. As noted in Chapter 1, usage-based research has shown that a learning mechanism, simulated by a computer program, can not only 'learn' from input but can also generalize, even making overgeneralization errors.

The competition model

Elizabeth Bates and Brian MacWhinney (1981) described the 'competition model' as an explanation for both first and second language acquisition that takes into account not only language form but also language meaning and language use. Through exposure to thousands of examples of language associated with particular meanings, speakers of a particular language come to understand how to use the 'cues' that signal specific functions. For example, the relationship between words in a sentence may be signalled by word order, grammatical markers, and the animacy of the nouns in the sentence. Most languages make use of multiple cues, but they differ in the primacy of each. This becomes clear in a situation where the meaning of a sentence is not immediately obvious. What helps you figure out the meaning? English uses word order as the most common indicator of the relationships between sentence components. Most English sentences have the order Subject–Verb–Object (SVO). That is, the typical English sentence mentions the subject first, then the verb, then the object.

Two- and three-year old English-speaking children can usually use cues of animacy and their knowledge of the way things work in the world to interpret odd sentences. Thus, if they hear a string of words such as 'Box push boy', they will act it out by making a boy doll push a tiny box, focusing on the fact that the 'boy' is the natural agent of action in this situation. However, the SVO pattern is so strong in English that, by the time they are four years old, children hearing this sentence will ignore the fact that boxes don't normally move on their own, and carefully demonstrate how the box pushes the boy. For English speakers, word order patterns are stronger than animacy cues at this point. At this age, children may attribute the SVO relationship to sentences in the passive voice. That is, 'The box was pushed by the boy' may be interpreted as 'The box pushed the boy.' Only later do they learn to pay attention to the grammatical markers that distinguish the active voice sentence from the passive word order.

In contrast, Spanish and Italian have more flexible word order, and speakers of these languages rely more on grammatical markers (for example, the agreement of subject and verb, the case marking of pronouns) or on the animacy of nouns to understand how sentence elements are related. When English speakers are learning these languages, they may have difficulty suppressing their tendency to rely on word order as the basis for interpretation. For example, an English speaking learner of Italian may find it confusing to hear sentences such as *Il giocattolo guarda il bambino* (the toy—is looking at—the boy). An Italian speaker, accustomed to more flexible word order, focuses on the animacy of the two nouns and concludes that the most reasonable interpretation is that the boy is looking at the toy. According to the competition model, second language acquisition requires that learners learn the relative importance of the different cues appropriate in the language they are learning (MacWhinney 1997).

ACTIVITY   Look at how different cues lead to sentence interpretation

Consider the following sentences:

1 The boy eats the apple.
2 The apple eats the boy.
3 The dog sees the ball.
4 The ball chases the dog.
5 The ball is chased by the dog.

1 Do they all follow the patterns of English grammar?

2 How can you tell which noun refers to the *agent* (the one who performs the action)?

3 In each sentence, what *cue* tells you which noun is the agent?

4 Is there more than one cue?

5 How are sentences 4 and 5 above different from each other?

6 According to the *competition model*, how might these sentences be interpreted by speakers of a language with a more flexible word order than English? What would those speakers focus on?

The cognitive perspective emphasizes the role of general human abilities to process and learn information—including language—on the basis of experience. In recent years, the term 'cognitive linguistics' has emerged and highlights the view that language is but one of the complex knowledge systems that humans acquire. Peter Robinson and Nick Ellis (2008) suggest that cognitive linguistics draws from and builds on a number of different approaches that have in common the hypothesis that language is learned through our perceptual and cognitive experiences and that like all other aspects of learning, language learning involves the discovery, categorization, and determination of patterns through the use of language.

Language and the brain

Another area of work within but not limited to the cognitive perspective is concerned with language learning and the brain. Some of the questions investigated include whether first and second languages are acquired and represented in the same areas of the brain and whether the brain processes second language input differently from first language input. For a long time the assumption was that language functions were located in the left hemisphere of the brain. Nonetheless, recent brain imaging studies show activation in different locations in both hemispheres of the brain during language processing. This is true for both first and second languages. However, differences have been observed, depending on the learners' age and level of proficiency. For example, when learners who acquire a second language later in life are given a grammatical task to complete, they show activation in the same neural areas that are activated for L1 processing but also activation in other areas of the brain. This is not the case with younger learners who show activation only in the areas for L1 processing (Beretta 2011). Other studies have measured the electrical activity in brain waves to explore differences in the processing of language input. Some of this research has shown that as an L2 learner's proficiency increases, the brain activity looks more like that of first language processing. There is also evidence that semantic processes are the first to look more like L1 processing patterns followed by syntactic processes as proficiency in the L2 increases (Hahne 2001).

While it is fascinating to think about connections between second language learning and the brain, it is important to keep in mind that this is a young discipline. Furthermore, the limited research that has been conducted has produced mixed findings. Therefore any implications of language and brain research for second language teaching are premature.

Second language applications: Interacting, noticing, processing, and practising

A number of hypotheses, theories, and models for explaining second language acquisition have been inspired by the cognitive perspective.

The interaction hypothesis

Evelyn Hatch (1978), Michael Long (1983, 1996), Teresa Pica (1994), Susan Gass (1997), and many others have argued that conversational interaction is an essential, if not sufficient, condition for second language acquisition. These researchers have studied the ways in which speakers modify their speech and their interaction patterns in order to help learners participate in a conversation or understand meaning in a new language. Long (1983) agreed with Krashen that comprehensible input is necessary for language acquisition. However, he focused on the question of how input could be made comprehensible. He argued that **modified interaction** is the necessary mechanism for making language comprehensible. That is, what learners need is opportunities to interact with other speakers, working together to reach mutual comprehension through **negotiation for meaning**. Through these interactions, interlocutors figure out what they need to do to keep the conversation going and make the input comprehensible to the less proficient speaker. According to Long, there are no cases of beginner-level learners acquiring a second language from native-speaker talk that has not been modified in some way.

Modified interaction does not always involve linguistic simplification. It may also include elaboration, slower speech rate, gesture, or the provision of additional contextual cues. Some examples of conversational modifications are:

1 *Comprehension checks*—efforts by the native speaker to ensure that the learner has understood (for example, 'The bus leaves at 6:30. Do you understand?').
2 *Clarification requests*—efforts by the learner to get the native speaker to clarify something that has not been understood (for example, 'Could you repeat please?'). These requests from the learner lead to further modifications by the native speaker.
3 *Self-repetition or paraphrase*—the more proficient speaker repeats his or her sentence either partially or in its entirety (for example, 'She got lost on her way home from school. She was walking home from school. She got lost.').

Long (1996) revised the **interaction hypothesis**, placing more emphasis on cognitive factors such as 'noticing' and corrective feedback during interaction. When communication is difficult, interlocutors must 'negotiate for meaning', and this negotiation is seen as the opportunity for language development. Related to this is Merrill Swain's (1985) **comprehensible output hypothesis**. She argued that when learners must produce language that their interlocutor can understand, they are most likely to see the limits of their second language ability and the need to find better ways to express their meaning. The demands of producing comprehensible output, she hypothesized, 'push' learners ahead in their development.

The noticing hypothesis

Richard Schmidt (1990, 2001) proposed the **noticing hypothesis**, suggesting that nothing is learned unless it has been 'noticed'. Noticing does not itself result in acquisition, but it is the essential starting point. From this perspective, comprehensible input does not lead to growth in language knowledge unless the learner becomes aware of a particular language feature.

Schmidt's original proposal of the noticing hypothesis came from his own experience as a learner of Portuguese. After months of taking classes, living in Brazil, and keeping a diary, he began to realize that certain features of language that had been present in the environment for the whole time began to enter his own second language system only when he had noticed them. This was because they were brought to his attention in class or some other experience made them salient. Drawing on psychological learning theories, Schmidt hypothesized that second language learners could not begin to acquire a language feature until they had become aware of it in the input. Susan Gass (1988) also described a learning process that begins when learners notice something in the second language that is different from what they expected or that fills a gap in their knowledge of the language.

The question of whether learners must be *aware* that they are 'noticing' something in the input is the object of considerable debate. According to information processing theories, anything that uses up our mental 'processing space', even if we are not aware of it or attending to it intentionally, can contribute to learning. From a usage-based perspective, the likelihood of acquisition is best predicted by the frequency with which something is available for processing, not by the learner's awareness of something in the input.

These questions about the importance of awareness and attention continue to be the object of research. Several researchers have found ways to track learners' attention as they engage in second language interaction. For example, Alison Mackey, Susan Gass, and Kim McDonough (2000) had learners watch and listen to themselves in videotaped interactions and asked questions leading them to explore what they were thinking as they participated in those interactions. Ron Leow (1997) developed crossword puzzles that learners had to solve while thinking aloud, thus providing some insight into what they noticed about language as they worked. Merrill Swain and Sharon Lapkin (1998) recorded learners in pair work and kept track of the language features they mentioned. These research designs cannot tell us if learners noticed things they did not mention. However, they do make it possible to identify some things that learners were aware of and to look at how this awareness is related to measures of their language knowledge. The extent to which learners' noticing of language features affects their second language development will come up again in our discussion of research on second language acquisition in the classroom in Chapters 5 and 6.

Input processing

In his research with American university students learning foreign languages, Bill VanPatten (2004) observed many cases of students misinterpreting sentences. For example, as predicted by the competition model discussed earlier in this chapter, when English speakers heard sentences in Spanish, they used word order to interpret the relationships among the nouns in the sentence. Thus, they interpreted '*La sigue el señor*' as 'She (subject pronoun) follows the man'. The correct interpretation is 'Her (object pronoun) follows the man' (subject of the sentence). In other words, the correct English translation would be 'The man follows her'. In order to understand that, students need to learn that in Spanish, a pronoun object often precedes the verb and that, rather than rely on the word order alone, it is essential to pay attention to whether the form of the pronoun indicates a subject or an object.

VanPatten argued that the problem arose in part from the fact that learners have limited processing capacity and cannot pay attention to form and meaning at the same time. Not surprisingly, they tend to give priority to meaning, overlooking some features of the language form. When the context in which they hear a sentence helps them make sense of it, that is a good strategy for understanding the general idea, but it may interfere with learners' progress in acquiring the language. In Chapter 6 we will see how VanPatten developed instructional procedures that require learners to focus on the specific language features in order to interpret the meaning, thus pushing them to acquire those features.

Processability theory

Jürgen Meisel, Harald Clahsen, and Manfred Pienemann (1981) studied the acquisition of German by a group of adult migrant workers who had little or no second language instruction. They analysed large samples of their speech and described the details of developmental sequences in their production of simple and complex sentences. They concluded that the sequence of development for features of syntax and morphology was affected by how easy these were to process. Ease of processing was found to depend to a large extent on the position of those features in a sentence. Features that typically occurred at the beginning or end of a sentence were easier to process (and learn) than those in the middle. All learners acquired the features in the same sequence, even though they progressed at different rates. The researchers also found that some language features did not seem to be affected by these constraints and could be learned and used by learners who were at different developmental stages. These were referred to as **variational features**.

Pienemann (1999, 2003) developed **processability theory** on the basis of research with learners of different languages in a variety of settings, both instructional and informal. One important aspect of his theory is the integration of developmental sequences with first language influence. He argues that his theory explains why learners do not simply transfer features from their first language at early stages of acquisition. Instead, they have to develop a certain level of processing capacity in the second language before they can use their knowledge of the features that already exist in their first language. We saw examples of this in the acquisition of negatives and questions in Chapter 2.

The role of practice

One component of language learning that has seen a renewal of interest within the cognitive perspective is practice. As we saw in discussions of the behaviourist perspective, an approach to learning that is based on drill and that separates practice from meaningful language use does not usually lead to communicative competence. This does not mean, however, that practice is not an essential component of language learning. Robert DeKeyser (1998) asserts that some classroom interpretations of behaviourism missed the point that practice is only effective if one practises the behaviour that one wishes to learn. As we will see in Chapter 6, the drills that characterized audiolingual instruction often failed to make the connection between the language patterns being drilled and the meaning(s) associated with them.

Researchers are now looking more closely at how practice converts declarative knowledge to procedural knowledge and then to automatic performance. Note that from the cognitive perspective, the practice needed for language development is not mechanical, and it is not limited to the production of language. Listening and reading are also affected by opportunities for practice. Lourdes Ortega (2007) has proposed three principles for practice in the foreign language classroom that she sees as compatible with the research carried out from what she calls the 'cognitive–interactionist' perspective:

1 Practice should be interactive.
2 Practice should be meaningful.
3 There should be a focus on task-essential forms.

Elizabeth Gatbonton and Norman Segalowitz (1988, 2005) have developed an approach to language teaching called ACCESS (Automatization in Communicative Contexts of Essential Speech Segments). It draws on the cognitive perspective and is based on classroom activities which, by their nature, require learners to use meaningful units of language repetitively in contexts where there are genuine exchanges of meaning. The goal is to provide opportunities for using these units with sufficient frequency that they will become automatic. Segalowitz (2010) has emphasized the importance of increasing the amount of language that can be used automatically, thus freeing more cognitive resources for learning new things. Paul Nation (2007) has suggested that automaticity, which he, like Segalowitz, refers to as 'fluency' may be the most neglected aspect of language teaching in contexts where instruction focuses primarily on meaning.

The sociocultural perspective

As we saw in Chapter 1, Vygotsky's theory assumes that cognitive development, including language development, arises as a result of social interactions. Unlike the psychological theories that view thinking and speaking as related but independent processes, sociocultural theory views speaking and thinking as tightly interwoven. Speaking (and writing) mediates thinking, which means that people can gain control over their mental processes as a consequence of internalizing what others say to them and what they say to others. This internalizing is thought to occur when an individual interacts with an interlocutor within his or her zone of proximal development (ZPD)—that is, in a situation in which the learner can perform at a higher level because of the support (scaffolding) offered by an interlocutor.

In some ways, this approach may appear to restate some of the hypotheses encountered elsewhere in this chapter. In fact, people sometimes wonder whether the ZPD is the same as Krashen's *i +1*. William Dunn and James Lantolf (1998) addressed this question in a review article, arguing that it is not possible to compare the two concepts because they depend on very different ideas about how development occurs. The ZPD is a metaphorical location or 'site' in which learners co-construct knowledge in collaboration with an interlocutor. In Krashen's *i +1*, the input comes from outside the learner and the emphasis is on the comprehensibility of input that includes language structures that are just beyond the learner's current developmental level. The emphasis in ZPD is on development and how learners co-construct knowledge based on their interaction with their interlocutor or in **private speech.**

Vygotskyan theory has also been compared to the interaction hypothesis because of the interlocutor's role in helping learners understand and be understood. These two perspectives differ primarily in the emphasis they place on the internal cognitive processes. In the interaction hypothesis, the emphasis is on the individual cognitive processes in the mind of the learner. Interaction facilitates those cognitive processes by giving learners access to the input they need to activate internal processes. In Vygotskyan theory, greater importance is attached to the conversations themselves, with learning occurring through the social interaction. Sociocultural theory holds that people gain control of and reorganize their cognitive processes during mediation as knowledge is internalized during social activity.

Second language applications: Learning by talking

Extending Vygotskyan theory to second language acquisition, Jim Lantolf (2000), Richard Donato (1994), and others are interested in showing how second language learners acquire language when they collaborate and interact with other speakers. Traditionally, the ZPD has been understood to involve an expert and a novice. However, recent work has broadened the term to include novice–novice or learner–learner interactions. An example of this is in Communication task B in Chapter 5 (p. 137). In that excerpt, the learners are struggling with French reflexive verbs as they try to construct a storyline from pictures. The example is from the work of Merrill Swain and Sharon Lapkin (2002), who have investigated sociocultural explanations for second language learning in Canadian French immersion programmes. Their work has its origins in Swain's comprehensible output hypothesis and the notion that when learners have to produce language, they must pay more attention to how meaning is expressed through language than they ordinarily do for the comprehension of language. Swain (1985) first proposed the comprehensible output hypothesis based on the observation that French immersion students were considerably weaker in their spoken and written production than in their reading and listening comprehension. She advocated more opportunities for learners to engage in verbal production (i.e. output) in French immersion classrooms. Since then, she and her colleagues have carried out extensive research to investigate the effects of output on second language learning.

Swain's early work on the output hypothesis was influenced by cognitive theory, but more recent work has been motivated by sociocultural theory. Using the term **collaborative dialogue**, Swain and Lapkin and their colleagues have carried out a series of studies to determine how second language learners co-construct linguistic knowledge while engaging in production tasks (i.e. speaking and writing) that simultaneously draw their attention to form and meaning. As shown in Communication task B in Chapter 5, learners were testing hypotheses about the correct forms to use, discussing them together and deciding what forms were best to express their meaning. Swain (2000) considers collaborative dialogues such as these as the context where 'language use and language learning can co-occur. It is language use mediating language learning. It is cognitive activity and it is social activity' (p. 97).

Therefore the difference between the sociocultural perspective and that of other researchers who also view interaction as important in second language acquisition is that sociocultural theorists assume that the cognitive processes begin as an external socially mediated activity and eventually become internalized. Other interactionist models assume that modified input and interaction provide learners with the raw material that is interpreted and analysed through internal cognitive processes.

Summary

In the end, what all theories of language acquisition are intended to account for is the ability of human learners to acquire language within a variety of social and instructional environments. All of the theories discussed in this chapter and in Chapter 1 use metaphors to represent something that cannot be observed directly.

Linguists working from an innatist perspective draw much of their evidence from studies of the complexities of proficient speakers' knowledge of language and from analysis of their own intuitions about language. Cognitive and developmental psychologists argue that it is not enough to know what the final state of knowledge is and that more attention should be paid to corpus-based studies of the input, as well as to the developmental steps leading up to the achievement of high levels of proficiency.

Recent cognitive perspectives have often involved computer simulations or controlled laboratory experiments where people learn specific sets of carefully chosen linguistic features, often in an invented language. Many linguists argue that this does not entitle psychologists to generalize to the complexities of the linguistic knowledge that learners eventually have.

Interactionists emphasize the role of negotiation for meaning in conversational interactions. This perspective and the sociocultural perspective provide insights into the ways in which learners can gain access to new knowledge about the language when they have support from an interlocutor. Some linguists challenge the interactionist position, arguing that much of what learners need to know is not available in the input, and so they put greater emphasis on innate principles of language that learners can draw on.

Both linguists and psychologists draw some of their evidence from neurological research. At present, most of the research on language representation in the brain and specific neurological activity during language processing is inconclusive. However, advances in technology are rapidly increasing opportunities to observe brain activity more directly. Such research will eventually contribute to reinterpretations of research that previously could examine only the observable behaviour of learners speaking or performing other language tasks.

Educators who are hoping that language acquisition theories will give them insight into language teaching practice are often frustrated by the lack of agreement among the 'experts'. The complexities of second language acquisition, like those of first language acquisition, represent puzzles that scientists will continue to work on for a long time. Research that has theory development as its goal has important long-term significance for language teaching and learning, but agreement on a 'complete' theory of language acquisition is probably, at best, a long way off. Even if such agreement were reached, there would still be questions about how the theory should be interpreted for language teaching practice.

While some teachers watch theory development with interest, they must still continue to teach and plan lessons and assess students' performance in the absence of a comprehensive theory of second language learning. A growing body of applied research draws on a wide range of theoretical orientations, sometimes explicitly stated, sometimes merely implied. This research may provide information that is more helpful in guiding teachers' reflections about pedagogy. In Chapters 5 and 6, we will examine language acquisition research that has focused on learning in the classroom.

Questions for reflection

1 Several theories for L2 learning have been proposed in this chapter. Is one of them more consistent with your own understanding of how languages are learned? If so, how have your experiences as a teacher or learner brought you to this view?

2 Schmidt's noticing hypothesis—that all second language learning in adults involves awareness of what is being learned—is somewhat controversial. That is, it has been argued that it is also possible to learn *incidentally*, without any awareness or even an intention to learn. However, second language learners certainly do have 'aha' moments when they suddenly understand something about how the target language works. Do you have any examples of *noticing* from your own language learning experiences, or from those of your students?

3 From the perspective of the interaction hypothesis, modified interaction is seen as an essential resource for second language learners. This is distinguished from modified (or simplified) input. Can you think of some examples of each? What are some of the features of modified interaction that you think are especially helpful to learners? Are there some features that may not support learning? What are the contexts in which second language learners are most likely to benefit from modified interaction? Do you think that simplified input is (also) important?

Suggestions for further reading

Dörnyei, Z. 2009. *The Psychology of Second Language Acquisition.* Oxford: Oxford University Press.

This overview of the theories that have been proposed to explain second language acquisition is both comprehensive and easy to read. Dörnyei provides detailed treatment of the theories that are discussed in this chapter, focusing particularly on those arising from the research in cognitive psychology. In addition, the book introduces the work in neurobiology that provides a new level of explanation for language acquisition and use.

Swain, M., P. Kinnear, and **L. Steinman.** 2010. *Sociocultural Theory and Second Language Education: An Introduction through Narratives.* Bristol: Multilingual Matters.

In this book the authors cover the key concepts of sociocultural theory (for example, mediation, zone of proximal development, private speech, collaborative dialogue) through the use of narratives. The narratives come from the voices of language learners and teachers from different educational contexts. The book is of particular interest to readers motivated to understand how sociocultural theory relates to the teaching and learning of second languages.

VanPatten, B. and **J. Williams** (eds.). 2007. *Theories in Second Language Acquisition: An Introduction.* Mahwah, NJ: Lawrence Erlbaum Associates.

VanPatten and Williams set out a list of observations that have arisen from research studies in second language acquisition. Then, well-known authors discuss how the theoretical framework in which they have done their own research would explain these observations. For example, there are chapters on Universal Grammar, sociocultural theory, skill acquisition theory, processability, and input processing. The chapters are brief (about 20 pages, including discussion questions and readings) and written in a style that is accessible to those with limited background in research and theory. The final chapter, by Lourdes Ortega, provides a concise overview of the different theories and identifies some ongoing challenges for explaining second language acquisition.

5 OBSERVING LEARNING AND TEACHING IN THE SECOND LANGUAGE CLASSROOM

Preview

In this chapter we explore different ways in which researchers have observed and described what goes on in second language classrooms. Before we do this, let us take a moment to reflect on the differences between classroom settings for language learning and other settings where people learn a new language without instruction.

As we saw in the activity in Chapter 2, learning a second language in a non-instructional setting is different from learning in the classroom. Many believe that learning 'on the street' is more effective. This belief may be based on the fact that most successful learners have had experience using the language outside the classroom. What is special about this 'natural' language learning? Can we create the same environment in the classroom? Should we? Or are there essential contributions that only instruction and not natural exposure can provide?

Natural and instructional settings

Natural acquisition contexts should be understood as those in which the learner is exposed to the language at work or in social interaction or, if the learner is a child, in a school situation where most of the other children are native speakers of the target language and where the instruction is directed toward native speakers rather than toward learners of the language. In such a classroom, much of a child's learning take places in interaction with peers as well as through instruction from the teacher.

In structure-based instructional environments, the language is taught to a group of second or foreign language learners. The focus is on the language itself, rather than on the messages carried by the language. The teacher's goal is to see to it that students learn the vocabulary and grammatical rules of the target language. Some students in structure-based classes may have opportunities to continue learning the target language outside the classroom; for others, the classroom is the only contact with that language. In some cases, the learners' goal may be to pass an examination rather than to use the language for daily communicative interaction beyond the classroom.

Communicative, content-based, and task-based instructional environments also involve learners whose goal is learning the language itself, but the style of instruction places the emphasis on interaction, conversation, and language use, rather than on learning *about* the language. The topics that are discussed in communicative and task-based instructional environments are often of general interest to the learner, for example, how to obtain a driver's license. In content-based language teaching (CBLT), the focus of a lesson is usually on the subject matter, such as history or mathematics, which students are learning through the medium of the second language. In these classes, the focus may occasionally be on the language itself, but the emphasis is on using the language rather than talking about it. The language that teachers use for teaching is not selected solely for the purpose of teaching a specific feature of the language, but also to make sure learners have the language they need to interact in a variety of contexts. Students' success in these courses is often measured in terms of their ability to 'get things done' in the second language, rather than on their accuracy in using certain grammatical features.

In natural acquisition settings

When people learn languages at work, in social interactions, or on the playground, their experiences are often quite different from those of learners in classrooms. Complete Table 5.1 on the next page. As you look at the pattern of + and – signs you have placed in the chart, you will probably find it matches the descriptions below.

- Language is not presented step by step. The learner is exposed to a wide variety of vocabulary and structures.
- Learners' errors are rarely corrected. If their interlocutors can understand what they are saying, they do not remark on the correctness of the learners' speech. They would probably feel it was rude to do so.
- The learner is surrounded by the language for many hours each day. Sometimes the language is addressed to the learner; sometimes it is simply overheard.
- The learner usually encounters a number of different people who use the target language proficiently.
- Learners observe or participate in many different types of language events: brief greetings, commercial transactions, exchanges of information, arguments, instruction at school and in workplace interactions.

ACTIVITY   **Compare learning contexts**

The chart in Table 5.1 is similar to the one in Table 2.1 in Chapter 2. In that chart, we compared the profiles of first and second language learners. In this one, we compare natural and instructional contexts for second language learning. Think about the characteristics of the four contexts represented by each column. For each context, decide whether the characteristics on the left are present or absent. Mark a plus (+) in the table if the characteristic is typical of that context. Mark a minus (–) if it is something you usually do not find in that context. Write '?' if you are not sure. Note that the 'Communicative instruction' column has been subdivided into teacher–student and student–student interaction. What happens when learners talk to each other? Is that different from what happens in teacher–student interaction?

Characteristics	Natural acquisition	Structure-based instruction	Communicative instruction	
			Teacher–student	Student–student
Learning one thing at a time				
Frequent feedback on errors				
Ample time for learning				
High ratio of native speakers to learners				
Variety of language and discourse types				
Pressure to speak				
Access to modified input				

Photocopiable © Oxford University Press

Table 5.1 Contexts for language learning

- Older children and adults may also encounter the written language in the use of video and web-based materials.
- Learners must often use their limited second language ability to respond to questions or to get information. In these situations, the emphasis is on getting meaning across clearly, and more proficient speakers tend to be tolerant of errors that do not interfere with meaning.
- Modified input is available in many one-to-one conversations. In situations where many native speakers are involved in the conversation, however, learners may have difficulty getting access to language they can understand.

In structure-based instructional settings

The events and activities that are typical of structure-based instruction differ from those encountered in natural acquisition settings. In grammar translation approaches, there is considerable use of reading and writing, as learners translate texts from one language to another, and grammar rules are taught explicitly. In audiolingual approaches there is little use of translation, and learners are expected to learn mainly through repetition and habit formation, although they may be asked to figure out the grammar rules for the sentences they have memorized.

- Linguistic items are presented and practised in isolation, one item at a time, in a sequence from what teachers or textbook writers believe is 'simple' to that which is 'complex'.
- Errors are frequently corrected. Accuracy tends to be given priority over meaningful interaction.
- Learning is often limited to a few hours a week.
- In situations of foreign language learning the teacher is often the only native or proficient speaker the student comes in contact with.
- Students experience a limited range of language discourse types. The most typical of these is the Initiation/Response/Evaluation (IRE) exchange where the teacher asks a question, a student answers, and the teacher evaluates the response. The written language students encounter is selected primarily to provide practice with specific grammatical features rather than for its content.
- Students often feel pressure to speak or write the second language and to do so correctly from the very beginning.
- Teachers may use the learners' native language to give instructions or for classroom management. When they use the target language, they tend to modify their language in order to ensure comprehension and compliance.

Language classrooms are not all alike. The conditions for learning differ in terms of the physical environment, the age and motivation of the students, the amount of time available for learning, and many other variables. Classrooms also differ in terms of the principles that guide teachers in their language teaching methods and techniques. Designers of communicative language teaching programmes have sought to replace some of the characteristics of structure-based instruction with those more typical of natural acquisition contexts.

In communicative instructional settings

In communicative and content-based instruction, the emphasis is on the communication of meaning, both between teacher and students and among the students themselves in group- or pair- work. Grammatical forms are focused on only in order to clarify meaning. The assumption is that, in focusing on meaning, learners will acquire the language in a way that is similar to natural acquisition.

- Input is simplified and made comprehensible by the use of contextual cues, props, and gestures, rather than through **structural grading**. Students provide each other with simplified and sometimes erroneous input.
- There is a limited amount of error correction on the part of the teacher, and meaning is emphasized over form. Students tend not to overtly correct each other's errors when they are engaged in communicative practice. Because the focus is on meaning, however, requests for

clarification may serve as implicit feedback. Negotiating for meaning may help students see the need to say something in a different way.

- Learners usually have only limited time for learning. In a typical teacher-fronted classroom with 25–30 students, individual students get very little opportunity to produce language in a 60-minute class, and when they do, it is usually in the form of a short response to a teacher's question. When students work in pairs or groups, they have opportunities to produce and respond to a greater amount and variety of language. Sometimes, however, subject-matter courses taught through the second language can add time for language learning. A good example of this is in immersion programmes where most or all the subject matter is taught to a group of students who are all second language learners.

- As in structure-based instruction, it is usually only the teacher who is a proficient speaker. Learners have considerable exposure to the inter-language of other learners, particularly in student–student interaction. This naturally contains errors that would not be heard in an environment where the interlocutors are native speakers, but it provides many more opportunities for students to use the target language than is the case in most teacher-fronted activities.

- A variety of discourse types may be introduced through stories, peer- and group-work, the use of 'authentic' materials such as newspapers and television broadcasts. Text materials may include both those modified for second language learners and those intended for native speakers. In the latter case, teachers use instructional strategies to help learners get the meaning, even if they do not know all the words and structures. In student–student interaction, learners may practise a range of sociolinguistic and functional features of language through role-play.

- There is little pressure to perform at high levels of accuracy, and there is often a greater emphasis on comprehension than on production, especially in the early stages of learning.

- Modified input is a defining feature of this approach to instruction. The teacher makes every effort to speak to students in a level of language they can understand. If students speak the same first language, they may have little difficulty in understanding each other. If they come from different language backgrounds, they may modify their language as they seek to communicate successfully.

General descriptions of classroom instruction such as those above cannot capture the individual characteristics of particular classrooms. For this reason, researchers have developed a number of ways to study classroom learning and teaching. We will discuss two approaches to classroom research in this chapter. We will look first at observation schemes, in which researchers anticipate the occurrence of particular events and behaviours and make note of them within pre-planned frameworks or checklists. Then we will look at classroom **ethnography**, an approach that requires the observer to describe what happens in the classroom, looking for patterns and relationships, but trying not to limit the observation to any predetermined categories or expectations.

Observation schemes

Many different observation schemes have been developed for use in second language classrooms. They differ in several respects, including the number of categories they contain, whether they focus on qualitative or quantitative descriptions, and whether they are used throughout a lesson or on selected samples of classroom interaction. The schemes also differ in relation to whether they are used by observers in 'real time' while they are in the classroom, or used later outside the classroom to analyse audio or video recordings or transcripts of such recordings.

One example of a scheme developed specifically for second language classrooms is the Communicative Orientation of Language Teaching (COLT) Observation Scheme described by Nina Spada and Maria Fröhlich (1995). COLT is divided into two parts. Part A describes teaching practices in terms of content, focus, and organization of activity types. When using Part A, the observer can record, for example, whether the pedagogical activities are teacher- or learner-centred, whether the focus is on language form or meaning, and whether there are opportunities for students to choose the topics for discussion. Part B describes specific aspects of the language produced by teachers and students, for example, how much (or how little) language students produce, whether their language production is restricted in any way, the kinds of questions teachers ask, and whether and how teachers respond to learners' errors.

The COLT scheme and others like it have been used primarily in classroom research that is intended to look at how differences in teaching practices are related to differences in second language learning. Observation schemes have also been used in the training of new teachers and in the professional development of experienced ones.

Below is an activity in which you are asked to use a set of pre-determined categories similar to those used in the COLT scheme to characterize the nature of interaction between teachers and students and between students and students.

Classroom comparisons: Teacher–student interactions

Excerpts from four transcripts of second language classroom interaction are given in this and the following section. The first two present teacher–student interaction. The transcripts come from classrooms that differ in their approach to second language teaching; one of them represents structure-based instruction; the other, a communicative approach. Structure-based approaches emphasize language form through either metalinguistic instruction (for example, grammar translation) or pattern practice (for example, audiolingual).

With each transcript, there is a chart where you can indicate whether certain things are happening in the interaction, from the point of view of the teacher and that of the students. Before you begin reading the transcripts, study the following interpretations of the categories used in the charts:

1 Errors: Are there errors in the language of either the teacher or the students?
2 Feedback on errors: When students make errors, do they receive feedback? From whom?
3 Genuine questions: Do teachers and students ask questions to which they don't know the answer in advance?
4 Display questions: Do teachers ask questions that they know the answers to so that learners can display their knowledge of the language (or lack of it)?
5 Negotiation for meaning: Do the teachers and students work to understand what the other speakers are saying? What efforts are made by the teacher? By the students?
6 Metalinguistic comments: Do the teachers and students talk about language, in addition to using it to transmit information?

In the following excerpts, T represents the teacher; S represents a student. (The first two examples come from unpublished data collected by P. M. Lightbown, N. Spada, and B. Barkman.)

Classroom A: A structure-based approach

(Students in this class are 15-year-old French speakers.)

	Teacher	Student
Errors		
Feedback on errors		
Genuine questions		
Display questions		
Negotiation for meaning		
Metalinguistic comments		

Photocopiable © Oxford University Press

T   OK, we finished the book—we finished in the book Unit 1, 2, 3. Finished. Workbook 1, 2, 3. So today we're going to start with

Unit 4. Don't take your books yet, don't take your books. In 1, 2, 3 we worked in what tense? What tense did we work on? OK?

S   Past.

T   In the past—What auxiliary in the past?

S   Did.

T   Did (writes on board '1–2–3 Past'). Unit 4, Unit 4, we're going to work in the present, present progressive, present continuous—OK? You don't know what it is?

S   Yes

T   Yes? What is it?

S   Little bit.

T   A little bit.

S   …

T   Eh?

S   Uh, present continuous

T   Present continuous? What's that?

S   e–n–g

T   i–n–g

S   Yes.

T   What does that mean, present continuous? You don't know? OK, fine. What are you doing, Paul?

S   Rien [nothing].

T   Nothing?

S   Rien—nothing.

T   You're not doing anything? You're doing something!

S   Not doing anything.

T   You're doing something!

S   Not doing anything.

T   You're doing something—Are, are you listening to me? Are you talking with Marc? What are you doing?

S   No, no—uh—listen—uh—

T   Eh?

S   to you.

T   You're listening to me.

S   Yes.

T   Oh. (writes 'What are you doing? I'm listening to you' on the board).

S   Je—[I …].

T   What are you—? You're excited.

S   Yes.

T   You're playing with your eraser (writes 'I'm playing with my eraser' on the board). Would you close the door please, Bernard? Claude, what is he doing?

S   Close the door.

T   He is closing the door (writes 'He's closing the door' on the board). What are you doing, Mario?

Classroom B: A communicative approach

(Students in this class are 10-year-old French speakers. In this activity, they are telling their teacher and their classmates what 'bugs' them. They have written 'what bugs them' on a card or paper that they hold while speaking.)

	Teacher	Student
Errors		
Feedback on errors		
Genuine questions		
Display questions		
Negotiation for meaning		
Metalinguistic comments		

Photocopiable © Oxford University Press

S   It bugs me when a bee string me.

T   Oh, when a bee stings me.

S   Stings me.

T   Do you get stung often? Does that happen often? The bee stinging many times?

S   Yeah.

T   Often? (Teacher turns to students who aren't paying attention) OK. Sandra and Benoît, you may begin working on a research project, hey? (Teacher turns her attention back to 'What bugs me')

S   It bugs me (inaudible) and my sister put on my clothes.

T   Ah! She borrows your clothes? When you're older, you may appreciate it because you can switch clothes, maybe. (Turns to check another student's written work) Mélanie, this is yours, I will check— OK. It's good.

S   It bugs me when I'm sick and my brother doesn't help me—my—my brother, 'cause he—me—.

T   OK. You know—when (inaudible) sick, you're sick at home in bed and you say, oh, to your brother or your sister: 'Would you please get me a drink of water?'—'Ah! Drop dead!' you know, 'Go play in the traffic!' You know, it's not very nice. Martin!

S   It bug me to have—

T   It bugs me. It bugzz me.

S   It bugs me when my brother takes my bicycle. Every day.

T   Every day? Ah! Doesn't your bro—(inaudible) his bicycle? Could his brother lend his bicycle? Uh, your brother doesn't have a bicycle?

S   Yeah! A new bicycle (inaudible) bicycle.

T   Ah, well. Talk to your mom and dad about it. Maybe negotiate a new bicycle for your brother.

S   (inaudible)

T   He has a new bicycle. But his brother needs a new one too.

S   Yes!

T   Hey, whoa, just a minute! Jean?

S   Martin's brother has—

T   Martin, who has a new bicycle? You or your brother?

S   My brother.

T   And you have an old one.

S   (inaudible)

T   And your brother takes your old one?

S   (inaudible) bicycle.

T   His bicycle! How old is your brother?

S   March 23.

T   His birthday?

S   Yeah!

T   And how old was he?

S   Fourteen.

T   Fourteen. Well, why don't you tell your brother that when he takes your bike you will take his bike? And he may have more scratches than he figures for. OK?

Characteristics of input and interaction

Compare the two charts you have completed so far. What kinds of second language input and opportunities for interaction are available to learners in each of the environments that these transcripts exemplify? How are they different?

Classroom A

1 Errors: Very few on the part of the teacher. However her speech does have some peculiar characteristics typical of this type of teaching, for example, the questions in statement form—often asked with dramatic rising intonation (for example, 'You don't know what it is?'). Students don't make too many errors because they say very little and what they say is usually limited by the lesson.

2 Feedback on errors: Yes, whenever students do make errors, the teacher reacts.

3 Genuine questions: Yes, a few, but they are almost always related to classroom management. No questions from the students.

4 Display questions: Yes, almost all of the teacher's questions are of this type. Interestingly, however, the students sometimes interpret display questions as genuine questions (T: What are you doing, Paul? S: Nothing.). The teacher wants students to produce a sentence—any sentence—in the 'present continuous' but the student worries that he's about to get in trouble and asserts that he is doing 'nothing'. This is a good example of how the teacher's pragmatic intent can be misinterpreted by the student, and of how strongly, even in this setting, students seek to find genuine meaning in language.

5 Negotiation for meaning: Very little, learners have no need to paraphrase or request clarifications, and no opportunity to determine the direction of the discourse; the teacher is focused only on the formal aspects of the learners' language. All the effort goes into getting students to produce a sentence with the present continuous form of the verb.

6 Metalinguistic comments: Yes, this is how the teacher begins the lesson and lets the students know what really matters!

Classroom B

1 Errors: Yes, students make errors. And even the teacher says some odd things sometimes. Her speech also contains incomplete sentences, simplified ways of speaking, and an informal speech style.

2 Feedback on errors: Yes, sometimes the teacher repeats what the student has said with the correct form (for example, 'he bugzz me'—emphasizing the third person singular ending). However, this correction is not consistent or intrusive as the focus is primarily on letting students express their meanings.

3 Genuine questions: Yes, almost all of the teacher's questions are focused on getting information from the students. The students are not asking questions in this exchange. However, they do sometimes intervene to change the direction of the conversation.

4 Display questions: No, because there is a focus on meaning rather than on accuracy in grammatical form.

5 Negotiation for meaning: Yes, from the teacher's side, especially in the long exchange about who has a bicycle!

6 Metalinguistic comments: No. Even though the teacher clearly hopes to get students to use the third person ending, she does not say so in these words.

You no doubt noticed how strikingly different these two transcripts are, even though the activities in both are teacher-centred. In the transcript from Classroom A, the focus is on form (i.e. grammar) and in Classroom B, it is on meaning. In Classroom A, the only purpose of the interaction is to practise the present continuous. Although the teacher uses real classroom events and some humour to accomplish this, there is no real interest in what students are doing. Rather the teacher is highlighting their ability to say what they are doing, using the correct verb form. There is a primary focus on correct grammar, display questions, and error correction in the transcript from Classroom A. In the transcript from Classroom B, the focus is on meaning, conversational interaction, and genuine questions, although there are some brief references to grammatical accuracy when the teacher feels it is necessary.

Classroom comparisons: Student–student interactions

This section presents some student–student interactions. The transcripts are based on the interactions between second language learners engaged in different communicative tasks.

As in the previous section, there is a chart with each transcript where you can indicate whether certain things are happening in the interaction.

Communication task A: Picture description

The following transcript is of two girls aged 11–12 years, both ESL learners in their first year of learning English in Australia. The first learner (S1) is from Hong Kong; the second (S2) is from Somalia. They are engaged in a task where S1 is describing a picture for S2 to draw. They are sitting at a table, separated by a small barrier, so that they can see each other's faces and hands (when they gesture), but not each other's picture. The picture S1 is drawing is a black outline containing stick figures—a boy flying a kite and a girl holding his hand. The stick figures are standing on some grass near a tree. Square brackets indicate non-target pronunciation. (This transcript comes from unpublished data collected by Alison Mackey, Rhonda Oliver, and Jennifer Leeman.)

	Student I	Student 2
Errors		
Feedback on errors		
Genuine questions		
Display questions		
Negotiation for meaning		
Metalinguistic comments		

Photocopiable © Oxford University Press

S1 And o-on the right, there is a [tree]. It's a- a, the ki-, the kite is up. (Points up in the air) This is the kite. (Points up again) This is the kite. (Points yet again) And the [tree] is up there.

S2 Three bird?

s1   Huh?

s2   Is a three bird?

s1   Huh?

s2   Up, up-up the kite?

s1   Yeah, the kite is u-, the kite is up and the [tree] is down. (Points directions)

s2   The [bird] down?

s1   The kite-, the [tree] is down.

s2   What's the [tee]?

s1   Huh?

s2   What's the [tree]? (Imitates Learner 1's production)

s1   Feel?

s2   Fell?
     Fell down? (Points down)

s1   No, it's not the fell down. No, it's just at the bottom.

s2   The bird?

s1   No, the tree.

s2   The tree? (Emphatic stress)

s1   Yes.

s2   It is left and right?

s1   It's right. (Points)

s2   It's long? It's [little]?

s1   It's—what?

s2   It's long and [little]?

s1   Um, a little-. It-, um, a middle size.

s2   Middle size tree?

s1   Yes.

s2   It's little. (Says as drawing the tree)

Communication task B: Jigsaw

The following transcript is of two students in a Grade 7 French immersion classroom. They are engaged in a jigsaw activity based on a series of eight pictures telling the story of a young girl being awakened by her alarm clock early in the morning. One student has pictures 1, 3, 5, and 7, and the other student has pictures 2, 4, 6, and 8. They take turns telling the story portrayed by the pictures and then they display all the pictures in sequence and write the story they have just told. Telling the story requires the use of a number of reflexive verbs in French. In the third person, the form *se* is placed between the subject and the finite verb. Thus, *elle se lève* (she gets up) and *elle se souvient* (she remembers) are correct. The learners are called Dara (D) and Nina (N). In the transcript incorrect uses of the reflexive verbs are in italics; other errors are not marked. (The data are from Swain and Lapkin 2002.)

	Dara	Nina
Errors		
Feedback on errors		
Genuine questions		
Display questions		
Negotiation for meaning		
Metalinguistic comments		

Photocopiable © Oxford University Press

D   Elle. [She]
D   Elle se souvient, non, *Elle souvient* qu'elle a un ... une pratique de chorale, alors elle se lève. [She remembers, no. She remembers that she has a choir practice so she gets up]
D   Tout à coup [Suddenly]
N   Elle ssse [She ssse]
D   *Elle souvient* [She remembers]
N   se souvient ou *souvient*? [Remembers or remembers?]
D   *Elle souvient* ... ahh, elle se souvient ... *Elle souvient* ... Elle se souvient, no. [She remembers ... ahh, she remembers ... She remembers ... She remembers, no]
N   pas ... [not]
D   *Elle souvient* qu'elle doit aller au band ...? [She remembers that she has to go to band]
N   Chorale. [Choir]
D   Chorale. [Choir]
N   Tout à coup *elle souvient* qu'elle ... doit aller à la chorale [All of a sudden she remembers that she has to go to choir]
D   [very softly] elle se souvient ... non. [She remembers ... no]
D   Alors, elle [So, she]
N   non, wait. Tout à coup elle ... se souvient? [no, wait ... all of a sudden she ... remembers?]
D   Je pense pas que c'est se souvient. [I don't think it's remember]
N   oh, souvient ... souvient. [oh remember ... remember]
D   *Elle souvient* qu'elle a le chorale. [She remembers that she has choir]
N   Qu'elle doit se préparer. [that she has to get ready]
D   Oui. [Yes]
N   pour le chorale ... non, tout à coup *elle souvient* qu'il y a une pratique de chorale. [for choir ... no, all of a sudden she remembers that there's a choir practice]

Characteristics of input and interaction

Compare the two charts you have completed. As before, what kinds of second language input and opportunities for interaction are available to learners in each of the environments that these transcripts exemplify? How are they different from each other and the teacher–student interactions you looked at previously?

Communication task A

1 Errors: There are many errors in the speech of both learners. This includes grammatical and pronunciation errors. These errors are present in several breakdowns in the learners' conversation.
2 Feedback on errors: There is no error correction in terms of form as the learners struggle to understand each other's meaning. The difficulty they are having in communication may serve as a kind of implicit feedback. That is, the fact that the interlocutor does not understand may signal that there is something wrong with what they have said.
3 Genuine questions: Yes, there are many genuine questions. Naturally, S2 asks most of these questions because she needs to get the information from S1 in order to draw the picture. S1 also asks some genuine questions and these are almost always to ask for clarification.
4 Display questions: No, there are no display questions because they are engaged in a real communication-gap exchange. S2 cannot see the picture that S1 is describing. Therefore all the questions asked are genuine questions.
5 Negotiation for meaning: Yes, indeed! Both learners are trying hard to understand each other, even though they often fail to do so. This involves many comprehension questions and clarification requests, as well as repetitions of each other's utterances, often with emphasis, trying to understand what the other learner has just said.
6 Metalinguistic comments: None.

Communication task B

1 Errors: Both learners make several grammatical errors, most notably the repeated failure to produce the reflexive form of the verb *se souvenir*.
2 Feedback on errors: There is no actual error correction provided. Neither learner is really sure what the correct form is. Instead, there is metalinguistic reflection and discussion as they try to figure out whether they are using the correct form of the verb *se souvenir*.
3 Genuine questions: The questions that are asked are genuine. The content is language form, but the students are genuinely sharing information about how to complete the task.
4 Display questions: There are no display questions. The students are actively collaborating to reconstruct the story and are asking genuine questions of each other.

5 Negotiation for meaning: At this point in the interaction, the students have agreed on the content of the story. Thus, there is more negotiation of form, that is, more discussion of whether they are using the correct forms to say what they've agreed they want to say.

6 Metalinguistic comments: Although they are not using words such as 'verb' or 'pronoun', the students are talking about language as they focus on trying to find the right form.

These two transcripts of student–student interaction are very different from each other. In the first communication task, the children are focused exclusively on meaning and on trying to understand each other in order to complete the information-gap activity. They are constantly using comprehension and clarification requests as they negotiate for meaning in this task. In the second student–student transcript, however, the learners are focused on both form and meaning. While reconstructing the story, they make several explicit statements about whether they are using the correct form of the reflexive verb *se souvenir* and continually question the grammatical accuracy of their use of this form as they continue to discuss the content of the story.

In the activities in the preceding pages, we have described and compared teacher–student and student–student interaction in terms of six observation categories. Some observation schemes use many more categories, covering a broad range of instructional practices and procedures. Others focus on one specific feature of classroom instruction and interaction. In the following sections, we review classroom research in which one particular feature of instruction has been examined. Five studies examine corrective feedback, four investigate teachers' use of questions and one describes the amount and distribution of time for L2 learning.

Corrective feedback in the classroom

Study 1: Recasts in content-based classrooms

Roy Lyster and Leila Ranta (1997) developed an observation scheme which describes different types of corrective feedback teachers give on errors and also examines student **uptake**—an indication that the student has noticed the feedback.. This scheme was developed in French immersion classrooms where second language students learn the target language via subject-matter instruction (i.e. content-based language teaching). It has also been used to describe feedback in other types of second language instruction.

They developed their scheme by observing the different types of corrective feedback provided during interaction in four French immersion classrooms with 9–11-year-old students. They began their observations by using a combination of some categories from Part B of the COLT scheme and other categories from models that had examined feedback in both first and second language learning. They adjusted some of the categories to fit their data, and they also developed additional categories. This resulted in the identification of six corrective feedback types, defined below. The definitions are taken from Lyster and Ranta (1997: pp. 46–8). The examples come from 10–11-year-old students in ESL classes that we have observed.

Explicit correction refers to the explicit provision of the correct form. As the teacher provides the correct form, he or she clearly indicates that what the student had said was incorrect (for example, 'Oh, you mean …', 'You should say …').

    s   The dog run fastly.
    т   'Fastly' doesn't exist. 'Fast' does not take -ly. That's why I picked 'quickly'.

Recasts involve the teacher's reformulation of all or part of a student's utterance, minus the error. Recasts are generally implicit in that they are not introduced by 'You mean', 'Use this word', or 'You should say.'

    s1 Why you don't like Marc?
    т   Why don't you like Marc?
    s2 I don't know, I don't like him.

Note that in this example the teacher does not seem to expect uptake from S1. It seems she is merely reformulating the question S1 has asked S2.

Clarification requests indicate to students either that their utterance has been misunderstood by the teacher or that the utterance is incorrect in some way and that a repetition or a reformulation is required. A clarification request includes phrases such as 'Pardon me …' It may also include a repetition of the error as in 'What do you mean by …?'

    т   How often do you wash the dishes?
    s   Fourteen.
    т   Excuse me. (Clarification request)
    s   Fourteen.
    т   Fourteen what? (Clarification request)
    s   Fourteen for a week.
    т   Fourteen times a week? (Recast)
    s   Yes. Lunch and dinner.

Metalinguistic feedback contains comments, information, or questions related to the correctness of the student's utterance, without explicitly providing the correct form. Metalinguistic comments generally indicate that there is an error somewhere (for example, 'Can you find your error?'). Also, metalinguistic information generally provides either some grammatical terminology that refers to the nature of the error (for example, 'It's masculine') or a word definition in the case of lexical errors. Metalinguistic questions also point to the nature of the error but attempt to elicit the information from the student (for example, 'Is it feminine?').

S   We look at the people yesterday.
T   What's the ending we put on verbs when we talk about the past?
S   e–d

Elicitation refers to at least three techniques that teachers use to directly elicit the correct form from the students. First, teachers elicit completion of their own utterance (for example, 'It's a …'). Second, teachers use questions to elicit correct forms (for example, … 'How do we say x in English?'). Third, teachers occasionally ask students to reformulate their utterance.

S   My father cleans the plate.
T   Excuse me, he cleans the ——?
S   Plates?

Repetition refers to the teacher's repetition of the student's erroneous utterance. In most cases, teachers adjust their intonation so as to highlight the error.

In this example, the repetition is followed by a recast:

S   He's in the bathroom.
T   Bathroom? Bedroom. He's in the bedroom.

In the next example, the repetition is followed by metalinguistic comment and explicit correction:

S   We is …
T   We is? But it's two people, right? You see your mistake? You see the error? When it's plural it's 'we are'.

Lyster and Ranta found that all teachers in the content-based French immersion classes they observed used recasts more than any other type of feedback. Indeed, recasts accounted for more than half of the total feedback provided in the four classes. Repetition of error was the least frequent feedback type provided. The other types of corrective feedback fell in between. Student uptake was least likely to occur after recasts and more likely to occur after clarification requests, metalinguistic feedback, and repetitions. Furthermore, elicitations and metalinguistic feedback not only resulted in more uptake, they were also more likely to lead to a corrected form of the original utterance.

Lyster (1998) has argued that students receiving content-based language teaching (where the emphasis is on meaning not form) are less likely to notice recasts than other forms of corrective feedback, because they may assume that the teacher is responding to the content rather than the form of their speech. Indeed, the double challenge of making the subject-matter comprehensible and enhancing knowledge of the second language itself within content-based language teaching has led Merrill Swain (1988) and others to conclude that 'not all content teaching is necessarily good language teaching' (p. 68). The challenges of content-based language teaching will be discussed further in Chapter 6.

Since Lyster and Ranta reported their findings, many more observation studies of corrective feedback in second or foreign language classrooms have been carried out. Some of them report similar results—that recasts are the most frequently occurring type of feedback and that they appear to go unnoticed by learners. However, others report that learners do notice recasts in the classroom. Below, two studies are described in which learners were observed to notice and to respond to recasts provided by their teachers.

Study 2: Recasts and private speech

In a study with adult foreign language learners of Japanese, Amy Ohta (2000) examined the oral language that learners addressed to themselves during classroom activities. She was able to obtain this private speech by attaching microphones to individual students during classroom interaction that focused on grammar and metalinguistic instruction. In this context, Ohta discovered that learners noticed recasts when they were provided by the instructor. Furthermore, learners were more likely to react to a recast with private speech when it was directed to another learner or to the whole class rather than when the recast was directed to their own errors. On the basis of these findings, she concluded that recasts do get noticed in classroom interaction even if they do not lead to uptake from the student who originally produced the error.

Study 3: Recasts in different instructional settings

Roy Lyster and Hirohide Mori (2006) compared learners' immediate responses to corrective feedback in French and Japanese immersion classrooms. They found that the teachers in both contexts used corrective feedback in similar ways. However, the effects of recasts on learners' uptake were different. In the Japanese immersion classes, learners frequently repaired their utterances after receiving recasts whereas learners in the French immersion classes rarely did. Instead, the greatest proportion of repair came after prompts, that is, the feedback types that indicated to students that a correction was needed and that encouraged them to self-correct.

In their efforts to understand these differences Lyster and Mori carried out a detailed analysis of the instructional characteristics in these classes. Using the COLT observation scheme described above to capture differences in the pedagogical practices, they discovered that there was an analytic orientation in the Japanese classrooms leading the teachers and learners to focus their attention on language form and accuracy. The orientation in the French immersion classes was more experiential with a greater focus on content and communication of messages. Lyster and Mori argued that because the Japanese learners' attention was regularly drawn to form, they were primed to notice the corrective function of recasts. In the more meaning-oriented French immersion classes, however, recasts were less likely to signal to the learner that the teacher was responding to a language error. Thus is likely that learners assumed that the teachers' recast was simply a confirmation of what they had said.

These findings and those from other research led Lyster and Mori to propose the **counterbalance hypothesis**. According to this hypothesis, feedback is more likely to be noticed if learners are oriented in a direction that is opposite to what they have become accustomed to in their instructional environment. One example of this would be that learners who receive L2 instruction that is focused on meaning/content need feedback that directs their attention to form more explicitly.

Study 4: Corrective feedback in context
Rhonda Oliver and Alison Mackey (2003) carried out a **descriptive study** of an Australian primary ESL classroom with 6–12-year-olds. They investigated whether teachers' provision and learners' use of corrective feedback differed depending on varying contexts for interaction in a lesson. They identified four contexts in which teachers and learners interacted:

1 content exchanges: the teacher imparted knowledge or asked questions about the content of the curriculum
2 management exchanges: the teacher talked about the organization of the lesson and appropriate classroom behaviour
3 communication exchanges: the emphasis was on students using English in meaningful ways, and
4 explicit language-focused exchanges: the emphasis was on grammar and the use of metalinguistic terminology.

Oliver and Mackey found that learners produced significantly more errors in the communication exchanges. Thus opportunities for feedback were greatest in this context. The researchers found that feedback was provided in all instructional contexts but that it was most frequent in the explicit language-focused exchanges, followed by content, communication, and management. When they examined how learners reacted to the corrective feedback, they found that learners modified their output most often within explicit language-focused exchanges, only some of the time in content and communication exchanges, and never in management exchanges. Interestingly, the types of corrective feedback also varied across contexts: recasts were used at a consistently high rate in management, communication, and content exchanges, but less so in explicit language-focused exchanges; explicit corrective feedback was rarely provided during content, management, and communication exchanges, and frequently during explicit language-focused contexts.

Oliver and Mackey's study emphasizes how differences in the instructional context affect teachers' feedback and learners' response to it. It is also important to keep in mind that different corrective feedback types can be interpreted differently depending on how they are delivered. Recasts are a case in point. In a study of corrective feedback in four different instructional contexts, Younghee Sheen (2006) observed many contrasting types of recasts, including recasts that were declarative versus interrogative, reduced versus non-reduced, single words or short phrases versus long phrases or clauses. Recasts can also differ according to whether they are delivered with or without stress or emphasis. In a study of adult learners of English, Shawn Loewen and Jenefer Philp (2006) found that recasts containing 'prosodic stress were thirteen times more likely to result in successful uptake' (p. 547), that is, uptake in which the student produced the corrected form. However, these interactions were not associated with improved performance on a subsequent test.

Other factors that may affect learners' reactions to different types of feedback include age and learning goals. For example, adults may be more likely to interpret recasts as feedback on language form, particularly if a high level of accuracy in the second or foreign language is one of their goals.

In this chapter we have examined the role of corrective feedback primarily in terms of learners' oral production. Most of this research has been concerned with the effects of corrective feedback in relation to learners' linguistic growth and more specifically, learners' grammatical development. There is also an extensive body of research that has investigated the role of corrective feedback on learners' written production. This research has been primarily concerned with whether corrective feedback can help learners improve their writing performance. Less attention has been given to whether and how written corrective feedback contributes to learners' linguistic development. One recent study which has done that is Younghee Sheen's research described in Study 5 below.

Study 5: Oral and written corrective feedback
Younghee Sheen (2010) compared the effects of two types of oral and written corrective feedback on adult ESL learners' accurate use of articles. The oral corrective feedback consisted of recasts or metalinguistic information; parallel written corrective types were direct correction or direct metalinguistic feedback. Five groups participated in the study, of which one was a **control group**. The other groups each received one of the following: 1) oral recasts, 2) oral metalinguistic feedback, 3) written direct correction, and 4) written direct metalinguistic feedback.

All groups participated in two 30-minute activities in which they were asked to read a story and then retell it either in the written or the oral mode. Learners in the oral corrective feedback group received either recasts or metalinguistic feedback every time they made an article error while they retold the story. Learners who wrote the story received their narratives with corrections for article errors two days later. To determine whether learners improved their ability to use articles correctly, their knowledge of articles was tested before the instructional treatment, immediately after the treatment, and again 3–4 weeks later. The tests included a speeded dictation, a written narrative, and an error-correction task. All groups, except for the one that received oral recasts, significantly outperformed the control group on all immediate and delayed post-tests. Sheen interprets these findings as evidence that the medium (oral versus written) in which corrective feedback is provided is less important than the explicitness of the corrective feedback (recasts versus metalinguistic feedback).

Questions in the classroom

Teachers' questioning behaviour has been the focus of a good deal of research in second language classrooms. Questions are fundamental in engaging students in interaction and in exploring how much they understand. Two types of questions that have been extensively examined are referred to as 'display' questions (to which the teacher already knows the answer) and 'genuine' or 'referential' questions (to which the teacher may not know the answer). The role they play in classroom interaction has been examined in a number of studies.

Study 6: Teachers' questions in ESL classrooms

Michael Long and Charlene Sato (1983) examined the forms and functions of questions asked by teachers in ESL classrooms and compared them with questioning behaviours observed outside the classroom between native and non-native speakers. They were particularly interested in differences between the quantity of 'display' and 'information' ('genuine' or 'referential') questions. Audio recordings made of the interactions between teachers and students in six adult ESL classes revealed that teachers asked more display questions than information questions. In the native speaker/non-native speaker conversations outside the classroom, referential questions were more frequent than display questions. The researchers concluded that teacher–learner interaction is a 'greatly distorted version of its equivalent in the real world' (p. 284), and they argued that the interactional structure of classroom conversation should be changed.

Even though language teaching methods have changed since the Long and Sato study, other classroom studies on teachers' questioning behaviour have also reported disproportionately higher numbers of display questions. In the context of communicative language teaching, teachers have been urged to use fewer display questions because they are thought to lead to short, simple responses that require little cognitive effort on the part of the learner. Instead, they have been encouraged to ask more referential (or genuine) questions since the latter are thought to require more cognitive processing and to generate more complex answers.

More recently, however, a re-evaluation of display questions has taken place. This is based on the observation that there are different ways in which display questions can be asked in classrooms. One is for the teacher to ask a series of questions in a drill-like format such as 'Do you have a brother?', 'Does he have a brother?', 'Do you have a sister?', 'Does she have a sister?' In this context, display questions do not have a meaningful or communicative purpose. In other contexts, however, display questions can serve important pedagogic and interaction functions. The study below describes teachers' use of display questions in a more positive light.

Study 7: Scaffolding and display and referential questions

In a case study of one teacher's adult ESL class, Dawn McCormick and Richard Donato (2000) explored how the teacher's questions were linked to her instructional goals. Working within sociocultural theory, the researchers chose the concept of scaffolding to investigate teacher questions as 'mediational tools within the dialogue between the teacher and students' (p. 184). As we saw in Chapter 1 and Chapter 4, scaffolding refers to a process in which, for example, a more knowledgeable (or expert) speaker helps a less knowledgeable (or novice) learner by providing an interactional framework that the learner can build on.

McCormick and Donato identified six functions of scaffolding (for example, drawing the novice's attention to the task, and simplifying or limiting the task demands). The researchers examined another function—the teacher's use of questions during scaffolded interactions—and how it contributed to class participation and learner comprehension. In the example below, they argue that the teacher's use of the display question 'Who usually lives in palaces?' serves an important pedagogic function because it draws the learners' attention to the word 'palace' through the display question and facilitates the learners' comprehension of the word.

> T   Palace?
> S1   Like castle?
> S2   Special place, very good.
> S3   Very nice.
> T   Castle, special place, very nice. Who usually lives in palaces?
> SS   Kings.
> T   Kings, and queens, princes and princesses.
> SS   Yeah
> S4   Maybe beautiful house?
> T   Big, beautiful house, yeah, really big.

McCormick and Donato suggest that questions should be examined within the framework of scaffolded interaction and with reference to the teacher's goals in a particular lesson or interaction.

Study 8: Open and closed questions

Another distinction similar to the one between display and genuine questions is that between open and closed questions. Closed questions typically have only one possible answer and they usually lead to simple one-word responses, making them quick and easy to respond to. Open questions have more than one possible answer and invite elaboration, typically leading to longer and more complex answers, including, for example, explanation and reasoning. In **content and language-integrated learning** (CLIL) classes in Austria, Christiane Dalton-Puffer (2006) observed and audio recorded the types of questions asked by English teachers, as well as the responses students gave to them. Students produced a greater quantity and quality of output after open questions. In addition, open questions that asked learners not just for facts but also for reasons or explanations led to the most complex linguistic outcomes. Dalton-Puffer concluded that asking more complex open questions would benefit learners in these CLIL classrooms but that this level of question/response interaction requires a high level of competence in the foreign language on the part of the teacher.

Study 9: Wait time and teachers' questioning practices

Another aspect of teachers' questioning behaviour is 'wait time'—the amount of time the teacher pauses after having asked a question to give the student time to respond. Joanna White and Patsy Lightbown (1984) did a quantitative analysis of wait time in audiolingual ESL classes. They found that teachers typically gave students no more than a second or two before they directed the question to another student or answered the question themselves. They also tended to repeat or paraphrase the question several times rather than silently wait for the student to formulate a response. Although such rapid question/answer patterns are typical of audiolingual classes, they also occur in communicative instruction. Finding a balance between placing too much pressure on students to respond quickly and creating awkward silences seems to be a real challenge.

Research has shown that when teachers are trained to give their students more time to respond to questions, not only do students produce more responses but their responses are also longer and more complex. Not surprisingly, this effect has been observed to be stronger with open/referential questions compared with closed/display questions (Long et al. 1985).

In classrooms with students at different age levels and in different kinds of instruction, finding the right balance can lead to students providing fuller answers, expanding their ideas, and more successfully processing the material to be learned.

Study 10: Time for learning languages in school

Earlier in this chapter we talked about the differences between learning a second language in the natural setting compared with the classroom (see Table 5.1). One of the major differences is the amount of time available for learning. In the natural setting there is ample time to learn whereas in the typical classroom setting, learners have limited time. One of the ways to provide more time for learning a second/foreign language is via content-based instruction. However, this is not always feasible or desirable (Lightbown 2012). Other alternatives include increasing the total instructional time or distributing time more intensively over the school year.

We know that it takes a great deal of time to learn a second language, but little research has been done to investigate how the distribution of instructional time affects L2 learning. Exceptions to this include the work of some Canadian researchers who have examined different amounts and distributions of time in English and French as a second language programmes. In one study in Quebec, learners receiving **intensive ESL** instruction for five hours every day for five months of one school year (in Grade 5 or 6) were compared to learners at the end of secondary school who had received the same total amount of instruction spread over 7–8 years of schooling. On a number of measures, the students who received the intensive instruction performed as well as or better than those whose instruction was delivered in what has been called a 'drip feed' approach (Lightbown and Spada 1994).

In subsequent research, comparisons were made between groups of Grade 5 and 6 students who participated in intensive English language instruction during a single school year, but with the time distributed differently: some students received five hours of English a day for five months; others received the same total number of hours, doing two and a half hours of English each day for 10 months. The researchers found that both groups benefited from the overall increase in hours of instruction with some additional advantages for learners receiving the more intensive instruction (Collins et al. 1999; Collins and White 2011). The advantages were evident not only in superior language abilities but also in attitudes toward the language and satisfaction with language learning experiences. Similar findings have been reported for different models of intensive and core French programmes (Netten and Germain 2004; Lapkin, Hart, and Harley 1998).

The classroom observation studies we have described in this chapter focus on specific features of classroom interaction. In these studies, the feature of interest was determined in advance of the observation on the basis of some hypothesis about what aspects of classroom instruction and interaction are important for learning, that is, whether a particular type of corrective feedback led to more learner repair, whether a particular type of question led to more learner output, and how the distribution of time affected learning outcomes. We now turn to a different approach to describing and interpreting instructional settings for second language learning.

Ethnography

Ethnography is a way of observing teaching and learning in second or foreign language classrooms without a set of predetermined categories. Instead, the observer takes extensive notes of the activities, practices, and interactions and looks for the patterns that emerge. This approach to classroom observation is similar to the way in which an anthropologist takes field notes in studying a group of people in their natural surroundings. In doing ethnographic research, the observer can either be a participant in the classroom activities, for example, as a teacher's aid, or as a non-participant, someone who sits quietly and unobtrusively in the background, observing and recording.

Ethnographic approaches to understanding teaching and learning involve qualitative studies that are much broader in scope than the studies using observation schemes described above. That is, ethnographies in second or foreign language classrooms do not focus solely on learning or on teaching but also on social, cultural, and political realities and their impact on learners' cognitive, linguistic, and social development. For example, Martha Crago's (1992) language socialization research with Inuit children led her to argue that if children come from a culture in which silence is a respectful and effective way to learn from an adult, their second language instructor needs to know this so that the children's behaviour is not misinterpreted as refusal to participate or inability to comprehend.

Here are summaries of three ethnographies carried out in second and foreign language classrooms: one in the South Pacific, one in Canada, and one in Europe.

Study 11: Language in the home and school
Karen Watson-Gegeo (1992) carried out a **longitudinal study** over several years with nine families in the Solomon Islands. She explored language-use practices in the home and in the school. Observations in the homes revealed environments that were rich and stimulating for both linguistic and cognitive development. Nevertheless, a large number of the children failed in school. A detailed analysis uncovered many differences in language use and values between the home and school setting. There was no use of the children's first language in school. Their first language was replaced with a restricted and often incorrect version of English. Although these language issues were contributing factors to the children's failure, a broader analysis of the social and cultural context revealed other, more influential factors at play. Evidently, part of the children's language socialization experience at home included parents negatively portraying their own experiences at school, expressing

fears about their children's ability to succeed and raising fundamental questions about the value of school in their lives. The researcher concludes that these factors were central in contributing to the children's lack of continued cognitive and linguistic development in school.

Study 12: Separation of second language learners in primary schools

In a longitudinal study, Kelleen Toohey (2000) observed a group of children aged 5–7 in kindergarten, Grade 1, and Grade 2 in Vancouver, Canada. The group included children who were native speakers of English, as well as children whose home language was Cantonese, Hindi, Polish, Punjabi, or Tagalog. All the children were in the same class, and English was the medium of instruction. Toohey identified three classroom practices that led to the separation of the ESL children. First, the ESL children's desks were placed close to the teacher's desk, on the assumption that they needed more direct help from the teacher. Some of them were also removed from the classroom twice a week to obtain assistance from an ESL teacher. Second, instances in which the ESL learners interacted more with each other usually involved borrowing or lending materials but this had to be done surreptitiously because the teacher did not always tolerate it. Finally, there was a 'rule' in the classroom that children should not copy one another's oral or written productions. This was particularly problematic for the ESL children because repeating the words of others was often the only way in which they could participate in conversational interaction. According to Toohey, these classroom practices led to the exclusion of ESL students from activities and associations in school and also in the broader community in which they were new members. Furthermore, such practices did not contribute positively to the children's ESL development.

Study 13: Sociopolitical change and foreign language classroom discourse

In an ethnographic study of English-medium content classes in Hungarian secondary schools, Patricia Duff (1995) examined the impact of sociopolitical changes on pedagogical practice. She compared the structure and participation patterns of two classroom activities. One is a traditional activity called a *felelés* which is a heavily ritualized recitation format closely associated with Soviet-oriented policies that were rejected after the fall of communism in the late 1980s. As a result, in many English-medium classes in Hungary, the *felelés* was replaced by a more open-ended activity called 'student lecture' in which students prepared and presented material to the class in a less ritualized way.

In an examination of the kind of language produced by students when participating in student lectures, Duff observed a large number of spontaneous comments and questions produced in English rather than Hungarian. She also noted how students appeared to incorporate feedback provided by the teacher (and other students) in their subsequent production, how the teacher and students worked together to negotiate meaning and form, and how they developed their fluency, accuracy, and comprehension skills in the process. On the basis of these findings, Duff concluded that sociopolitical transformation affects classroom practice and ultimately second language learning.

Summary

In this chapter we have reviewed some of the ways in which different features of second language instruction can be described and interpreted. We have presented descriptions and examples of how classrooms differ in terms of their overall instructional focus and provided examples of different ways in which classroom observation has been carried out. We have included summaries of studies examining specific pedagogical features (i.e. corrective feedback and question types) as well as those examining the broader social, cultural, and political context and its relationship to second or foreign language learning.

We have also provided examples of charts and taxonomies that can be used to observe and describe different aspects of the interactions that take place between teachers and students in the classroom setting. We encourage you to try out one of these tools to observe and describe the interactions in your own classroom or that of a colleague. The information you gain from engaging in this small-scale research may help you make decisions about your own pedagogical practice.

In the next chapter, we will examine different views about how languages are best learned in classroom settings and examine some research relevant to these positions.

Questions for reflection

1 Do you think you may have a preference for using a particular type of corrective feedback in your teaching? For example, would you consider yourself to be a 'recaster' or a 'prompter' or do you think you use a range of different feedback types? What could you do to find out?

2 Are you teaching in multilingual classrooms where many of your students have a first language other than the language of instruction? Do you group these students together to respond to their needs or do you integrate them with the rest of the class? What do you think are the advantages/disadvantages of either decision?

3 The charts that you used to analyse the teacher–student talk and student–student talk in this chapter include six features (for example, errors, genuine questions, negotiation for meaning). Do you think there are other features that should be included in this chart? You can base your decision on the transcripts provided in this chapter or on your own teaching experience.

Suggestions for further reading

Spada, N. and **M. Fröhlich.** 1995. *The Communicative Orientation of Language Teaching Observation Scheme: Coding Conventions and Applications.* Sydney: Macmillan.

This book describes the origins and purposes of the Communicative Orientation of Language Teaching (COLT) observation scheme. COLT describes the pedagogical practices and verbal interactions that take place between teachers and students with the aim of describing the instruction as being more or less communicatively oriented. It also provides detailed guidelines and illustrations for using COLT including how to collect data, how to code the data, and how to analyse it. Also included are descriptions of how COLT has been used in second/foreign language classrooms throughout the world.

Toohey, K. 2000. *Learning English at School: Identity, Social Relations and Classroom Practice.* Clevedon: Multilingual Matters.

This book addresses a common educational practice in many countries in the world in which children from minority language backgrounds are taught in mainstream English-medium classes. Through a longitudinal description of a group of children learning English from kindergarten to the end of Grade 2 in a Canadian school, the reader is introduced to a range of social and critical perspectives on education and how they can be applied to child second language learning. The book provides important insights and useful guidance about how teachers and schools can support minority language children in their efforts to become educated through the medium of English.

Wajnryb, R. 1992. *Classroom Observation Tasks: A Resource Book for Language Teachers and Trainers.* Cambridge: Cambridge University Press.

This book is mainly addressed to teachers to illustrate how they can use observation to learn about their own teaching. Readers are guided through a variety of different tasks and shown how to observe, analyse, and reflect on various aspects of instruction including learners, language, lessons, and teaching strategies.

6 SECOND LANGUAGE LEARNING IN THE CLASSROOM

Preview

In this chapter, we examine six proposals for second and foreign language teaching, provide examples from classroom interaction to illustrate how the proposals get translated into classroom practice, and discuss research findings that help to assess their effectiveness. The labels we have given these proposals are:

1 Get it right from the beginning
2 Just listen … and read
3 Let's talk
4 Get two for one
5 Teach what is teachable
6 Get it right in the end

Proposals for teaching

Many theories have been proposed for the best way to learn a second language in the classroom. Even more teaching methods and materials have been developed to implement these theories. But the only way to answer the question 'What is the best way to promote language learning in classrooms?' is through research that specifically investigates relationships between teaching and learning.

To assess proposals for classroom practice, we need to use a range of research approaches, from large-scale quantitative to in-depth qualitative studies. As we saw in Chapter 5, quantitative research may be essentially descriptive. However, it may also be experimental, involving careful control of the variables that may influence learning. The goal of **experimental studies** is usually to identify specific variables that may affect learning similarly in different environments and find ways of measuring these effects. These studies often involve large numbers of learners in an effort to avoid the possibility that the unusual behaviour of one or two individuals might lead to a misleading conclusion about learners in general.

Qualitative research, including ethnographies and case studies, often involves small numbers, perhaps one class or only one or two learners in that class. The emphasis is not on what is most general but rather on a thorough understanding of what is particular about what is happening in this classroom. As pointed out by Ann Burns (2010) and others, while quantitative and qualitative research are important in assessing theoretical proposals, **action research** carried out by teachers in their own classrooms is also essential to answer specific local questions. In this chapter we focus mainly on experimental studies. These are studies that were designed to test hypotheses about how teaching affects second language learning. Readers are encouraged to follow up with further reading but also to explore related questions through research activities within their own teaching and learning environments.

1 *Get it right from the beginning*

'Get it right from the beginning' is probably the proposal that characterizes more second and foreign language instruction than any other kind. Although communicative language teaching has come to dominate in some environments, the structure-based approaches discussed in Chapter 5, especially grammar translation, remain widespread.

The grammar translation approach has its origin in the teaching of classical languages (for example, Greek and Latin). Students were presented with vocabulary lists, often accompanied by translation equivalents, and grammar rules. The original purpose of this approach was to help students read literature rather than to develop fluency in the spoken language. It was also thought that this approach provided students with good mental exercise to help develop their intellectual and academic abilities.

In a typical grammar translation activity, students read a text together line by line and are asked to translate it from the target language into their native language. Students may answer comprehension questions based on the passage, often in their first language. The teacher draws attention to a specific grammar rule that is illustrated by the text (for example, a certain verb form). Following this, the students are given an exercise in which they are asked to practise the grammar rule, for example, by filling in the blanks with the appropriate verb form in a series of decontextualized sentences that may or may not be related to the text they have read and translated.

Audiolingual instruction arose in part as a reaction to the grammar translation approach. The argument was that, unlike grammar translation teaching, in which students learned about the language, audiolingual teaching would lead students to actually speak the language (Brooks 1960; Lado 1964). In Chapter 4, we saw that the audiolingual approach was based on behaviourism and contrastive analysis. The examples below reflect audiolingual teaching. It is evident that, even though the emphasis is on the oral language, students rarely use the language spontaneously. Teachers avoid letting beginning learners speak freely out of concerns that this would allow them to make errors. The errors, it is said, could become habits. So it is better to prevent these bad habits before they happen and 'Get it right from the beginning.'

Example 1

(A group of 15-year-old students involved in an exercise based on the simple present of English verbs.)

> S1 And uh, in the afternoon, uh, I come home and uh, uh, I uh, washing my dog.
> T I wash.
> S1 My dog.
> T Every day you wash your dog?
> S1 No. [ben]
> S2 Il n'a pas de chien! (= He doesn't have a dog!)
> S1 Non, mais on peut le dire! (= No, but we can say we do!)

(Unpublished data from P. M. Lightbown and B. Barkman)

Clearly, in this case, the student's real experience with his dog (or even the fact that he did or did not have a dog) was irrelevant. What mattered was the correct use of the simple present verb!

Example 2

(A group of 12-year-old learners of English as a foreign language.)

> T   Repeat after me. Is there any butter in the refrigerator?
> CLASS   Is there any butter in the refrigerator?
> T   There's very little, Mom.
> CLASS   There's very little, Mom.
> T   Are there any tomatoes in the refrigerator?
> CLASS   Are there any tomatoes in the refrigerator?
> T   There are very few, Mom.
> CLASS   There are very few, Mom.

(Unpublished data from P. M. Lightbown and B. Barkman)

Pure repetition. The students have no reason to get involved or to think about what they are saying. Indeed, some students who have no idea what the sentences mean will successfully repeat them anyway, while their minds wander off to other things.

Research findings

Many adult learners, especially those with good metalinguistic knowledge of their own language, express a preference for structure-based approaches. Learners whose previous language learning experience was in grammar translation classes may also prefer such instruction. As we saw in Chapter 3, learners' beliefs about the kind of instruction that is best can influence their satisfaction and success. The grammar translation approach is useful for the study of grammar and vocabulary and can be valuable for understanding important cultural texts. The audiolingual approach with its emphasis on speaking and listening was used successfully with highly motivated adult learners in intensive training programmes for government personnel in the United States. However, there is little classroom research to support such approaches for students in ordinary school programmes that must serve the needs of students who bring different levels of motivation and aptitude to the classroom. In fact, it was the frequent failure of traditional grammar translation and audiolingual methods to produce fluency and accuracy in second language learners that led to the development of more communicative approaches to teaching in the first place.

Supporters of communicative language teaching have argued that language is not learned by the gradual accumulation of one grammatical feature after another. They suggest that errors are a natural and valuable part of the language learning process. Furthermore, they believe that the motivation of learners is often stifled by an insistence on correctness in the earliest stages of second language learning. These opponents of the 'Get it right from the beginning' proposal argue that it is better to encourage learners to develop 'fluency' before 'accuracy'.

Some researchers and educators have reacted to the version of communicative language teaching that advocates an exclusive focus on meaning. They argue that allowing learners too much 'freedom' without correction and explicit instruction will lead to early fossilization of errors. Once again we hear the call for making sure that learners 'Get it right from the beginning'.

Unfortunately, it is difficult to test whether an emphasis on form in the early stages of second language learning will, in the long run, lead to better results than those achieved when the emphasis is on meaning in the early stages. To test that hypothesis, it would be necessary to compare groups that are similar in all respects except for the type of instruction they receive. However, it is not easy for researchers to find proper comparison groups. This is because there are many parts of the world where one finds predominantly structure-based approaches to language teaching, and in these settings there are no (or very few) classrooms where the teaching places an emphasis on meaning. On the other hand, with the widespread adoption of communicative language teaching in other parts of the world, it is difficult to find classrooms that are exclusively structure-based. Nonetheless, some findings from second language classroom research do permit us to assess the effects of instruction that is strongly oriented to the 'Get it right from the beginning' approach. These include descriptive studies of the interlanguage development of second language learners in audiolingual programmes (Study 14), and comparisons of the development of second language proficiency between groups of students receiving different combinations of form- and **meaning-based instruction** (Study 15).

Study 14: Audiolingual pattern drill
In the late 1970s, Patsy Lightbown (1983a/b) carried out a series of longitudinal and cross-sectional investigations into the effect of audiolingual instruction on interlanguage development. The investigations focused on French-speaking learners aged 11–16 in Quebec, Canada. Students in these programmes typically participated in the types of rote repetition and **pattern practice drill** we saw in Examples 1 and 2.

The learners' acquisition of certain English grammatical morphemes (for example, plural -*s* and the progressive -*ing*) was compared with the acquisition of grammatical morphemes observed in the interlanguage of uninstructed second language learners (see Chapter 2, p. 46). The results showed differences between the developmental sequences we saw there and the relative accuracy with which these classroom learners produced them. These findings suggested that the type of instruction students had experienced—isolated pattern practice drills—resulted in a developmental sequence that appeared to be different from that of learners in more natural learning environments.

For a time after their instruction had focused on it, learners reliably produced a particular grammatical morpheme in its obligatory contexts. For example, after weeks of drilling on present progressive, students usually supplied both the auxiliary *be* and the *-ing* ending (for example, 'He's playing ball'). However, they also produced one or more of the morphemes in places where they did not belong ('He's want a cookie'). The same forms were produced with considerably less accuracy in obligatory contexts when they were no longer being practised in class and when the third person singular simple present *-s* was being drilled instead. At this point, many students appeared to revert to what looked like a developmentally earlier stage, using no tense marking at all (for example, 'He play ball'). These findings provided evidence that an almost exclusive focus on accuracy and practice of particular grammatical forms does not mean that learners will be able to use the forms correctly outside the classroom drill setting, nor that they will continue to use them correctly once other forms are introduced. Not surprisingly, this instruction, that depended on repetition and drill of decontextualized sentences, did not seem to favour the development of comprehension, fluency, or communicative abilities either.

Study 15: Grammar plus communicative practice
In one of the earliest experimental studies of communicative language teaching, Sandra Savignon (1972) studied the linguistic and communicative skills of 48 college students enrolled in French language courses at an American university. The students were divided into three groups: a 'communicative' group, a 'culture' group, and a control group. All groups received about four hours per week of audiolingual instruction where the focus was on the practice and manipulation of grammatical forms. In addition, each group had a special hour of different activities. The 'communicative' group had one hour per week devoted to communicative tasks in an effort to encourage practice in using French in meaningful, creative, and spontaneous ways. The 'culture' group had an hour devoted to activities, conducted in English, designed to 'foster an awareness of the French language and culture through films, music, and art'. The control group had an hour in the language laboratory doing grammar and pronunciation drills similar to those they did in their regular class periods.

Tests to measure learners' linguistic and communicative abilities were administered before and after instruction. The tests of linguistic competence included a variety of grammar tests, teachers' evaluations of speaking skills, and course grades. The tests of communicative competence included measures of fluency and of the ability to understand and transmit information in a variety of tasks, which included: discussion with a native speaker of French, interviewing a native speaker of French, reporting facts about oneself or one's recent activities, and describing ongoing activities in French.

At the end of the period of instruction, there were no **significant differences** between groups on the linguistic competence measures. However, the communicative group scored significantly higher than the other two groups on the four communicative tests developed for the study. Savignon interpreted these results as support for the argument that second language programmes that focus only on accuracy and form do not give students sufficient opportunity to develop communication abilities in a second language. Even more important in the context of the 'Get it right from the beginning' approach was the evidence that opportunities for freer communication did not cause learners to do less well on measures of linguistic accuracy.

Interpreting the research

The studies reviewed above provide evidence to support the intuitions of teachers and learners that instruction based on the 'Get it right from the beginning' proposal has important limitations. Learners receiving audiolingual or grammar-translation instruction are often unable to communicate their messages and intentions effectively in a second language. Experience has also shown that primarily or exclusively structure-based approaches to teaching do not guarantee that learners develop high levels of accuracy and linguistic knowledge. In fact, it is often very difficult to determine what students know about the target language. The classroom emphasis on accuracy often leads learners to feel inhibited and reluctant to take chances in using their knowledge for communication. The results from these studies provide evidence that learners benefit from opportunities for communicative practice in contexts where the emphasis is on understanding and expressing meaning.

It is important to emphasize that in the Savignon study, all students continued to receive their regular, grammar-focused instruction. They differed only in terms of the presence or absence of an additional communicative practice component. In other words, this study offers support for the argument that meaning-based instruction is advantageous, not that form-based instruction is not. The contributions of communicative practice and grammar-focused instruction will be discussed in more detail in relation to the 'Get it right in the end' proposal.

2 *Just listen ... and read*

'Just listen ... and read' is based on the hypothesis that language acquisition takes place when learners are exposed to comprehensible input through listening and/or reading. As noted in Chapter 4, the individual whose name is most closely associated with this proposal is Stephen Krashen (1985, 1989). This is a controversial proposal because it suggests that second language learners do not need to produce language in order to learn it, except perhaps to get other people to provide input by speaking to them. According to this view, it is enough to hear (or read) and understand the target language.

Read Example 3 to get a feel for how this theory of classroom second language learning can be implemented in a classroom. This description shows that one way to obtain comprehensible input is to provide learners with listening and reading comprehension activities with no (or very few) opportunities to speak or interact with the teacher or other learners in the classroom.

Example 3
It is time for English class at a primary school in a French-speaking community in New Brunswick, Canada. The classroom looks like a miniature language lab, with about thirty small desks, on each of which there is a cassette player and a set of large earphones. Around the room, shelves and racks display scores of books. Each book is packaged with an audiocassette that contains a recording of its content. The materials are not strictly graded, but some sets of books are very simple, and other sets are grouped so that they are gradually more challenging. There are pre-school children's books with a picture and a word or two on each page; illustrated stories with a few sentences per page; picture dictionaries; ESL textbooks for children; illustrated science books about animals, weather, vehicles, etc. Students (aged 8–10) enter the classroom, select the material they want, and take it to their individual workspace. They insert the cassette, put on their earphones, and open their books. They hear and read English for the next 30 minutes. For some of the time the teacher walks around the classroom, checking that the machines are running smoothly, but she does not interact with the students concerning what they are doing. Some of the students are listening with closed eyes; others read actively, mouthing the words silently as they follow each line with a finger. The classroom is almost silent except for the sound of tapes being inserted and removed or chairs scraping as students go to the shelves to select new tapes and books.

Research findings
Research relevant to the 'Just listen … and read' proposal includes studies of comprehension-based teaching and extensive reading (Day et al. 2011). We will also look at some **comprehension-based instruction** in which the input is manipulated in ways that are intended to increase the likelihood that students will pay attention to language form as well as meaning.

Study 16: Comprehension-based instruction for children
Example 3 was a description of a real programme implemented in experimental classes in a French-speaking region in Canada. From the beginning of their ESL instruction at age eight, students only listened and read during their daily 30-minute ESL period. There was no oral practice or interaction

in English at all. Teachers did not 'teach' but provided organizational and technical support. Thus, learners received native-speaker input from tapes and books but they had virtually no interaction in English with the teacher or other learners. They guessed at meaning by using the pictures or by recognizing cognate words that are similar in French and English. Occasionally they could refer to translation equivalents of a few words, taped inside a book's back cover.

Patsy Lightbown and her colleagues investigated the second language development of hundreds of children in this comprehension-based programme and compared their learning with that of students in the regular ESL programme, which was mainly an audiolingual approach. All the students in both programmes had classes that lasted 30 minutes per day. After two years, learners in the comprehension-based programme knew as much English as (and in some cases more than) learners in the regular programme. This was true not only for comprehension but also for speaking, even though the learners in the experimental programme had never practised spoken English in their classes (Lightbown et al. 2002; Trofimovich et al. 2009).

The students' English language abilities were reassessed three years later, when they were in Grade 8. Some students had continued in the comprehension-only programme throughout that time. On comprehension measures and on some measures of oral production, they continued to perform as well as students in the regular programme. On other measures, some groups of students in the regular programme had made greater progress, especially in writing. Those students were in classes where the regular programme included not only audiolingual instruction but also other speaking and writing components, teacher feedback, and classroom interaction.

Study 17: Reading for words
Finding reading material for primary school students learning a second language is challenging. Finding reading material for adults in early stages of second language acquisition is challenging too, but graded readers specially designed for adult ESL learners are increasingly available. These simplified literary classics, biographies, romances, and thrillers offer interesting and age-appropriate content, while the vocabulary and writing style remain simple. Marlise Horst (2005) used simplified readers in a study of vocabulary development among adult immigrants who were enrolled in an ESL programme in a community centre in Montreal, Canada. The 21 participants represented several language backgrounds and proficiency levels. In addition to the activities of their regular ESL class, students chose simplified readers that were made available in a class library. Over a six-week period, students took books home and read them on their own.

Horst developed individualized vocabulary measures so that learning could be assessed in terms of the books each student actually read. She found that there was vocabulary growth attributable to reading, even over this short period, and that the more students read, the more words they learned. She concluded that substantial vocabulary growth through reading is possible, but that students must read a great deal (more than just one or two books per semester) to realize those benefits. As we saw in Chapter 2, when we interact in ordinary conversations, we tend to use mainly the 1,000 or 2,000 most frequent words. Thus, reading is a particularly valuable source of new vocabulary. Students who have reached an intermediate level of proficiency may have few opportunities to learn new words in everyday conversation. It is in reading a variety of texts that students are most likely to encounter new vocabulary. The benefit of simplified readers is that students encounter a reasonable number of new words. This increases the likelihood that they can figure out the meaning of new words (or perhaps be motivated to look them up). If the new words occur often enough, students may remember them when they encounter them in a new context.

Other research that explores the 'Just listen ... and read' proposal includes studies in which efforts have been made to draw second language learners' attention to language forms in the input, for example, by providing high-frequency exposure to specific language features through an **input flood**, highlighting the features through **enhanced input**, and/or providing **processing instruction**. All of these are described in more detail below but the emphasis in all cases is on getting learners to notice language forms in the input, not on getting them to practise producing the forms. The next three studies are examples of this research.

Study 18: Input flood

Martha Trahey and Lydia White (1993) carried out a study with young French-speaking learners (aged 10–12) in intensive ESL classes in Quebec such as those described in Chapter 5, Study 10. The goal of the research was to determine whether high-frequency exposure to a particular form in the instructional input would lead to better knowledge and use of that form by the students. The linguistic form investigated was adverb placement in English (see Chapter 2, p. 58). For approximately 10 hours over a two-week period, learners read a series of short texts in which they were exposed to literally hundreds of instances of adverbs in English sentences—so many that the investigators referred to this study as an 'input flood'. There was no teaching of adverb placement, nor was any error correction provided. Instead, students simply read the passages and completed a variety of comprehension activities based on them.

Although learners benefited from this exposure to sentences with adverbs in all the correct positions, their learning was incomplete. They improved in their acceptance of sentences with word order that is grammatical in English but not in French ('The children quickly leave school'). However, they continued to accept sentences that are grammatical in French but not in English ('The children leave quickly school'). The students' inability to recognize that adverbs in this position are ungrammatical in English suggests that the input flood could help them add something new to their interlanguage, but did not lead them to get rid of an error based on their first language. As noted in Chapter 2, Lydia White (1991) argued that although exposure to language input provides learners with positive evidence (information about what is grammatical in the second language), it fails to give them negative evidence (information about what is not grammatical). Positive evidence is not enough to permit learners to notice the absence in the target language of elements that are present in their interlanguage (and their first language). Thus, more explicit information about what is not grammatical in the second language may be necessary for learners' continued development. This is discussed in more detail in the section 'Get it right in the end'.

Study 19: Enhanced input
Michael Sharwood Smith (1993) coined the term 'input enhancement' to refer to a variety of things that might draw learners' attention to features in the second language, thus increasing the chances that they would be learned. In a study involving enhanced input, Joanna White (1998) examined the acquisition of possessive determiners (specifically 'his' and 'her'; see Chapter 2, p. 53) by French-speaking learners aged 11–12 in intensive ESL classes. Students received approximately 10 hours of exposure to hundreds of possessive determiners through a package of reading materials and comprehension activities provided over a two-week period. The major difference between this study and Trahey and White's input flood is that typographical enhancement was added. That is, every time a possessive determiner appeared in the texts, it was in bold type, underlined, italicized, or written in capital letters. The hypothesis was that this would lead the learners to notice the possessive determiners as they read the texts.

White compared the performance of learners who had read the typographically enhanced passages with that of learners who read the same texts without enhancement. She found that both groups improved in their knowledge and use of these forms and that there was little difference between them. In interpreting these findings, White questions whether the enhancement was sufficiently explicit to draw the learners' attention to possessive determiners. That is, even though the forms were highlighted by the use of bold type, capital letters, etc., students did not learn how to choose the possessive determiner to match the gender of the possessor. In subsequent research, White found that learners made more progress when they were given a simple rule and then worked together to find the correct possessive determiners (Spada, Lightbown, and White 2005).

Enhancing the input

Study 20: Processing instruction

Bill VanPatten (2004) and his colleagues have investigated the effects of processing instruction, another approach to comprehension-based learning. In processing instruction, learners are put in situations where they cannot comprehend a sentence by depending solely on context, prior knowledge, or other clues. Rather they must focus on the language itself. In one of the first studies, adult learners of Spanish as a foreign language received instruction on different linguistic forms, for example, object pronouns (VanPatten and Cadierno 1993). As noted in Chapter 4, VanPatten found that English-speaking learners of Spanish tended to treat the object pronouns, which precede the verb in Spanish, as if they were subject pronouns. Thus, a sentence such as *La sigue el señor* (literally 'her (object) follows the man (subject)') was interpreted as 'She follows the man'.

Two groups were compared in the study, one receiving processing instruction, the other following a more traditional approach. The processing instruction group received explicit explanations about object pronouns and did some activities that drew their attention to the importance of noticing that object pronouns could occur before the verb. Then, through a variety of focused listening and reading exercises, learners had to pay attention to how the target forms were used in order to understand the meaning. For example, they heard or read *La sigue el señor* and had to choose which picture—a man following a woman or a woman following a man—corresponded to the sentence. A second group of learners also received explicit information about the target forms but instead of focusing on comprehension practice through processing instruction, they engaged in production practice, doing exercises to practise the forms being taught. After the instruction, learners who had received the comprehension-based processing instruction not only did better on the comprehension tasks than learners in the production group, they also performed as well on production tasks.

Interpreting the research

Research on comprehension-based approaches to second language acquisition shows that learners can make considerable progress if they have sustained exposure to language they understand. The evidence also suggests, however, that comprehension-based activities may best be seen as an excellent way to begin learning and as a supplement to other kinds of learning for more advanced learners.

Comprehension of meaningful language is the foundation of language acquisition. **Active listening** and reading for meaning are valuable components of classroom teachers' pedagogical practices. Nevertheless, considerable research and experience challenge the hypothesis that comprehensible input is enough. VanPatten's research showed that forcing students to rely on specific linguistic features in order to interpret meaning increased the chances that they would be able to use these features in their own second language production.

Another response to comprehension-based approaches is Merrill Swain's (1985) comprehensible output hypothesis. She argues that it is when students have to produce language that they begin to see the limitations of their interlanguage (see Chapter 4). However, as we will see in the discussion of the 'Let's talk' proposal, if learners are in situations where their teachers and classmates understand them without difficulty, they may need additional help in overcoming those limitations.

3 Let's talk

Advocates of the 'Let's talk' proposal emphasize the importance of access to both comprehensible input and conversational interactions with teachers and other students. They argue that when learners are given the opportunity to engage in interaction, they are compelled to negotiate for meaning, that is, to express and clarify their intentions, thoughts, opinions, etc., in a way that permits them to arrive at mutual understanding. This is especially true when the learners are working together to accomplish a particular goal, for example in task-based language teaching (TBLT). According to the interaction hypothesis, negotiation leads learners to acquire the language forms—the words and the grammatical structures—that carry the meaning they are attending to. This is the theoretical view underlying the teacher–student behaviour in the transcript from Classroom B and from the student–student interaction in Communication task A in Chapter 5.

Negotiation for meaning is accomplished through a variety of modifications that naturally arise in interaction, such as requests for clarification or confirmation, repetition with a questioning intonation, etc.

Look for negotiation for meaning in the examples below and compare this with the examples given for the 'Get it right from the beginning' proposal.

Example 4
(A group of 12-year-old ESL students are discussing a questionnaire about pets with their teacher.)

> s   And what is 'feed'?
> t   Feed? To feed the dog?
> s   Yes, but when I don't have a ...
> t   If you don't have a dog, you skip the question.

Example 5
(Students from Classroom B, as they settle in at the beginning of the day.)

> t   How are you doing this morning?
> s1   I'm mad!
> s2   Why?
> t   Oh boy. Yeah, why?
> s1   Because this morning, my father say no have job this morning.
> t   Your father has no more job this morning? Or you have no job?
> s1   My father.

How different these examples are from the essentially meaningless interaction often observed in classrooms where the emphasis is on 'getting it right from the beginning'. Such genuine exchanges of information must surely enhance students' motivation to participate in language learning activities.

But do they, as advocates of this position claim, lead to successful language acquisition? Note, for example, that, although the conversation proceeded in a natural way, the student in Example 4 never did find out what 'feed' meant.

Research findings
Most of the early research that examined the 'Let's talk' proposal was descriptive in nature, focusing on such issues as: How does negotiation in classrooms differ from that observed in natural settings? How do teacher-centred and student-centred classrooms differ in terms of conversational interaction? Do task types contribute to different kinds of interactional modifications? Several studies also examined relationships between modifications in conversational interaction and comprehension.

In the mid-1990s researchers began to directly explore the effects of interaction on second language production and development over time. Most of these studies have been carried out in laboratory settings and are motivated by Michael Long's (1996) updated version of the interaction hypothesis (see Chapter 4). Compared with the original version stating that conversational interaction promotes second language development (Long 1983), the updated version integrates learner capacities that contribute to second language learning (for example, attention) and features of interaction that are most likely to facilitate learning. Corrective feedback has been identified as one feature that is believed to play a crucial role in helping learners to make connections between form and meaning. In fact, as we will see later in this chapter, research relevant to the updated interaction hypothesis is more in line with the 'Get it right in the end' proposal.

Study 21: Learners talking to learners
In one of the early descriptive studies on learner interaction, Michael Long and Patricia Porter (1985) examined the language produced by adult learners performing a task in pairs. There were 18 participants: 12 non-native speakers of English whose first language was Spanish, and six native English speakers. The non-native speakers were intermediate or advanced learners of English.

Each individual learner participated in separate discussions with a speaker from each of the three levels. For example, an intermediate-level speaker had a conversation with another intermediate-level speaker, another with an advanced-level speaker, and another with a native speaker of English. Long and Porter compared the speech of native and non-native speakers in conversations, analysing the differences across proficiency levels in conversation pairs. They found that learners talked more with other learners than they did with native speakers. Also, learners produced more talk with advanced-level learners than with intermediate-level partners, partly because the conversations with advanced learners lasted longer.

Long and Porter examined the number of grammatical and vocabulary errors and false starts and found that learner speech showed no differences across contexts. That is, intermediate-level learners did not make any more errors with another intermediate-level speaker than they did with an advanced or native speaker. This was an interesting result because it called into question the argument that learners need to be exposed to a native-speaking model (i.e. teacher) at all times to ensure that they produce fewer errors. Overall, Long and Porter concluded that although learners cannot always provide each other with the accurate grammatical input, they can offer each other genuine communicative practice that includes negotiation for meaning. Supporters of the 'Let's talk' proposal argue that it is precisely this negotiation for meaning that is essential for language acquisition.

Study 22: Learner language and proficiency level

George Yule and Doris Macdonald (1990) investigated whether the role that different proficiency-level learners play in a two-way communication task led to differences in their interactive behaviour. They set up a task that required two learners to communicate information about the location of different buildings on a map and the route to get there. One learner, referred to as the 'sender', had a map with a delivery route on it, and this speaker's job was to describe the delivery route to the 'receiver' so that he or she could draw the delivery route on a similar map. The task was made more challenging by the fact that there were minor differences between the two maps.

To determine whether there would be any difference in the interactions according to the relative proficiency of the 40 adult participants, different types of learners were paired together. One group had high-proficiency learners in the 'sender' role and low-proficiency learners in the 'receiver' role; the other group had low-proficiency 'senders' paired with high-proficiency 'receivers'.

When low-proficiency learners were senders, interactions were considerably longer and more varied than when high-proficiency learners were the senders. The explanation for this was that high-proficiency senders tended to act as if the lower-level receiver had little contribution to make in the completion of the task. As a result, the lower-level receivers were almost forced to play a passive role and said very little. When lower-level learners were the senders however, much more negotiation for meaning and a greater variety of interactions between the two speakers took place. Based on these findings, Yule and Macdonald suggest that teachers should sometimes place more advanced students in less dominant roles in paired activities with lower-level learners.

Study 23: The dynamics of pair work

In a longitudinal study with adult ESL learners in an Australian university, Neomy Storch (2002) observed the patterns of interaction between 10 pairs of students completing different tasks over one semester. She identified four distinct patterns of interaction: 'collaborative' interaction consisted of two learners fully engaged with each other's ideas; 'dominant–dominant' interaction was characterized by an unwillingness on the part of either learner to engage and/or agree with the other's contributions; 'dominant–passive' consisted of one learner who was authoritarian and another who was willing to yield to the other speaker; and 'expert–novice' interaction consisted of one learner who was stronger than the other but actively encouraged and supported the other in carrying out the task. To investigate whether the four types of interaction led to differences in learning outcomes, Storch identified learning events that occurred during the interactions (for example, learning that the definite article is used with the names of some countries). Then she looked at whether that language knowledge was maintained in a subsequent task. Storch found that learners who participated in the collaborative and expert–novice pairs maintained more of their L2 knowledge over time. Learners who participated in the dominant–dominant and dominant–passive pairs maintained the least. Storch interprets this as support for Vygotsky's theory of cognitive development (see Chapter 4) and the claim that when pair work functions collaboratively and learners are in an expert–novice relationship, they can successfully engage in the co-construction of knowledge.

Study 24: Interaction and second language development

Alison Mackey (1999) asked adult learners of ESL to engage in different communicative tasks, for example, story completion and picture sequencing with native speakers of English. The tasks were designed to provide contexts for learners to produce questions. Prior to participating in the tasks, the learners were assessed in terms of the stage they had reached in learning questions, as described in Chapter 2. They were then divided into five groups. The learners in Group 1, referred to as 'Interactors,' carried out the tasks with native speakers, who modified their language as they sought to clarify meaning for the learners. Learners in Group 2 received the same modified input as learners in Group 1 but they were not as advanced in their acquisition of question forms and thus were referred to as the 'Interactor Unreadies.' Learners in Group 3, the 'Observers,' were asked to listen to the learner and the native speaker as they carried out the task but they did not interact in any way. Learners in Group 4, the 'Scripteds' carried out the same tasks with the native speakers but the native speakers used language that had been simplified and scripted in such a detailed manner that communication breakdowns did not occur and thus no negotiation for meaning took place. There was also a control group of learners who did not participate in any of the tasks but completed all the tests.

Both Interactors and Interactor Unreadies demonstrated more sustained progress in their question formation development than learners who did not engage in interaction (i.e. Observers, Scripteds, and Control). The Observers and the Scripteds were similar to the Control group learners, who changed very little. Mackey also notes that the significant increase in development for the Interactors was maintained on the delayed post-tests administered one month after the treatment tasks. These results are interpreted as support for the hypothesis that negotiated interaction leads to L2 development.

Study 25: Learner–learner interaction in a Thai classroom

In a study relevant to the updated version of the interaction hypothesis, Kim McDonough (2004) investigated the use of pair- and small-group activities in English as a foreign language classes in Thailand. Students engaged in interactional activities in which they discussed environmental problems in their country. The topic was chosen as one that would generate contexts for the use of conditional clauses such as 'If people didn't leave water running while brushing their teeth, they would save an estimated 5–10 gallons each time' (p. 213). Learners were audio-recorded as they discussed the environmental problems.

The recorded conversations were examined to see the extent to which students used interactional features that are believed to facilitate second language learning, for example, negative feedback (i.e. clarification requests, explicit correction, and recasts) and modified output (i.e. a learner's more accurate/complex reformulation of his or her previous utterance). Learners were tested on their ability to produce conditional clauses in a pre-test, an immediate post-test, and a delayed post-test.

McDonough found that learners who had used more negative feedback and modified output in their interactions significantly improved in the accuracy of their conditional clauses. Those who made less use of these features did not. McDonough also explored opinions about the usefulness of pair work and small-group activities, asking whether such activities contributed to learning. She found that the students did not perceive pair- and group-activities as useful for learning English. This was true both for students who seemed to have made effective use of the interaction for learning and those who had not. The fact that learners were sceptical of the benefits of group- and pair-work activities suggests a need to take account of learners' beliefs about learning (see Chapter 3) and to share with them our reasons for using these activities.

Interpreting the research

Research based on the interaction hypothesis has investigated factors that contribute to the quality and quantity of interactions between second language learners. It has provided some useful information for teaching. Certainly, the studies by Long and Porter, Yule and Macdonald, and Storch contribute to a better understanding of how to organize group and pair work more effectively in the classroom. The Mackey and McDonough studies are two examples of research that have measured second language development in relation to different aspects of conversational interaction. Mackey's study used one-on-one pair-work activities between trained native speakers and non-native speakers focusing on a single grammatical feature in a laboratory context. Thus it is difficult to relate the findings to the kind of interactions that take place in classrooms. The McDonough study helps to fill this gap because it is a classroom study that also demonstrates the benefits of interaction on second language learning over time.

Recently, a number of laboratory studies have also examined the effects of different interactional features on specific aspects of second language learning over time. Several studies have shown that implicit corrective feedback (for example, recasts) in pair-work situations is beneficial. A recent review of this research confirms that the positive effects for recasts are strongest in the laboratory setting (Mackey and Goo 2007). This may be because recasts are more salient in pair work, particularly if only one form is recast consistently (Nicholas, Lightbown, and Spada 2001).

In McDonough's classroom study, recasts (and other forms of corrective feedback) were more likely to have been noticed because the Thai learners were accustomed to traditional grammar instruction and a focus on accuracy. This is not always the case, however. As we learned in Chapter 5, when the instructional focus is on expressing meaning through subject-matter instruction, the teachers' recasts may not be perceived by the learners as an attempt to correct their language form but rather as just another way of saying the same thing. Later in this chapter we will look at classroom studies related to the 'Get it right in the end' position that have investigated the effects of more explicit corrective feedback on second language learning.

4 *Get two for one*

In content-based language teaching, learners acquire a second or foreign language as they study subject matter taught in that language. It is implemented in a great variety of instructional settings, for example, immersion programmes and the content and language-integrated learning (CLIL) programmes in Europe described in Study 8 in Chapter 5. Other educational programmes such as the European Schools extend this further by offering instruction in two or more languages in addition to students' home language. The expectation of this approach is that students can get 'two for one', learning the subject matter content and the language at the same time.

In immersion and CLIL programmes, students choose (or their parents choose for them) to receive content-based instruction in a second language. In many educational situations, however, no other option is available. For example, in some countries, the only language of schooling is the language of a previous colonial power. In others, educational materials are not available in all local languages, so one language is chosen as the language of education. In countries of immigration, students often have access to schooling only through the majority language. Other students may have access to **bilingual education** programmes that allow some use of a language they already know, but the transition to the majority language is usually made within a year or two.

Research findings

In many contexts for content-based instruction, it is simply assumed that students will develop both their academic skills and second language ability.

In recent years, researchers have sought to examine this assumption more critically.

Study 26: French immersion programmes in Canada

Research in Canadian French immersion programmes is often cited in support of the 'Get two for one' proposal. Most immersion programmes are offered in primary and secondary schools, but some universities also offer content-based instruction that expands opportunities for students to use their second language in cognitively challenging and informative courses. What have the studies shown?

In terms of popularity and longevity, French immersion has been a great success. Thousands of English-speaking Canadian families have chosen this option since its first implementation in the 1960s (Lambert and Tucker 1972), both in areas where French is spoken in the wider community and in those where French is rarely heard outside the classroom. Numerous studies have shown that French immersion students develop fluency, high levels of listening comprehension, and confidence in using their second language. They also maintain a level of success in their academic subjects that is comparable to that of their peers whose education has been in English (Genesee 1987). Over the years, however, educators and researchers began to express concern about students' failure to achieve high levels of performance in some aspects of French grammar, even after several years of full-day exposure to the second language in these programmes.

Some researchers argue that the difficulty French immersion learners experience in their L2 production shows that comprehensible input is not enough (Harley and Swain 1984). They claim that the learners engage in too little language production because the classes are largely teacher-centred. Students are observed to speak relatively little and rarely required to give extended answers. This permits them to operate successfully with their incomplete knowledge of the language because they are rarely pushed to be more precise or more accurate. When students do speak, communication is usually satisfactory in spite of numerous errors in their speech because the learners' interlanguages are influenced by the same first language, the same learning environment, and the same limited contact with the target language outside the classroom. Teachers also tend to understand students' interlanguage, so there is rarely a need to negotiate for meaning. Such successful communication makes it difficult for an individual learner to work out how his or her use of the language differs from the target language.

Another explanation for students' lack of progress on certain language features is their rarity in French immersion instruction. For example, Merrill Swain (1988) observed that even history lessons, where past tense verbs might be expected to occur, were often delivered in the 'historical present' (for example, 'The ships go down to the Caribbean; they pick up sugar and they take it back to England ...'). Roy Lyster (1994) found that the use of the second person pronoun *vous* to politely address an individual was used so rarely in classes that even after years of immersion instruction, students did not use it appropriately. Elaine Tarone and Merrill Swain (1995) noted that learners with only classroom exposure to the language did not have access to the speech styles that would be typical of interaction among native speakers of the same age. Increasingly, it was suggested that subject matter instruction needed to be complemented by instruction that focused on language form, including pragmatic features of the language. In some experimental studies, learners did benefit from **form-focused instruction** on particular language features (see the 'Get it right in the end' proposal).

Study 27: Late immersion under stress in Hong Kong

In the 1960s the educational system in Hong Kong moved from one in which students studied either exclusively in English or in Cantonese to one in which the majority of students studied in Cantonese in primary school (Grades 1–6) and in English at secondary school (Grades 7–13). These late English immersion programmes were popular with Chinese parents who wanted their children to succeed professionally and academically in the international community. They were also seen as being consistent with the Hong Kong government's goal of maintaining a high level of Chinese–English bilingualism.

In reviewing some of the research on teaching and learning behaviours in late English immersion classes in Hong Kong secondary schools, Keith Johnson (1997) raised concerns about the ability of the educational system to meet the demands for such programmes. He noted that students lacked the English proficiency needed to follow the secondary level curriculum successfully. He also observed teachers' difficulties in effectively delivering the content because of limitations in their own English proficiency. He argued that several pedagogic behaviours contributed to the inability of learners to make adequate linguistic progress in these English immersion programmes. One of them was teacher talk that consisted of English, Chinese, and 'Mix' (a combination of English and Chinese).

Observational classroom studies revealed that Chinese and Mix predominated in the speech of teachers and that students interacted with the teacher and with each other in English only in minimal ways. Many students came to the first year of secondary school without any literacy skills in English. To compensate for this, teachers employed a variety of strategies to help students comprehend texts. They reduced the vocabulary load, simplified the grammar, encouraged the use of bilingual dictionaries, and provided students with supplementary notes and charts in Chinese to assist their comprehension. Johnson observed that, while 'the texts are not translated, they are essentially pre-taught so that by the time students come to read the texts for themselves the more able students at least are sufficiently familiar with the content to be able to deal with them' (p.177). Although these strategies helped students understand the content, they may not have helped them learn to use the syntactic and discourse structures in the second language to establish form–meaning relationships. Therefore it is not surprising that the standards of reading in English at age 15 were reported to be significantly lower than those for Chinese. At the same time, however, the educational outcomes for Hong Kong students in content subjects continued to be high, comparable to, and in some areas superior to, achievements in other developed countries. In addition, the levels of Chinese L1 reading proficiency remained high.

In spite of professional development efforts to help teachers achieve the dual goals of language and content instruction, Philip Hoare and Stella Kong (2008) find that many teachers in the Hong Kong immersion programmes continue to have difficulty implementing immersion pedagogy. They attribute this in part to the pressure teachers feel in a society where performance on examinations is paramount. To ensure that their students do well on the content exams, teachers often feel that they must teach in Chinese or in a simplified English that does not give students access to the language that is appropriate for high-level academic work.

Study 28: Dual immersion

In recent years, legislation has limited the availability of bilingual education for most minority language students in the United States. In most states, English language learners' education must take place entirely in English, or with only minimal support for learning through their first language. As we saw in Chapter 1, the result of this approach is often subtractive bilingualism. Children gradually lose their first language or fail to develop it for academic purposes. In addition, they often fall behind in their academic work because they do not yet have the English language skills needed for dealing with the grade-level subject matter.

Some jurisdictions allow 'dual immersion' as an exception to the strict enforcement of instruction through English only. In dual immersion, minority language students learn English in classrooms where English-speaking children also learn the minority language students' home language. Patsy Lightbown (2007) observed classroom interaction and learning outcomes in a school where an equal number of native English- and native Spanish-speaking students shared the classrooms. Starting in kindergarten, half their instruction was delivered in English by an English native speaker and half in Spanish by a native speaker of that language. Teachers coordinated closely to ensure that the subject matter instruction in the two languages was complementary rather than redundant. Students' performance on a variety of measures administered through Grade 3 showed that the programme was beneficial for their development of English language skills, and Spanish-speaking students made especially rapid progress in reading. Of particular importance was the fact that students also continued to develop their Spanish language skills in ways that were not available to students whose instruction was either in English only or in transitional bilingual classes where there was very little support for their home language.

In other dual immersion programmes, the number of students and the amount of time are distributed differently, often with more time devoted to the teaching and learning of English, but sometimes with an early emphasis on the minority language that resembles the Canadian French immersion programmes, that is, where the English-speaking students receive nearly all their early instruction in their second language. This approach is preferred in settings where it is not possible to have a substantial number of students from the minority language. Indeed, a number of different models of dual immersion have been developed, but they all are based on the principle that the continued development of a child's home language is a strong foundation on which to build second language abilities (Howard et al. 2007).

In recent years, several research reviews have examined the evidence for different approaches to educating English language learners in the United States (August and Shanahan 2008; Genesee et al. 2006). The research confirms better outcomes, in both English language learning and subject matter knowledge, for minority language students in programmes that support the students' home languages than for those in English only or 'early exit' bilingual programmes where they receive only token opportunities to continue learning through their home language. Kathryn Lindholm-Leary (2001) also found benefits for the majority language students in dual immersion programmes, where they share the challenges and achievements of second language learning with minority language students. She suggests that this approach 'has the potential to eradicate the negative status of bilingualism in the US' (p.1).

Study 29: Inuit children in content-based programmes
In an aboriginal community in Quebec, Canada, Nina Spada and Patsy Lightbown (2002) observed the teaching and learning of school subjects and language with Inuit children. The children had been educated in their first language, Inuktitut, from kindergarten to Grade 2 (aged 5–7). Then, except for occasional lessons in Inuit culture, their education was in one of Canada's official languages, French or English. Nearly all students had some difficulty coping with subject matter instruction in their second language.

In a case study of one French secondary-level class, they observed instructional activities, analysed instructional materials, and assessed students' ability to understand and to produce written French. In the observation data from a social studies lesson, it was evident that the teacher had to work very hard to help students understand a text on beluga whales. He did this in many ways—by paraphrasing, repeating, simplifying, checking for comprehension, gestures, etc. Despite his efforts it was clear that most students understood very little of the text. In their French language classes, these same students also lacked the terminology they needed to talk about grammatical gender in relation to adjective agreement.

When the students' performance on a wide range of measures was examined to assess their knowledge of French (for example, vocabulary recognition, reading comprehension, writing), it was evident that the students did not have the French language skills they needed to cope with the demands of typical secondary-level instruction. Furthermore, even though many of the students were able to speak French informally outside class, their oral abilities were limited when they had to discuss more complex academic subject matter. As we saw in Chapter 1, teachers are sometimes misled by students' ability to use the language in informal settings, concluding that their academic difficulties could not be due to language problems.

The students' lack of age-appropriate academic French is a serious problem. Solving it will involve complex educational, social, and cultural questions. One pedagogical element that might contribute to a solution is a better balance between language and subject matter instruction, focusing on the language that the students need to succeed in school. Another possibility is that further development of the learners' L1 literacy would better prepare them for second language and subject matter learning. There is another good reason to support students' development of Inuktitut. There are increasing concerns that Inuktitut will be lost as future generations shift to English or French as their preferred language. An educational system that encourages the development of both first and second languages may ensure the survival of this heritage language (Taylor, Caron, and McAlpine 2000).

Interpreting the research

Content-based language teaching has many advantages. In general, it increases the amount of time for learners to be exposed to the new language. It creates a genuine need to communicate, motivating students to acquire language in order to understand the content. For older students, there is the advantage of content that is cognitively challenging and interesting in a way that is often missing in foreign language instruction, especially where lessons are designed around particular grammatical forms.

Nevertheless, there are also some problems with content-based instruction. Our research with Inuit children adds further evidence to Jim Cummins' (1984) claim that students need 5–7 years before their ability to use the language for cognitively challenging academic material has reached an age-appropriate level. For students from disadvantaged minority groups, this delay in coming to grips with schooling can have lasting effects, as we saw in the discussion of subtractive bilingualism in Chapter 1. Majority language students in immersion programmes—in Canada and in Hong Kong—seem to do well in learning subject matter, and it is also noteworthy that they receive a substantial amount of subject matter instruction through their first language over the full course of their academic careers. Similarly, dual immersion programmes allow students from each language group to continue development of the home language and to continue learning subject matter content in that language. However, although students in content-based language instruction are able to communicate with some fluency in the second language, they often fall short of the high levels of linguistic accuracy that their years of schooling in the language might predict.

In recent years, proponents of content-based instruction have stressed the need to recall that content-based language teaching is still language teaching. For example, Jana Echevarria, Mary Ellen Vogt, and Deborah Short (2004) have done research and developed teacher education programmes that show the effectiveness of lessons that have both content objectives and language objectives.

5 *Teach what is teachable*

Manfred Pienemann (1988) and his colleagues have tried to explain why it often seems that some things can be taught successfully whereas other things, even after extensive or intensive teaching, seem to remain unacquired. Their research provides evidence that some linguistic structures, for example, basic word order in sentences (both simple and complex) develop along a predictable developmental path. These are labelled **developmental features**. The developmental stages of English questions that we saw in Chapter 2 are based on this research. According to Pienemann (1988) any attempt to teach a Stage 4 word-order pattern to learners at Stage 1 will not work because learners have to pass through Stage 2 and get to Stage 3 before they are ready to acquire what is at Stage 4. As we saw in 'Get it right from the beginning', students may produce certain structures after they have been taught them in class, but cease to use them later because they are not fully integrated into their interlanguage systems. The underlying cause of the stages has not been fully explained, but processability theory (see Chapter 4) suggests that they may be based at least in part on learners' developing ability to notice and remember elements in the stream of speech they hear.

Researchers supporting this view also claim that certain other aspects of language—for example, individual vocabulary items—can be taught at any time. Learners' acquisition of these variational features appears to depend on factors such as motivation, the learners' sense of identity, language aptitude, and the quality of instruction, including how learners' identities and cultures are acknowledged in the classroom.

In Example 6 below, we see a teacher trying to help students with the word order of questions. The students seem to know what the teacher means, but the level of language the teacher is offering them is beyond their current stage of development. Students are asking Stage 3 questions, which the teacher recasts as Stage 5 questions. The students react by simply answering the question or accepting the teacher's formulation.

Example 6

Students in an intensive ESL class (11–12-year-old French speakers) interviewing a student who had been in the same class in a previous year (see Classroom B in Chapter 5).

> s1   Mylène, where you put your 'Kid of the Week' poster?
> t   Where did you put your poster when you got it?
> s2   In my room.

(Two minutes later)

> s3   Beatrice, where you put your 'Kid of the Week' poster?
> t   Where did you put your poster?
> s4   My poster was on my wall and it fell down.

In Example 7, the student is using the 'fronting' strategy that is typical of Stage 3 questions. The teacher's corrective feedback leads the student to imitate a Stage 4 question.

Example 7

(The same group of students engaged in 'Famous person' interviews.)

> s1   Is your mother play piano?
> t   'Is your mother play piano?' OK. Well, can you say 'Is your mother play piano?' or 'Is your mother a piano player?'
> s1   'Is your mother a piano player?'
> s2   No.

In Example 8, the teacher draws the student's attention to the error and also provides the correct Stage 4 question. This time, however, the feedback is not followed by an imitation or a reformulation of the question, but simply by an answer.

Example 8
(Interviewing each other about house preferences)

    S1 Is your favourite house is a split-level?
    S2 Yes.
    T   You're saying 'is' two times dear. 'Is your favourite house a split-level?'
    S1 A split-level.
    T   OK.

In Example 9 the student asks a Stage 3 question, and the teacher provides a Stage 4 correction that the student imitates. The interaction suggests that the student is almost ready to begin producing Stage 4 questions. Note, however, that the student does not imitate the possessive 's, something that French speakers find very difficult.

Example 9
('Hide and seek' game)

    S Do the boy is beside the teacher desk?
    T Is the boy beside the teacher's desk?
    S Is the boy beside the teacher desk?

Research findings

The 'Teach what is teachable' view suggests that while variational features of the language can be taught successfully at various points in the learners' development, developmental features are best taught according to the learners' internal schedule. Furthermore, although learners may be able to produce more advanced forms on tests or in very restricted pedagogical exercises, instruction cannot change the 'natural' developmental course. The recommendation is to assess the learners' developmental level and teach what would naturally come next. Let us examine some studies that have tested this hypothesis.

Study 30: Ready to learn

Manfred Pienemann (1988) investigated whether instruction permitted learners to 'skip' a stage in the natural sequence of development. Two groups of Australian university students of German who were at Stage 2 in their acquisition of German word order were taught the rules associated with Stage 3 and Stage 4 respectively. The instruction took place over two weeks and during this time learners were provided with explicit grammatical rules and exercises for Stage 3 and 4 constructions. The learners who received instruction on Stage 3 rules moved easily into this stage from Stage 2. However, those learners who received instruction on Stage 4 rules either con-tinued to use Stage 2 rules or moved only into Stage 3. That is, they were not able to 'skip' a stage in the developmental sequence. Pienemann interprets his results as support for the hypothesis that for some linguistic structures, learners cannot be taught what they are not developmentally ready to learn.

Study 31: Readies, unreadies, and recasts

Alison Mackey and Jenefer Philp (1998) investigated whether adult ESL learners who were at different stages in their acquisition of questions could advance in their production of these forms if they received implicit negative feedback (i.e. recasts) in conversational interaction. As described in Chapter 5, recasts are paraphrases of a learner's incorrect utterance that involve replacing one or more of the incorrect components with a correct form while maintaining a focus on meaning. The researchers were interested in discovering whether adult learners who received modified interaction with recasts were able to advance in their production of question forms more than learners who received modified interaction without recasts. Furthermore, they wanted to explore whether learners who were at more advanced stages of question development ('readies') would benefit more from interaction with recasts than learners at less advanced stages of question development ('unreadies'). The results revealed that the 'readies' in the interaction plus recasts group improved more than the 'readies' in the interaction without recasts group. However, the 'unreadies' who were exposed to recasts did not show more rapid improvement than those who were not exposed to recasts.

Study 32: Developmental stage and first language influence

Nina Spada and Patsy Lightbown (1999) have also investigated the acquisition of questions in relation to learners' developmental 'readiness'. French-speaking students (aged 11–12) in intensive ESL classes received high-frequency exposure to question forms that were one or two stages beyond their developmental level. Learners who were judged on oral pre-tests to be at Stage 2 or 3 were given high frequency exposure to Stage 4 and 5 questions in the instructional input.

The materials that contained the more advanced question forms were designed to engage the learners mainly in comprehension practice. There was no student production and thus no corrective feedback, nor was there any explicit instruction on question formation. The researchers wanted to know whether Stage 3 learners (i.e. those considered to be developmentally 'ready') would benefit more from the high-frequency exposure to Stage 4 and 5 questions than the Stage 2 learners, who were not yet developmentally 'ready'.

Learners' performance on an oral post-test measure indicated no advantage for the Stage 3 learners. In fact, there was little progress for either group. However, on a task that required learners to judge the grammaticality of written questions there was evidence that all students had some knowledge of Stage 4 and 5 questions. A more detailed examination of the learners' performance on this task showed that students tended to accept Stage 4 and 5 questions when the subject of the sentence was a pronoun (for example, 'Are you a good student?' or 'When are you going to eat breakfast?'). When the subject of the sentence was a noun, however, there was a tendency for students to reject higher stage questions (for example, 'Are the students watching TV?' or 'What is your brother doing?'). This pattern in the students' performance appears to be related to a question rule in their first language that we saw in Chapter 2. That is, in French, questions with nouns in subject position are not inverted (for example, **Peut-Jean venir chez moi?* = 'Can John come to my house?'). In French questions with pronoun subjects, however, inversion is permitted (for example, *Peut-il venir chez moi?* = 'Can he come to my house?').

These results indicate that instruction timed to match learners' developmental 'readiness' may move them into more advanced stages, but their performance may still be affected by other factors. In this study first language influence seems to be responsible for the learners' inability to generalize their knowledge of inversion to all questions.

Interpreting the research

The results of these studies suggest that targeting instructional or interactional input to learners when they are developmentally ready to progress further in the second language can be beneficial. However, other factors such as type of input and first language influence can interact with learners' developmental readiness in complex ways. If we compare the types of instructional/interactional input across the three studies, Pienemann provided the most explicit instruction to learners who were both 'ready' and 'unready'. The results showed that learners who were 'ready' moved into the next stage of development, whereas learners who were not 'ready' did not. The results of the Mackey and Philp study also offer some support for the teachability hypothesis but reveal that developmental readiness is not the only predictor of success. The fact that the 'readies' benefited more from recasts than the 'unreadies' suggests that the type of instructional/interactional input is also important. The Spada and Lightbown study shows how the learners' first language may interact with developmental readiness in contributing to learning outcomes. Furthermore, in that study there was no explicit instruction on questions. Learners were simply exposed to a high frequency of correctly formed higher-stage questions in the input. Thus, they received increased 'exposure' but no 'instruction', and, in the end, they did not show as much developmental change as learners who received focused instruction.

Some research appears to offer counter-evidence to the claim that it is beneficial to teach what is developmentally next. This includes several studies that have used the accessibility hierarchy (see Chapter 2) to describe second language learners' progress in their acquisition of relative clauses. Results of these studies suggest that when low-level learners (for example, those who use relative clauses only in subject position) are taught relative clauses that are several stages beyond their current level, they not only learn what is taught, they also acquire the relative clause position(s) between the one taught and the one(s) they already knew. In some instances they even learn how to use relative clauses beyond the level they were taught (Ammar and Lightbown 2005; Eckman, Bell, and Nelson 1988; Hamilton 1994).

At first glance, this research seems to contradict Pienemann's claim that learners should be taught what is 'next'. However, it is also possible that the developmental paths of different linguistic features are based on different sorts of processing abilities. For example, Catherine Doughty (1991) suggested that once learners have learned to use relative clauses in one position (usually the subject position), there is no constraint on their ability to learn the others. What all the studies of relative clause teaching and learning have in common is that learners acquire the relative clauses in an order very similar to the accessibility hierarchy. That is, whether or not they learn what is taught, they make progress by learning subject, then direct object, then indirect object, and so on.

The 'Teach what is teachable' position is of great potential interest to syllabus planners as well as teachers. However, it must be emphasized that a description of a learner's developmental path is not in itself a template for a syllabus. There are numerous practical reasons for this, not least the fact that only a small number of language features have been described in terms of a developmental sequence. While Pienemann's work on processability theory (see Chapter 4) provides insights into the principles that may make some features more difficult than others, those principles are not easily translated into instructional sequences.

As Patsy Lightbown (1998) has suggested, the 'Teach what is teachable' research is important primarily for helping teachers understand why students don't always learn what they are taught—at least not immediately. The research also shows that instruction on language that is 'too advanced' may still be helpful by providing learners with samples of language that they will be able to incorporate into their interlanguage when the time is right. However, many other factors need to be taken into consideration in choosing language features to focus on. We will return to this point after we discuss the final proposal for language teaching, 'Get it right in the end.'

6 *Get it right in the end*

Proponents of the 'Get it right in the end' proposal recognize an important role for form-focused instruction, but they do not assume that everything has to be taught. Like advocates of the 'Let's talk', 'Two for one', and the 'Just listen … and read' positions, they have concluded that many language features—from pronunciation to vocabulary and grammar—will be acquired naturally if learners have adequate exposure to the language and a motivation to learn. Thus, while they view comprehension-based, content-based, task-based, or other types of essentially meaning-focused instruction as crucial for language learning, they hypothesize that learners will do better if they also have access to some form-focused instruction. They argue that learners will benefit in terms of both efficiency of their learning and the level of proficiency they will eventually reach.

Advocates of this proposal also agree with those who support the 'Teach what is teachable' view that some things cannot be taught if the teaching fails to take the student's readiness (stage of development) into account. This proposal differs from the 'Teach what is teachable' proposal, however, in that it emphasizes the idea that some aspects of language must be taught and may need to be taught quite explicitly. There are a number of situations in which guidance—form-focused instruction or corrective feedback—is expected to be especially important. For example, when learners in a class share the same first language, they will make errors that are partly the result of transfer from that shared language. Because the errors are not likely to lead to any kind of communication breakdown, it will be virtually impossible for learners to discover the errors on their own.

Examples 10, 11, and 12 are taken from a classroom where a group of 12-year-old French speakers are learning English. In Example 10, they are engaged in an activity where the words in sentences are reordered to form new sentences. The following sentence has been placed on the board: 'Sometimes my mother makes good cakes'.

Example 10

T	Another place to put our adverb?
S1	After makes?
T	After makes.
S2	Before good?
T	My mother makes sometimes good cakes.
S3	No.
T	No, we can't do that. It sounds yucky.
S3	Yucky!
T	Disgusting. Horrible. Right?
S4	Horrible!

This is hardly a typical grammar lesson! And yet the students' attention is being drawn to an error that virtually all of them make in English.

Proponents of 'Get it right in the end' argue that what learners focus on can eventually lead to changes in their interlanguage systems, not just to an appearance of change. However, the supporters of this proposal do not claim that focusing on particular language points will prevent learners from making errors or that they will begin using a form as soon as it is taught. Rather, they suggest that the focused instruction will allow learners to notice the target features in subsequent input and interaction.

Form-focused instruction as it is understood in this position does not always involve metalinguistic explanations, nor are learners expected to be able to explain why something is right or wrong. They claim simply that the learners need to notice how their language use differs from that of a more proficient speaker. As we will see in the examples below, teachers who work in this approach look for the right moment to create increased awareness on the part of the learner—ideally, at a time when the learner is motivated to say something and wants to say it as clearly and correctly as possible.

Example 11

(The students are practising following instructions; one student instructs, the others colour.)

s1 Make her shoes brown.
t   Now, her shoes. Are those Mom's shoes or Dad's shoes?
s2 Mom's.
t   Mom's. How do you know it's Mom's?
s1 Because it's her shoes.

As we saw in Chapter 4, French-speaking learners of English have difficulty with 'his' and 'her' because French possessives use the grammatical gender of the object possessed rather than the natural gender of the possessor in selecting the appropriate possessive form. The teacher is aware of this and—briefly, without interrupting the activity—helps the learners notice the correct form.

Example 12

(The students are playing 'hide and seek' with a doll in a doll's house, asking questions until they find out where 'George' is hiding. Although a model for correct questions has been written on the board, the game becomes quite lively and students spontaneously ask questions that reflect their interlanguage stage.)

s1 Is George is in the living room?
t   You said 'is' two times, dear. Listen to you—you said 'Is George is in?' Look on the board. 'Is George in the' and then you say the name of the room.
s1 Is George in the living room?
t   Yeah.
s1 I win!

Note that the teacher's brief intervention does not distract the student from his pleasure in the game, demonstrating that focus on form does not have to interfere with genuine interaction.

Proponents of 'Get it right in the end' argue that it is sometimes necessary to draw learners' attention to their errors and to focus on certain linguistic (vocabulary or grammar) points. However, it is different from the 'Get it right from the beginning' proposal in acknowledging that it is appropriate for learners to engage in meaningful language use from the very beginning of their exposure to the second language. They assume that much of language acquisition will develop naturally out of such language use, without formal instruction that focuses on the language itself.

Research findings

A great deal of research has examined issues related to this proposal. This includes both descriptive and experimental studies.

Study 33: Form-focus experiments in intensive ESL

Since the 1980s, researchers have investigated the effects of form-focused instruction and corrective feedback on the developing English of French-speaking students participating in intensive ESL classes in Quebec. For five months in either Grade 5 or Grade 6, students (aged 10–12) spent most of every school day learning English through a variety of communicative inter-active activities.

In descriptive studies involving almost 1,000 students in 33 classes, Patsy Lightbown and Nina Spada (1990, 1994) observed that teachers rarely focused on language form. The emphasis of the teaching was on activities that focused on meaning rather than form, opportunities for spontaneous interaction, and the provision of rich and varied comprehensible input. In these classes, learners developed good listening comprehension and communicative confidence in English. However, they continued to have problems with linguistic accuracy and complexity.

In experimental studies with a smaller number of classes, the effects of form-focused instruction and corrective feedback were examined with respect to adverb placement and question formation. In the first study, Lydia White selected adverb placement for investigation because of the differences between English and French that have already been discussed (see Chapter 2 and Study 17 in 'Just listen … and read'). The hypothesis was that learners would persist in using adverb placement rules consistent with French (their first language) if they were not explicitly told how rules for adverb place-ment differ in English and French. Questions were selected for the second study because they have been extensively investigated in the literature and considerable comparison data were available, particularly with regard to developmental stages (see Chapter 2).

Both experimental and comparison groups were tested before and after the period of special instruction. Throughout the period of the experiments, all students continued to participate in the regular communicative activities that were typical of their instruction. The researchers gave each teacher a set of pedagogical materials to be used for the special form-focused instruction. The experimental groups received approximately eight hours of instruction on adverbs or questions over a two-week period. This included some explicit teaching of the rules associated with each structure as well as corrective feed-back during the practice activities.

Learners who received explicit instruction on adverb placement dramatically outperformed the learners who did not. This was found on all the post-tests (immediately following instruction and six weeks later). In the follow-up tests a year later, however, the gains made by the learners who had received the adverb instruction had disappeared and their performance on this structure was like that of uninstructed learners (White 1991).

In the question study the instructed group also made significantly greater gains than the uninstructed group on the written tasks immediately following instruction. Furthermore, they maintained their level of knowledge on later testing (six weeks and six months after instruction). The instruction also contributed to improvement in oral performance that was sustained over time (White, Spada, Lightbown, and Ranta 1991).

The difference in long-term effects of the two studies may be due to a difference in the availability of the target forms in the classroom input to which learners were exposed. Analysis of classroom language showed that adverbs were extremely rare in classroom speech, giving learners little opportunity to maintain their newly-acquired knowledge through continued exposure and use. In contrast, there were hundreds of opportunities to hear and use questions every day in the classroom. Once learners had been given some focused instruction, it seems they were able to continue to advance in their knowledge and use of questions (Spada and Lightbown 1993).

In several of the studies carried out in intensive ESL programmes, there is evidence of the strong influence of the learner's first language on their second language development. In Study 32, we described the tendency of intensive ESL learners to reject inversion in questions when the subject is a noun but to accept inversion when the subject is a pronoun, consistent with their first language. The influence of the learners' first language in their acquisition of the possessive determiners 'his' and 'her' was also observed with this group of learners (see Chapter 2 and Study 18). This led to the question of whether form-focused instruction that includes explicit contrastive information about how the first and second language differ would help in their development of question formation and possessive determiners. In a study to explore this, learners who received instruction on possessive determiners improved more in their knowledge and use of this feature than did learners who received instruction on question forms. This finding appeared to be related to differences between the form–meaning connections of these two features. That is, a misused possessive determiner ('He's going home with her mother') is more likely to lead to a communication breakdown than an ill-formed question (for example, 'Where he's going?'). Results like these point to the importance of considering how instruction may affect language features in different ways (Spada, Lightbown, and White 2005; White 2008).

As we saw in the discussion of the 'Get two for one' proposal, there is growing evidence that learners in content-based programmes such as French immersion need more opportunities to focus on form and receive corrective feedback. A number of studies have explored the question of how this can best be accomplished.

Study 34: Focusing on gender in French immersion

Birgit Harley (1998) examined the effects of instruction with young children in French immersion programmes. Six classes of Grade 2 children (7–8 years old) were given focused instruction on a language feature that is known to be a persistent problem for French immersion students—grammatical gender. For 20 minutes a day over a five-week period these children carried out many activities based on children's games (for example, 'I spy') that were modified to draw their attention to gender distinctions and which required them to choose between feminine and masculine articles (*une* or *un, la* or *le*). Students were also taught how certain noun endings provide clues about gender (for example, *-ette* in *la bicyclette* for feminine, and *-eau* in *le bateau* for masculine).

The students were pre-tested on their knowledge of grammatical gender via listening and speaking tests before the instruction began and the same tests were administered immediately after instruction and then again five months later. Learners who received instruction were much better at recognizing and producing accurate gender distinctions for familiar nouns than those who did not receive instruction. However, the instruction did not enable learners to generalize their learning to new nouns. Harley's interpretation of this is that too much new vocabulary was introduced in the later teaching activities and this meant that teachers spent more time teaching the meaning of words than the noun endings and their relationship to gender. Therefore, 'the input on noun endings was simply not available in sufficient quantity and intensity for the majority of students to establish the predictive relevance of the noun endings in question' (p. 169).

Study 35: Focusing on sociolinguistic forms in French immersion

Roy Lyster (1994) examined the effects of form-focused instruction on the knowledge and use of sociolinguistic style variations in three classes of Grade 8 French immersion students (about 13 years old). One of the main features examined in his study was the distinction between the use of second person pronouns *tu* and *vous*. In addressing an individual, *tu* is used to indicate informality and familiarity while *vous* is used as a marker of respectful politeness, or social distance between speakers. Prior to instruction, immediately after, and again one month later, the learners were tested on their ability to produce and recognize these forms (in addition to others) in appropriate contexts.

The instruction took place for about 12 hours over a five-week period. During this time, students in the experimental classes were given explicit instruction and engaged in guided practice activities that included role-plays in a variety of formal and informal contexts and corrective feedback from teachers and peers. Students in the two comparison classes continued with their regular instruction without any focused teaching or guided practice in using sociolinguistically appropriate forms. On the immediate post-test, learners in the experimental classes performed significantly better than learners in the comparison classes on both written and oral production tasks and the multiple-choice test, and these benefits were maintained when learners were tested a month later.

Study 36: Focusing on verb forms in content-based science classrooms

Catherine Doughty and Elizabeth Varela (1998) carried out a study with a group of ESL learners in their science classes. One class of middle-school students (11–14 years old) from a variety of first language backgrounds received corrective feedback on past tense and conditional verb forms in English. For several weeks, while students were engaged in oral and written work related to a series of science reports, the teacher provided corrective feedback on their errors in past tense and conditional forms—both explicitly and implicitly. Students' ability to use these forms was assessed before and after the experimental period and again two months later. Their performance was compared to that of a group of students who were in another science class doing the same science reports but who did not receive corrective feedback on the verb forms.

Students who received the corrective feedback made more progress in using past and conditional forms than the comparison group both immediately after the period of focused feedback and two months later. Their progress was assessed in terms of both increased accuracy and the presence of interlanguage forms that showed students were doing more than repeating forms they had heard.

Study 37: Recasts and prompts in French immersion classrooms

In Chapter 5, we saw some of Roy Lyster's descriptive research on the different types of corrective feedback provided by teachers in Canadian French immersion programmes and learners' immediate responses (uptake) to that feedback. More recently, Lyster (2004) explored the effects of form-focused instruction and feedback type on second language learning in an experimental study with Grade 5 students in French immersion classes. There were three experimental groups and a comparison group. The experimental groups received approximately nine hours of explicit instruction over a five-week period, during which their attention was drawn to grammatical gender and the fact that word endings can give a clue to grammatical gender in French (see Study 34). Students in two of the experimental groups also received corrective feedback in the form of either recasts or prompts when they produced errors in grammatical gender. These feedback types differ in that recasts provide learners with the correct model, whereas prompts signal the need for a correction and require the student to produce the target form through clarification requests, elicitation, and metalinguistic clues (see Chapter 5 for definitions and examples of these different types of feedback). The third experimental group received the instruction but no corrective feedback, and the comparison group received neither instruction nor corrective feedback. All groups continued their regular French immersion programme of content-based instruction throughout the study and they were all tested before the instructional treatment, immediately after, and again three months later.

On the post-tests all three experimental groups (i.e. those who received instruction) were significantly more accurate than the comparison group in assigning grammatical gender. In addition, the instruction + prompts group did significantly better than the instruction + recasts group on the written measures. However, there were no significant differences between the three experimental groups in terms of learners' performance on the oral tasks. Lyster interprets this finding as a task effect. That is, because of the time-consuming nature of oral tasks, only a randomly selected sub-sample of students participated in this part of the study. These students met with the researcher in three intensive one-on-one sessions. In order to ensure the accuracy of the data, the researcher encouraged students to speak as clearly as possible because previous research had shown that learners sometimes used a 'hybrid article' that could be interpreted as either masculine or feminine. This emphasis on the clear articulation of articles provided all learners with individualized attention on the target feature and thus may be the reason why all three groups performed similarly on the oral measure.

Study 38: Focus on form through collaborative dialogue
Motivated by sociocultural theory and the idea that language learning occurs in dialogue, Merrill Swain and Sharon Lapkin (2002) observed the language development of two Grade 7 French immersion students as they wrote a story collaboratively. Later, in a 'noticing' activity, the students compared what they had written with a reformulated version of the story. The students also took part in a stimulated recall of their noticing activity. Swain and Lapkin wanted to find out what students noticed about differences between their original version and the reformulated one and whether they made revisions to their original stories based on their collaborative talk about the reformulated version.

The talk that learners produced in all phases of the research was recorded, transcribed and coded for **language-related episodes** (LREs), 'any part of the dialogue where learners talk about the language they produced, and reflect on their language use' (p. 292). An excerpt of the learners' collaborative talk from this study is presented in Chapter 5, Communication Task B. The LREs were coded in terms of whether they focused on lexical, grammatical, or discourse features. The researchers used the original story that the two learners created together as a pre-test and the stories that each learner constructed as a post-test. Both learners were much more accurate on the post-test version of the story. The researchers conclude that the multiple opportunities for learners to engage in collaborative talk on the language features in question led them to a greater understanding of their correct use.

Study 39: Focus on form in task-based instruction

In a descriptive study investigating the importance of the teacher's role in task-based instruction, Virginia Samuda (2001) explored ways of guiding adult ESL learners' attention to form–meaning relationships by focusing on expressions of possibility and probability (for example, 'might', 'could', 'it's possible'). In a task design that took learners through a 'meaning to form to meaning progression', learners were first asked to work in groups to speculate on the identity of an unknown person (for example, age, gender, occupation) by looking at a set of objects thought to have come from that person's pocket. In carrying out this task, learners were observed to produce expressions of probability and possibility such as 'It's possible that he smokes' and 'maybe it's a girl', but few instances of modal auxiliaries (for example, 'must', 'may') were used.

In the second phase of the task, the students were asked to come together as a whole group to tell each other what they had decided. During this phase, the teacher acted as a co-communicator and maintained the focus on meaning but gradually shifted to form by using the language that the learners had produced on their own and providing them with alternative ways of expressing uncertainty. Initially, this was done implicitly. For example if a learner said something like 'We think uh 50 per cent he smokes', the teacher said 'So you're not certain that he smokes?' After each group had presented, the teacher provided a more explicit focus. She drew the learners' attention to other ways of expressing possibility and probability by overtly talking about language form as shown in the excerpt below (p. 131).

ST   Businessman

T   Businessman ninety? OK So you're 90 per cent certain he's a businessman, right? Here's another way to say this. You think it's 90 per cent certain, so you think he must be a businessman. He must be a businessman (writes it on the board). So this (points to 'must be' on board) is showing how certain how sure you are. Not 100 per cent, but almost 100 per cent. 90 per cent.

In the final stage of the task, the students prepared and presented a poster based on their conclusions about the identity of the unknown person to the whole class. During this time, the teacher responded to the content and not the form of their work. When the researcher examined the differences between expressions of probability and possibility that the students used in the first stage of this task and compared it with the final stage, there was evidence of improvement in that many more instances of modal auxiliaries were present in the learners' speech.

Study 40: The timing of form-focused instruction

Nina Spada and her research team carried out a study to examine whether there may be a better time in the instructional sequence to draw learners' attention to form (Spada et al. 2012). Two classes of intermediate-level adult ESL learners were provided with 12 hours of instruction that differed in terms of whether attention to form was embedded in communicative activities or separated from communicative practice. They are referred to as integrated and isolated form-focused instruction. The target feature was the passive construction and learners were tested on their knowledge of it before instruction, immediately after instruction, and again three weeks later.

A second question motivating the research was whether the two types of instruction might lead to different kinds of L2 knowledge. This question was informed by transfer-appropriate processing theory and the idea that we are more likely to remember something we have learned if the cognitive processes that are activated during the learning process are the same as those activated during retrieval (see Chapter 4). Thus, the researchers were interested in whether learners who obtained their knowledge of the passive while participating in communicative interaction (i.e. integrated FFI) were better at retrieving that knowledge on an oral communication task than the learners who received isolated FFI. Similarly, they wanted to explore whether learners who obtained their knowledge of the passive structure in grammar activities that were separated from communicative practice (i.e. isolated FFI) were better at retrieving their knowledge on a written grammar test than the learners who received integrated FFI.

Learners in both the integrated and isolated FFI classes improved significantly on both language measures over time. The findings also revealed some support for TAP in that learners who received integrated FFI outperformed the isolated FFI learners on the oral communication task and the learners who received isolated FFI outperformed the integrated learners on the written grammar test.

The overall results of this study point to the complementarity of the two types of instruction, likely due to the fact that they both provide a focus on form and meaning, albeit at different times.

ACTIVITY   Match pedagogical activities with teaching proposals

Below are brief descriptions of 12 pedagogical activities. Match each activity with the teaching proposal it represents and explain how you reached that conclusion. For example, an activity such as 'Fill in the blanks with the correct form of the verb' represents the 'Get it right from the beginning' proposal because such grammatical exercises are typical of the grammar translation approach with its emphasis on rule learning and accuracy. Keep in mind that in some cases, an activity is compatible with more than one teaching proposal. For example, if the sentences in the 'Fill in the blanks' activity came from an earlier draft of a letter written for a communicative activity, it might be consistent with the 'Get it right in the end' proposal because it integrates attention to language form in a meaning-based activity.

1 Role-play a conversation between a travel agent and a tourist. ①/④

2 Memorize a dialogue about buying airline tickets. ①

3 Underline the past tense verbs while reading a story. ②

4 Arrange illustrations in the correct sequence after listening to a story. ②

5 Work with a partner to write a story based on a cartoon strip. ③

6 Rearrange a set of scrambled words to form correct questions. ⑥

7 Debate or discuss a topic that was featured in a newspaper article. ③/④

8 Watch an episode of *Sesame Street*. ②

9 Demonstrate and describe the steps in a science experiment. ④

10 Interview a mystery guest and try to discover his or her occupation. ⑤

11 Play a game of 'Simon Says'. ? ②

12 Work in small groups to choose the ideal candidate for a job. ③- 5

Interpreting the research

The overall results of the studies described above provide support for the hypothesis that form-focused instruction and corrective feedback can help learners improve their knowledge and use of particular grammatical features. There is also compelling evidence that more explicit attention to form is particularly useful within communicative and content-based second and foreign language programmes. This has been confirmed in reviews and **meta-analyses** of many studies that have investigated the contribution of form-focused instruction to L2 learning (Norris and Ortega 2000; Spada 2011). Some results also show, however, that the effects of instruction are not always long-lasting. This may be related to whether there is continued exposure to a linguistic feature in the regular classroom input after the experimental treatment ends.

We have also seen that form-focused instruction may be more effective with some language features than with others. For example, the successful learning of the *tu/vous* distinction in Lyster's (1994) study could be due to the fact that learning *tu* and *vous* is essentially a matter of learning two important vocabulary items and thus may have been less difficult to learn than syntactic features that affect meaning in less obvious ways. In the intensive ESL research, learners may have been more successful after instruction on possessive determiners than questions because there is a stronger form–meaning connection with possessive determiners than with questions.

Other language features for which form-focused instruction may play a crucial role are those that are influenced by the learners' first language, particularly when there are misleading similarities between L1 and L2. The difficulty may be increased in second language classrooms where learners share the same first language and reinforce each other's first language-based errors.

Finally, the rules associated with some language features are more complex than others. For example, the article system in English is both complex and abstract and notoriously difficult to teach and learn. Thus, learners may be better off learning about articles via exposure in the input. On the other hand a simple 'rule of thumb' such as 'put an -*s* at the end of a noun to make it plural' may be a better target for instruction. In a recent **meta-analysis** of the effects of type of instruction on 'complex' and 'simple' language features, however, Spada and Tomita (2010) report that explicit instruction promoted learning for both types of language features.

Research on integrated and isolated FFI is a reminder that the timing of form-focused instruction may also make a difference in L2 learning. Samuda's study with adult ESL learners is a good example of integrated FFI, illustrating how teachers can effectively direct students' attention to form within task-based instruction. The finding that isolated and integrated FFI may lead to different kinds of L2 knowledge is intriguing and resonates with the experience of many teachers. That is, teachers of second/foreign languages know that explicit rule-based grammar teaching without communicative practice is likely to lead to a fairly good knowledge of the rules of grammar but not the ability to use the rules in meaningful and spontaneous language production. These differences in L2 knowledge have been variously referred to as declarative versus procedural and learning versus acquisition, as discussed in Chapter 4, or as explicit versus implicit knowledge. Explicit knowledge is typically described as conscious and analysed, whereas implicit knowledge is considered to be intuitive and unanalysed.

Some theorists and researchers claim that L2 instruction can lead to explicit knowledge only. Furthermore, they argue that the results from meta-analyses showing positive effects for L2 instruction are due to the fact that the tests used to assess learners' progress in the majority of studies have measured explicit knowledge using, for example, discrete-point grammar tests. Fortunately, recent research has included a greater variety of language measures to tap into learners' intuitive L2 knowledge such as oral communication tasks and time-pressured tasks that require learners to retrieve their knowledge quickly without having time to 'think about it'. Nonetheless, we won't have a clear answer to the question of what type of knowledge results from L2 instruction until valid and reliable tests of both implicit and explicit knowledge are used in a larger number of studies (Ellis et al. 2009).

Similar issues have been raised about research on corrective feedback but the central focus of this work has been on investigating whether certain types of corrective feedback are more effective than others. The results from Lyster's study in French immersion programmes suggests that learners benefit more from feedback that pushes them to self-correct (i.e. prompts) than from feedback that provides the correct form (i.e. recasts). Research in other contexts, however, has produced different results. For example, the majority of laboratory studies of corrective feedback report benefits for recasts over other types of corrective feedback including prompts (Mackey and Goo 2007). These conflicting findings are likely related to differences in context—the laboratory is a more controlled environment than the classroom, where there are competing demands on learners' attention. As a result, learners may notice certain types of feedback in the one-on-one laboratory interactions more than they do in communicative or content-based classes, where the primary focus is on meaning.

As discussed in Chapter 5, the specific pedagogical activity in which corrective feedback is provided also plays an important role in terms of whether learners recognize it as corrective feedback. The timing of corrective feedback may also be important in L2 learning. To date little research has explored whether it is preferable, for example, to provide feedback during or after communicative practice. One study of this issue was carried out by James Hunter (2012). He investigated the effectiveness of feedback that the teacher provided *after* students had participated in student-led conversations. His findings show that such an approach can result in a higher proportion of repair than feedback provided in whole-class teacher-led activities.

Recently there have been a number of meta-analyses of studies investigating the effectiveness of L2 corrective feedback on L2 oral production. The results are mixed, with some reporting benefits for recasts over other types of feedback (Li 2010) and others reporting advantages for prompts over recasts (Lyster and Saito 2010). Until there is greater consensus on the contributions of different types of corrective feedback on L2 learning, a prudent approach would be to provide learners with a variety of different types of corrective feedback and to keep in mind the counterbalance hypothesis presented in Chapter 5, which suggests that more explicit corrective feedback may be effective in contexts where the learners' attention is focused on meaning/content while implicit feedback may be sufficient to attract learners' attention in contexts where the focus of instruction is typically on language form.

Assessing the proposals

Although there is still much work to do, it seems evident that proposals representing an almost exclusive focus on form or those representing an almost exclusive focus on meaning alone can not be recommended. Approaches that provide attention to form within communicative and content-based interaction receive the most support from classroom research.

We know that some exceptionally gifted learners will succeed in second language learning regardless of the teaching method. In the schools of the world, grammar translation is no doubt the most widely applied method and most of us have met individuals whose advanced proficiency in a foreign language developed out of their experience in such classes. Similarly, audiolingual instruction has produced highly proficient second language speakers. However, we also know—from personal experience and research findings—that these methods leave many learners frustrated and unable to participate in ordinary conversations, even after years of classes. Grammar translation and audiolingual approaches will continue to be used, but the evidence suggests that 'Get it right from the beginning' does not correspond to the way the majority of successful second language learners have acquired their proficiency. On the other hand, in throwing out contrastive analysis, feedback on error, and metalinguistic explanations and guidance, the 'communicative revolution' may have gone too far.

There is increasing evidence that learners continue to have difficulty with basic structures of the language in programmes that offer little or no form-focused instruction. This calls into question extreme versions of the 'Just listen … and read' and 'Get two for one' proposals. While there is good evidence that learners make considerable progress in both comprehension and production in comprehension-based programmes, we do not find support for the hypothesis that language acquisition will take care of itself if second language learners simply focus on meaning in comprehensible input. Comprehension-based approaches are most successful when they include guided attention to language features as a component of instruction.

The 'Let's talk' proposal raises similar concerns. Opportunities for learners to engage in conversational interactions in group and paired activities can lead to increased communicative competence and the ability to manage conversations in a second language. However, the research also shows that learners may make slow progress on acquiring more accurate and sophisticated language if there is no focus on form. This is especially true in classes where students' shared language and learning backgrounds allow them to communicate successfully in spite of their errors. Because 'Let's talk' emphasizes meaning and attempts to simulate 'natural' communication in conversational interaction, the students' focus is naturally on what they say, not how to say it. Furthermore, when feedback on error takes the form of recasts, learners may interpret it as a continuation of the conversation rather than focus on form. Thus, programmes based on the 'Let's talk' approach are incomplete on their own, and learners' gains in confidence and conversational skills may not be matched by their development of more accurate and complex language.

It is important to emphasize that the evidence to support a role for form-focused instruction and corrective feedback does not suggest a return to the 'Get it right from the beginning' approach. Research has shown that learners do benefit considerably from communicative interaction and instruction that is meaning-based. The results of research in French immersion, other content-based language teaching, and communicative ESL are strong indicators that learners develop higher levels of fluency through primarily meaning-based instruction than through rigidly grammar-based instruction. The problem is that certain aspects of linguistic knowledge and performance are not fully developed in such programmes.

Research investigating the 'Teach what is teachable' proposal is not yet at a point where it is possible to say to teachers: 'Here is a list of linguistic features and the order in which they will be acquired. You should teach them in this order'. The number of features that researchers have investigated in experimental studies within this framework is far too small. On the other hand, there has been no strong evidence that teaching according to the developmental sequences is necessary or even desirable or that it will improve the long-term results in language learning. What is most valuable about this proposal is that it serves to help teachers set realistic expectations about the ways in which learners' interlanguage may change in response to instruction. The implications of 'Teach what is teachable' may be seen primarily in the fact that genuine progress in second language development must be measured in ways that include, but are not limited to, increased accuracy in language production.

According to the 'Get it right in the end' proposal, classroom activities should be built primarily on creating opportunities for students to express and understand meaningful language. However, this proposal is based on the hypothesis that form-focused instruction and corrective feedback are also essential for learners' continued growth and development. The challenge is to find the balance between meaning-based and form-focused activities. The right balance is likely to be different according to the characteristics of the learners. The learners' age, metalinguistic sophistication, prior educational experiences, motivation, and goals, as well as the similarity of the target language to a language already known need to be taken into account when decisions are made about the amount and type of form focus to offer.

Classroom data from a number of studies offer support for the view that form-focused instruction and corrective feedback provided within the context of communicative and content-based programmes are more effective in promoting second language learning than programmes that are limited to a virtually exclusive emphasis on comprehension, fluency, or accuracy alone. Thus, we would argue that second language teachers can (and should) provide guided, form-focused instruction and corrective feedback in certain circumstances. For example, teachers should not hesitate to correct persistent errors that learners seem not to notice without focused attention. Teachers should also be especially aware of errors that the majority of learners in a class are making when they share the same first language background. They should not hesitate to provide contrastive information about how a particular structure in a learner's first language differs from the target language. Teachers might also try to become more aware of language features that are just beginning to emerge in the second language development of their students and provide some guided instruction in the use of these forms. It can also be useful to encourage learners to take part in the process by creating activities that draw their attention to the forms they use in communicative activities, by developing contexts in which they can provide each other with feedback, and by encouraging them to ask questions about language.

Decisions about when and how to provide form focus must take into account differences in learner characteristics, of course. Quite different approaches would be appropriate for, say, trained linguists learning a fourth or fifth language, young children beginning their schooling in a second language environment, both younger and older immigrants who cannot read and write their own language, and adolescents studying a foreign language for a few hours a week at school.

Summary

Many teachers are aware of the need to balance form focus and meaning focus, and they may feel that recommendations based on research simply confirm their current classroom practice. Although this may be true to some extent, it is hardly the case that all teachers have a clear sense of how best to accomplish their goal. It is not always easy to step back from familiar practices and say, 'I wonder if this is really the most effective way to go about this?' Furthermore, it can be difficult to try out classroom practices that go against the prevailing trends in their educational contexts. Many teachers still work in environments where there is an emphasis on accuracy that virtually excludes spontaneous language use in the classroom. At the same time, the introduction of communicative language teaching methods has sometimes resulted in a complete rejection of attention to form and error-correction in second language teaching. But it is not necessary to choose between form-based and meaning-based instruction. Rather, the challenge is to find the best balance between these two orientations.

Classroom-based research on second language learning and teaching has given us partial answers to many questions. Through continuing research and experience, researchers and teachers will fill in more details, always recognizing that no single answer will be adequate for all learning environments. Among the questions we will continue to ask are these:

- How can classroom instruction provide the right balance of meaning-based and form-focused instruction?
- Which features of language will respond best to form-focused instruction, and which will be acquired without explicit focus if learners have adequate access to the language?
- Which learners will respond well to metalinguistic information and which will require some other way of focusing attention on language form?
- When is it best to draw learners' attention to form—before, after, or during communicative practice?
- How should corrective feedback on language form be offered?
- When should learners be allowed to focus their attention on the content of their utterances?

Continued classroom-centred research, including the action research by teachers in their own classrooms, will provide further insights into these and other important issues in second language teaching and learning.

Questions for reflection

1 Keeping in mind that individual learner differences play an important role in second language learning, do you think a particular learner profile might be more compatible with one of the teaching proposals than another?

2 If you were going to experiment with a new approach to teaching in your classroom, which of the six proposals described in this chapter would you choose? Why?

3 This chapter concludes with the suggestion that 'Get it right in the end' is the best approach. Is this consistent with your own views? Why/why not?

Suggestions for further reading

Ellis, R. 2012. *Language Teaching Research and Language Pedagogy.* Malden, MA: Wiley-Blackwell.

In this volume, Ellis focuses on research that is designed specifically to investigate the role of teaching in second language learning. He reviews both the methods and the findings from a vast number of studies. Ellis approaches the task from his dual perspectives as a researcher and as editor of the journal *Language Teaching Research*, which publishes the work of scholars and educators who are investigating language teaching around the world. Throughout the book, links are made between the research and its implications for language pedagogy.

Hedge, T. 2000. *Teaching and Learning in the Language Classroom.* Oxford: Oxford University Press.

This is a useful reference book for the classroom teacher. It covers a wide range of topics relevant to the teaching and learning of second/foreign languages. It is divided into four sections: a framework for teaching and learning, teaching the language system, developing the language skills, planning, and assessing learning. Each chapter moves from theoretical to practical considerations and there is extensive use of tasks, activities, and teaching materials to motivate readers to reflect on the ideas presented in relation to their own practice.

Lyster, R. 2007. *Learning and Teaching Language through Content: A Counterbalanced Approach.* Amsterdam: John Benjamins.

This book provides a comprehensive description and analysis of language teaching and learning in content-based classrooms. With a primary but not exclusive focus on research in French immersion programmes in Canada, Roy Lyster synthesizes decades of empirical work that has sought solutions to the challenges of teaching language and content simultaneously. The author's experience as both teacher and researcher is evident in the useful connections made between theory and practice.

Nation, I. S. P. and **J. Macalister.** 2010. *Language Curriculum Design.* New York: Routledge.

Paul Nation has proposed four 'strands' that are seen as essential—and of equal importance—in a language teaching programme. The four strands are: meaning-focused input, meaning-focused output, language-focused learning, and fluency development. Together they represent a balanced approach to language teaching that is compatible with research on classroom learning. Originally based on Nation's research in vocabulary learning, the four strands may also be seen as the elements of a lesson, a syllabus, or even a curriculum. Nation (2007) introduces the ideas, and this book elaborates on the full range of issues related to curriculum design.

7 POPULAR IDEAS ABOUT LANGUAGE LEARNING REVISITED

Preview

In this chapter, we return to the 18 statements that you responded to in the Introduction and summarize some of the related research and theory that we have discussed in this book, sharing some of our own views about these popular opinions.

ACTIVITY   **Review your opinions**

In the Introduction, we asked you to indicate how strongly you agreed with some popular ideas about language learning. Before you continue reading this chapter, go back and complete the questionnaire again. Compare the responses you gave then and those you would give now. Have your views about second language acquisition been changed or confirmed by what you've read in the preceding chapters?

Reflecting on the popular ideas: Learning from research

1 Languages are learned mainly through imitation

It is difficult to find support for the argument that languages are learned mainly through imitation, because first and second language learners produce many novel sentences that they could not have heard before. These sentences are based on their developing understanding of how the language system works. This is evident in children's sentences such as 'I'm hiccing up and I can't stop', and 'It was upside down but I turned it upside right', and with second language learners who say 'The cowboy rided into town', or 'The man that I spoke to him is angry'. These examples and many others provide evidence that language learners do more than internalize a large list of imitated and memorized sentences. They also identify patterns in the language and extend them to new contexts.

If we use a narrow definition of imitation (the immediate repetition of all or part of another speaker's utterance) we find that some children imitate a great deal as they acquire their first language. Even these children, however, do not imitate everything they hear. Instead, they selectively imitate certain words or structures that they are in the process of learning. Furthermore, children who do little overt imitation learn language as quickly and as well as those who imitate more. Thus, this type of imitation may be an individual learning strategy but it is not a universal characteristic of language learners.

Some second language learners also find it useful to imitate samples of the new language. Classroom researchers have observed students who repeat what they hear others say, and some advanced learners who are determined to improve their pronunciation find it helpful to spend time carefully listening to and imitating language in a language laboratory or tutorial. However, for beginning learners, the imitation and rote memorization that characterizes audiolingual approaches to language teaching is not effective if learners do not also use the sentences and phrases they are practicing in meaningful interaction. Learners need to do more than recite bits of accurate language in drills and dialogues.

Nevertheless, recent findings from corpus linguistics have provided a new appreciation for formulaic language use. We know from the discussion of usage-based theories discussed in Chapter 4 that a great deal of natural language use is predictable on the basis of the frequency with which words or phrases occur together. Learners create strong associations between language features that tend to occur together. Thus, language is partly learned in chunks larger than single words. However, this internalization of the input does not depend on the learner's imitation of all or part of another person's utterance in a rote-repetition fashion. It is the combined exposure to language features in the input and their use in meaningful exchanges that leads to learning.

2 Parents usually correct young children when they make grammatical errors

There is considerable variation in the extent to which parents correct their children's speech. The variation is based partly on the children's age and partly on the parents' social, linguistic, and educational background. When children are very young, parents rarely comment on grammatical errors, although they may correct lapses in politeness or the choice of a word that doesn't make sense. As children reach school age, parents may correct the kinds of non-standard speech that they hope their children will outgrow, for example, 'Me and Fred are going outside now'.

Extensive observations of parents and children show that, as a rule, parents tend to focus on meaning rather than form when they correct children's speech. Thus, they may correct an incorrect word choice, an incorrect statement of the facts, or a rude remark, but they do not often react to errors that do not interfere with communication. What this tells us is that children cannot depend on consistent corrective feedback in order to learn the basic structure (the word order, the grammatical morphemes, the intonation patterns) of their language. Fortunately, they appear to be able to acquire the adult form of the language with little or no explicit feedback.

The case for second language learners is more complex. On the one hand, both children and adults can acquire a great deal of language without any formal instruction or feedback on error. On the other hand, the evidence suggests that, without corrective feedback and guidance, second language learners may persist in using certain ungrammatical forms for years.

3 Highly intelligent people are good language learners

The kind of intelligence that is measured by IQ tests is often a good predictor of success in classrooms where the emphasis is on learning *about* the language (for example, grammar rules). People who do well on IQ tests may do well on other kinds of tests as well. However, in natural language learning settings and in classrooms where interactive language use is emphasized, research has shown that learners with a wide variety of intellectual abilities can be successful language learners. This is especially true if the emphasis is on oral communication skills rather than metalinguistic knowledge.

Most important, it must be recalled that language learning involves a great many different skills and abilities that are not measured by IQ tests. Students should not be excluded from opportunities to learn another language on the grounds that they do not have the academic ability to succeed. In many educational contexts, students from immigrant or minority groups have no choice about learning a second language. What is essential is to find ways to engage the different abilities that students bring to the learning environment.

4 The best predictor of success in second language acquisition is motivation

Everyone agrees that learners who want to learn tend to do better than those who don't. But we must not interpret this too rigidly. Sometimes, even highly motivated learners encounter great challenges in language learning. We know, for example, that learners who begin learning a second language as adults rarely achieve the fluency and accuracy that children do in first language acquisition. This should not be taken as evidence that adult second language learners are not motivated to learn. It may be a reflection of changes that come with age or of other individual differences such as language learning aptitude, how the instruction interacts with individual learners' styles and preferences for learning, how much time the learner can devote to learning the new language, and what opportunities the learner has to use the language outside the classroom.

Teachers have no influence over learners' intrinsic motivation for learning a second language. Students come to classrooms from different backgrounds and life experiences, all of which have contributed to their motivation to learn and their attitudes toward the target language and the community with which it is associated. The principal way that teachers can influence learners' motivation is by making the classroom a supportive environment in which students are stimulated, engaged in activities that are appropriate to their age, interests, and cultural backgrounds, and, most importantly, where students can experience success. This in turn can contribute to positive motivation, leading to still greater success.

5 The earlier a second language is introduced in school programmes, the greater the likelihood of success in learning

The decision about when to introduce second or foreign language instruction must depend on the objectives of the language programme in the particular social context of the school. When the objective is native-like performance in the second language, then it may be desirable to begin exposure to the language as early as possible, as long as learners have extensive exposure to and opportunities to use the second language in a variety of contexts. The research evidence is fairly strong that those who begin second language learning at an early age are most likely to eventually be indistinguishable from native speakers.

However, even in cases where native-like proficiency is targeted, it is important to recognize certain disadvantages of an early start for second language learning. When an early start means that children have little opportunity to continue to develop their first language, the resulting subtractive bilingualism may have lasting negative consequences.

For children from minority-language backgrounds, programmes promoting the development of the first language both at home and at school may be more important for long-term success in the second language than an early start in the second language itself. Research shows that a good foundation in the child's first language, including the development of literacy, is a sound base to build on. Children who can begin their schooling in a language they already know will have more self-confidence, will be able to learn more effectively in the early school years, and will not lose valuable time in a period of limbo during which they struggle just to understand what is happening in the classroom.

For many children, there is no opportunity to have their early schooling in their first language. They are members of small minority groups where it is not practical for schools to offer them an educational programme in their first language, or they live in jurisdictions where legislation has mandated a single language of education for all children, regardless of their background. For these children, it is crucial to have sensitive educators who respect the children's difficulty, who encourage parents to maintain the home language, and who understand that second language learning takes time and effort.

For foreign language instruction or for second language instruction where the level of proficiency that is targeted is not native-like performance by all students, the situation is quite different. When the goal of the educational programme is basic communicative skill for all students, and where there is a strong commitment to maintaining and developing the child's first language, it can be more efficient to begin second language teaching later. Older children (for example, 10-year-olds) are able to catch up quickly with those who began earlier (for example, at 6–7 years old) in programmes offering only a few hours a week of instruction. This is especially true if the foreign language course includes a period of more intensive exposure to the new language.

All school programmes should be based on realistic estimates of how long it takes to learn a second language. One or two hours a week—even for seven or eight years—will not produce advanced second language speakers. This 'drip-feed' approach often leads to frustration, as learners feel that they have been studying 'for years' without making much progress. Sadly, they are often right about this.

6 Most of the mistakes that second language learners make are due to interference from their first language

First, we should recognize that knowledge of one or more languages can contribute positively to many aspects of second or foreign language learning. If the languages are relatively close cousins (for example, English and German, Spanish and French), there is much that learners already 'know'—including the alphabet, cognate words, as well as some basic principles of syntax.

On the other hand, the transfer of patterns from the native language is one of the major sources of errors in learner language. When errors are caused by learners' perception of some partial similarity between the first and second languages, they may be difficult to overcome, especially when learners are frequently in contact with other learners who make the same errors.

Aspects of the second language that are different from the first language will not necessarily be acquired later or with more difficulty than those aspects that are similar. Second language learning is not simply a process of putting second-language words into first-language sentences. In fact, learners may not always be able to take advantage of similarities unless they are pointed out to them. Learners can be overly discriminating, failing to take advantage of similarities because they assume, sometimes incorrectly, that the languages must be different.

However, the first language is not the only influence on second language learning. Learners from different backgrounds often make the same kinds of errors, and some of these errors are remarkably similar to those made by first language learners. In such cases, second-language errors are evidence of the learners' efforts to discover the structure of the target language itself rather than attempts to transfer patterns from their first language.

7 The best way to learn new vocabulary is through reading

This statement is true but it does not tell the whole story. Children expand their vocabulary dramatically during their school years, and reading is the major source of this growth. Second language learners can also increase their vocabulary knowledge through reading, but few second language learners will read the amount of target language text that a child reads in the course of more than a decade of schooling.

Research evidence suggests that second language learners benefit from opportunities to read material that is interesting and important to them. However, those who also receive guidance from instruction and develop good strategies for learning and remembering words will benefit more than those who simply focus on getting the main ideas from a text. What is perhaps most striking in the research is the evidence that in order to successfully guess the meanings of new words in a text, a reader usually needs to know more than 90 per cent of the words in that text.

8 It is essential for learners to be able to pronounce all the individual sounds in the second language

Research on pronunciation has shown that second language speakers' ability to make themselves understood depends more on their ability to reproduce the phrasing and stress patterns—the 'melody' of the language—than on their ability to articulate each individual sound. Another important emphasis in current research is the undeniable fact that most languages of the world are spoken in many different varieties. Thus, it no longer seems appropriate to insist that learners be taught only one language variety or that only native speakers of a particular variety are the best teachers. Rather, learners need to learn to understand and produce language varieties that will permit them to engage in communicative interaction with the interlocutors they are most likely to encounter.

9 Once learners know 1,000 words and the basic structure of a second language, they can easily participate in conversations with native speakers

It is true that most conversational language involves only a relatively limited number of words and sentence types. However, learners will find it easier to understand and to make themselves understood if they also have an under-standing of some of the pragmatic features of the new language. For example, it is useful for them to focus their attention on such things as how speakers show respect, apologize, or make requests. The cultural differences in these types of interactions sometimes lead to communication breakdown or mis-understandings, even when the words and the sentence structures are correct.

10 Teachers should present grammatical rules one at a time, and learners should practise each one before going on to another

Second language learning is not simply linear in its development. Learners may use a particular form accurately at Stage x (suggesting that they have learned that form), fail to produce the form (or make errors when they attempt it) at Stage y, and produce it accurately again at Stage z. The decline in accuracy at stage y may show that learners are incorporating new informa-tion about the language into their interlanguage. We saw, for example, how learners may ask correct formulaic questions such as 'What's that?' or 'How do you say *proche* in English?' and then produce questions like 'What you're doing with that?' at a later time. Language development is not just adding one rule after another. Rather, it involves processes of integrating new lan-guage forms and patterns into an existing interlanguage, readjusting and restructuring until all the pieces fit.

Some structure-based approaches to teaching are based on the false assump-tion that second language development is an accumulation of rules. This can be seen in the organization of textbooks that introduce a particular language feature in the first unit and reinforce it in several subsequent units, and then move on the next feature, with only rare opportunities for learners to practise the ones previously taught. This isolated presentation and practice of one structure at a time does not provide learners with an opportunity to discover how different language features compare and contrast in normal language use. It is also likely that, without opportunities to continue hearing, seeing, and using them, the language features learned in the first unit will have been forgotten long before the last.

11 Teachers should teach simple language structures before complex ones

Research has shown that no matter how language is presented to learners, certain structures are acquired before others. This suggests that it is neither necessary nor desirable to restrict learners' exposure to structures that are per-ceived in linguistic terms to be 'simple'—particularly when this involves the isolated presentation, ordering, and practice of 'simple' to 'complex' features.

At the same time, there is no doubt that second language learners benefit from the efforts of native speakers and fluent bilinguals to modify their speech to help them understand. The language used in modified interaction may contain a variety of linguistic structures, some 'simple' and some 'complex'. However, it also includes a range of adjustments that enable second language learners to engage in interactions with native and more advanced speakers of the second language more easily—more repetition, slower rate of delivery, paraphrasing, etc.

Teachers must also be aware, however, that some linguistic forms are so rare in classroom language that learners have little opportunity to hear, use, and learn them if the teacher does not make a point of providing them. These are not necessarily difficult or complex forms. As we saw in Chapter 6, some 'simple' language forms turn out to be extremely rare in classroom language, even in content-based instruction.

12 Learners' errors should be corrected as soon as they are made in order to prevent the formation of bad habits

Errors are a natural part of language learning. This is true of the development of a child's first language as well as of second language learning by children and adults. Errors reflect the patterns of learners' developing interlanguage systems—showing gaps in their knowledge, overgeneralization of a second language rule, or an inappropriate transfer of a first language pattern to the second language.

Teachers have a responsibility to help learners do their best, and this includes the provision of explicit, form-focused instruction and feedback on error. When errors are persistent, especially when they are shared by almost all students in a class, it is important to bring the problem to their attention. This does not mean that learners should be expected to adopt the correct form or pattern immediately or consistently. If the error reflects a developmental stage, the instruction or feedback may be useful only when the learner is ready for it. It may be necessary to repeat feedback on the same error many times.

Of course, excessive feedback on error can have a negative effect on motivation; teachers need to be sensitive to their students' reactions to correction. The amount and type of correction that is offered will also vary according to the specific characteristics of the students, as well as their relationship with the teacher and with each other. Children and adults with little education in their first language will not benefit greatly from sophisticated metalinguistic explanations, but university students who are advanced learners of the language may find such explanations of great value. Immediate reaction to errors in an oral communication setting may embarrass some students and discourage them from speaking while others welcome such correction as exactly what is needed to help them notice a persistent error at just the moment when it occurs.

13 Teachers should use materials that expose students only to language structures they have already been taught

Such a procedure can provide comprehensible input of course, but—given a meaningful context—learners can comprehend the general meaning of oral or written texts that contain vocabulary and structures they have not 'mastered'. Thus, restricting classroom second language materials to those that contain little or nothing that is new may have several negative consequences. There will undoubtedly be a loss of motivation if students are not sufficiently challenged. Students also need to develop strategies for dealing with 'real' or 'authentic' material if they are eventually going to be prepared for language use outside the classroom. They do this first with the teacher's guidance and then independently. Restricting students to step-by-step exposure to the language extends their dependency.

When a particular language feature is introduced for the first time, or when the teacher feels there is a need for correction of a persistent problem, it is appropriate to use narrow-focus materials that isolate one element in a context where other things seem easy. But it would be a disservice to students to use such materials exclusively or even predominantly. We should remember that learners who successfully acquire a second language outside classrooms certainly are exposed to a great variety of forms and structures they have not mastered.

14 When learners are allowed to interact freely (for example, in group or pair activities), they copy each other's mistakes

The language that learners hear and read serves as input to their language development. The cognitive processes that allow them to learn from input are not 'shut down' when they are interacting with other learners. Thus, when learners interact with each other, they may provide some incorrect input. Furthermore, when learners come from the same first language background and are at roughly the same level of proficiency, they are likely to understand each other very well, eliminating the need for negotiation for meaning that might lead them to replace their interlanguage patterns with more target-like ones. Nevertheless, the benefits of pair and group work far outweigh the disadvantages, especially if the tasks are properly designed.

If the activities are well designed and learners are appropriately matched, pair and group work provides far more practice in speaking and participating in conversations than a teacher-centred class ever could. Somewhat surprisingly, research has shown that learners do not produce any more errors in their speech when talking to learners at similar levels of proficiency than they do when speaking to learners at more advanced levels or to native speakers. The research also shows, however, that learners at similar levels cannot ordinarily provide each other with information that would help to correct those errors. Nonetheless, tasks can be devised in such a way that learners working together can discover not only how to express or interpret meaning but also how to discover the correct patterns in the second language. In order for this to happen, the tasks must be carefully planned to give learners access to the new language they need.

Group and pair work is a valuable addition to the variety of activities that encourage and promote second language development. Used in combination with individual work and teacher-centred activities, it plays an essential role in language teaching and learning.

15 Students learn what they are taught

Teachers know from experience that students don't learn everything they are taught! Fortunately, learners also learn a great deal that no one ever teaches them. They are able to use their own internal learning abilities to discover many of the patterns and associations that underlie the language they are learning. In this sense, students learn much more than they are explicitly taught.

Some teaching methods typically give learners the opportunity to learn only a restricted number of words and sentence types. Even when the language teaching method provides much richer language input, the fact that something is taught or made available in the input does not mean learners will acquire it right away. For example, some aspects of the second language emerge and evolve according to developmental sequences, and learners may be more likely to learn certain language features when they are developmentally ready. Thus, attempts to teach aspects of language that are too far away from the learner's current stage of development can be frustrating. Other language features, for example, vocabulary, can be taught at any time, as long as the learners are interested in the opportunity to learn and the teaching methods are appropriate to the learner's age, interests, needs, experiences, and learning styles.

16 Teachers should respond to students' errors by correctly rephrasing what they have said rather than by explicitly pointing out the error

This kind of feedback, referred to as 'recasts' has been found to be by far the most common type of feedback in second language classrooms. This has been shown to be true for learners at different ages and in different instructional settings—from audiolingual to communicative and content-based instruction. A recast has the advantage of not interrupting the flow of interaction. It is seen as indirect and polite, a way of giving students the information they need without embarrassing them.

Research in classes with a general focus on grammar and accurate language use shows that learners are responsive to this kind of feedback. Research in which learners interact individually with interlocutors has also shown that recasts are perceived as corrective feedback, even though learners may not always know exactly which language features the feedback is focused on. However, in content-based instruction (for example, immersion classes) and in communicative instruction with younger learners, recasts often appear to be misinterpreted. Learners seem to hear them as confirmation of meaning rather than as correction of form. In these situations, recasts have been found to be more effective if the teacher has a method of signalling to the student— tone of voice, gesture, or facial expression—that says to the student, 'I think I understand what you are saying, and I'm showing you how you can say it better'.

17 Students can learn both language and academic content (for example, science and history) simultaneously in classes where the subject matter is taught in their second language

The advantages of content-based instruction are numerous. Motivation is increased when the material that is used for language teaching has an inherent value to the students: it creates a genuine, immediate need to learn the language. Content-based instruction is also often associated with the opportunity to spend more time in contact with the language, without losing out on instruction in other subject matter. In addition, the range of vocabulary and language features that students encounter in learning academic subjects is more varied than that which is typically available in second and foreign language classes.

Research has confirmed that students in content-based and immersion classes develop comprehension skills, vocabulary, and general communicative competence in the new language. Teachers and researchers have also found, however, that the ability to understand the content and to function in classroom interaction does not ensure that students will continue to improve in certain aspects of their second language, especially in areas of accuracy on language features that do not usually interfere with meaning. Thus, for example, students can spend years in French immersion without achieving accuracy in marking nouns for gender or verbs for tense. Experimental studies in which an element of form-focused instruction was added to the content-based instruction have shown that, with guidance, students can improve in these areas as well. Both students and teachers need to keep in mind that content-based instruction is also language teaching.

18 Classrooms are good places to learn about language but not for learning how to use language

Some structure-based approaches to language teaching have tended to treat language as a set of grammar rules or as separate bits of information that need to be learned before learners can use the language as a communicative tool. Other approaches such as communicative language teaching, content-based, and task-based instruction start from the principle that we learn language by using it to achieve a goal, for example, understanding a story, making a medical appointment, writing a science report, or joining the fun on the playground. With this in mind, classroom activities are designed to prepare students to continue learning outside the classroom, by giving them experience in language *uses* that are like those they will encounter there.

As we saw in Chapter 6, some theorists argue that second language instruction can only lead to knowledge *about* language (explicit knowledge) and question whether instruction can lead to the ability to *use* the language spontaneously and fluently (implicit knowledge) in a wide range of communicative contexts. Contemporary approaches to L2 instruction target the development of both types of L2 ability by ensuring that students use the language in meaningful interaction inside the classroom and that they learn effective strategies for using the language outside the classroom when they have opportunities to do so.

ACTIVITY   **Support your opinion**

Choose two or three of the 'popular ideas' that you find especially important. For each of these, identify and discuss how one or more of the research studies you have read about in this book has strengthened your agreement/ disagreement with the statement or has led you to change your views.

Conclusion

Knowing more about second language acquisition research will not tell you what to do in your classroom tomorrow morning. We hope, however, that this book has provided you with information that encourages you to reflect on your experience in teaching. We hope, in addition, that this reflection will contribute to a better understanding of your responsibilities as a teacher and your students' abilities and responsibilities as language learners.

As we have seen, language learning is affected by many factors. Among these are the personal characteristics and experiences of the learner, the social and cultural environment both inside and outside the classroom, the structure of the native and target languages, opportunities for interaction with speakers of the target language, and access to corrective feedback and form-focused instruction. It is clear that teachers do not have control over all these factors. Nevertheless, a better understanding of them will permit teachers and learners to make the most of the time they spend together in the twin processes of teaching and learning a second language.

GLOSSARY

The glossary contains items that have a special or technical meaning in second language acquisition research and second language teaching. The definitions are intended to reflect the terms as *we use them in this book*.

accessibility hierarchy: A ranking of relative clauses developed by Keenan and Comrie (1977). Different languages use relative clauses to modify nouns in different grammatical roles. According to the accessibility hierarchy, for example, most languages allow relative clauses for sentence subjects, while fewer languages allow them for the object of comparison.

accuracy order: The relative accuracy of grammatical forms in learner language. For example, learners are often more accurate in using plural *-s* than in using possessive *'s*. Some researchers have inferred that an accuracy order is equivalent to a developmental sequence.

action research: Research carried out by teachers, often in their own classrooms or in collaboration with other teachers. The research goals and questions are local and specific to their own teaching environment.

active listening: A teaching technique in which students not only listen but also show their comprehension by their responses.

additive bilingualism: Learning a second language without losing the first.

American Sign Language (ASL): The gestural language used by many North Americans who are deaf or who interact with others who are deaf. It is a true language, with complex rules of structure and a rich vocabulary, all expressed through motions of the hands and body.

audiolingual approach: An approach to second or foreign language teaching that is based on the behaviourist theory of learning and on structural linguistics, especially the contrastive analysis hypothesis. This instructional approach emphasizes the formation of habits through the repetition, practice, and memorization of sentence patterns in isolation from each other and from contexts of meaningful use.

auditory discrimination: The ability to distinguish language sounds, for example minimal pairs such as *ship/sheep*.

behaviourism: A psychological theory that all learning, whether verbal or non-verbal, takes place through the establishment of habits. According to this view, when learners imitate and repeat the language they hear in their surrounding environment and are positively reinforced for doing so, habit formation (or learning) occurs.

bilingual education: Schooling in which students receive instruction in two (or more) languages, usually their home language and a second language.

bilingualism: The ability to use more than one language. The word itself does not specify the degree of proficiency in either language.

brain imaging: A variety of techniques that allow researchers to observe and track activity in the brain.

child-directed speech: The language that caretakers address to children. In some cases, this language is simpler than that which is addressed to adults. In some cultures, it is also slower, higher pitched, more repetitive, and includes a large number of questions.

chunk: A unit of language that is often perceived or used as a single unit. Chunks include formulaic expressions such as *Thank you* or *What's that?* but also bits of language that frequently occur together, for example, *ice cream cone* or *significant difference*.

classroom observation scheme: A tool (often in the form of a grid) that consists of a set of predetermined categories used to record and describe teaching and learning behaviours.

cognate: A word in one language that comes from the same origin as a word in another language and has the same meaning, for example, 'nation' in English and *nation* in French or *vaca* and *vache* (cow) in Spanish and French. The term *false cognate* is used to refer to words that may come from the same origin but have evolved to have different meanings, for example, *librairie* (bookstore) in French does not have the same meaning as *library* in English.

cognitive: Relating to how the human mind receives, processes, stores, and retrieves information. The focus is on internal learning mechanisms that are believed to be used for learning in general, not just language learning alone.

cognitive maturity: The ability to engage in problem-solving, deduction, and complex memory tasks.

collaborative dialogue: A conversation between learners in which they work together to solve a problem, for example, reconstructing a story they have heard. While the focus is on the task, learners may also focus on the elements of language that they need to complete the task.

communicative competence: The ability to use language in a variety of settings, taking into account relationships between speakers and differences in situations. The term has sometimes been interpreted as the ability to convey messages in spite of a lack of grammatical accuracy.

communicative language teaching (CLT): CLT is based on the premise that successful language learning involves not only a knowledge of the structures and forms of a language, but also the functions and purposes that a language serves in different communicative settings. This approach to teaching emphasizes the communication of meaning in interaction rather than the practice and manipulation of grammatical forms in isolation.

competence: Linguist Noam Chomsky used this term to refer to knowledge of language. This is contrasted with performance, which is the way a person actually uses language—whether for speaking, listening, reading, or writing. Because we cannot observe competence directly, we have to infer its nature from performance.

comprehensible input: A term introduced by Stephen Krashen to refer to language that a learner can understand. It may be comprehensible in part because of gestures, contextual information, or prior knowledge/experience.

comprehensible output hypothesis: The hypothesis that successful second language acquisition depends on learners producing language (oral or written). Swain (1985) proposed this hypothesis in response to Krashen's (1985) comprehensible input hypothesis.

comprehension-based instruction: A general term to describe a variety of second language programmes in which the focus of instruction is on comprehension rather than production.

connectionism: A theory of knowledge (including language) as a complex system of units that become interconnected in the mind as they are encountered together. The more often units are heard or seen together, the more likely it is that the presence of one will lead to the activation of the other.

content and language-integrated learning (CLIL): An approach to content-based language teaching that has been developed primarily in secondary schools in Europe.

content-based language teaching (CBLT): Second language instruction in which lessons are organized around subject matter rather than language points. For example, in immersion programmes, students study science, history, mathematics, etc. in their second language.

contrastive analysis hypothesis (CAH): The expectation that learners will have less difficulty acquiring target language patterns that are similar to those of the first language than those that are different.

control group: In experimental studies, a group of learners that differs from the experimental group only in terms of the single variable that the researcher is investigating. Performance of the control group is used to show that the variable in question is the best (or only) explanation for changes in the experimental group. Also sometimes referred to as 'comparison group'.

corpus (plural: corpora): A principled collection of oral or written language samples that can usually be accessed and explored with computer-based tools. Some of the most famous corpora contain millions of words from, for example, newspapers. Samples of the language produced by learners have also been collected for second language acquisition research.

corpus linguistics: An approach to the study of language that is based on the analysis of language corpora. See corpus.

corrective feedback: An indication to a learner that his or her use of the target language is incorrect.

correlation: A statistical procedure that compares the relative frequency or size of different variables in order to determine whether there is a relationship between them.

counterbalance hypothesis: The hypothesis that learners' attention will be drawn to classroom events that are different from those they are accustomed to.

critical period hypothesis (CPH): The proposal that there is a limited period during which language acquisition can occur.

cross-linguistic influence: The effect on knowledge of one language by the knowledge of another. This term is preferred over previous terms such as *interference* to indicate that knowledge of one language can be beneficial to learning another. The term also reflects the fact that the influence can go from a known language to the one being learned but also from the new language to one already known.

cross-sectional study: A study in which participants at different ages and/or stages of development are studied. This contrasts with longitudinal studies.

declarative knowledge: Information that we have and know we have. An example would be a rule such as 'the verb must agree with the subject to form a correct sentence'. In some skill learning theories, it has been hypothesized that all learning begins with declarative knowledge. This contrasts with *procedural knowledge*.

descriptive study: Research that does not involve any manipulation, change, or intervention in the phenomenon being studied. The researcher's goal is to observe and record what is happening. This contrasts with experimental study.

developmental features: Those aspects of a language which, according to Pienemann and his colleagues, develop in a particular sequence, regardless of input variation, learner motivation, or instructional intervention.

developmental sequence: The order in which certain features of a language (for example, negation) are acquired in language learning. Also called developmental stages or order of acquisition.

display question: A question to which the asker already knows the answer. Teachers often ask these questions (for example, *What colour is your shirt?*) to get the learner to display his or her knowledge of the language.

enhanced input: Input that is altered in an effort to make some language features more salient to learners. It can be more or less explicit, ranging from explicit metalinguistic comments to typographical enhancement (bold type or underlining) or exaggerated stress in speaking.

ethnography: Descriptive research in which the observer seeks to understand a group or community from within its own perspective. The research requires extensive periods of observation as well as consultation with group members to validate the observer's descriptions.

experimental study: Research designed to test a hypothesis about the impact of one or more specific variables on another variable. A strictly experimental study would have 'experimental' and 'control' groups that differ from each other only in the presence or absence of the variable(s) of interest. In educational research, it is often difficult to create all of the conditions that permit a study to be termed as a 'genuine' experimental study. In this book, the term is used in a non-technical sense to refer to research in which an attempt has been made to investigate a single variable in an educational setting.

field independent/field dependent: This distinction has been used to describe people who differ in their tendency to see the forest or the trees. That is, some people (called field independent) are very quick to pick out the hidden figures in a complicated drawing. Others (called field dependent) are more inclined to see the whole drawing and have difficulty separating it into parts.

first language (L1, mother tongue, native language): The language first learned. Many children learn more than one language from birth and may be said to have more than one 'first' language.

foreigner talk: The modified or simplified language that some native speakers address to second language learners. A special category of foreigner talk is teacher talk.

foreign language learning: This refers to the learning of a language, usually in a classroom setting, in a context where the target language is not widely used in the community (for example, learning French in China). This is sometimes contrasted with 'second language learning', where the language being learned is used in the community (for example, learning Italian in Florence).

form-focused instruction: Instruction that draws attention to the forms and structures of the language within the context of communicative interaction. This may be done by giving metalinguistic information, simply highlighting the form in question, or by providing corrective feedback.

formulaic: Expressions or phrases that are often perceived and learned as unanalysed wholes. For example, a child or second language learner may first hear 'What's that?' as a single unit of language rather than as three units.

fossilization: This term is used to describe a persistent lack of change in interlanguage patterns, even after extended exposure to or instruction in the target language.

function words: Words that are used mainly as linking or supporting words for nouns, verbs, adjectives, and adverbs. For example, prepositions ('to', 'for', 'by') and articles ('a', 'the') are two types of function words. They have little or no meaning when they occur alone, but they have an important effect on the meanings of the words they accompany.

generalization: Extending a pattern learned in one context to another one. See also overgeneralization.

genuine question: A question to which the asker does not know the answer in advance (for example, *What did you do last weekend?*). Also called 'referential' or 'information' questions. Contrasts with display question.

grammar translation: An approach to second language teaching characterized by the explicit teaching of grammar rules and the use of translation exercises.

grammatical morphemes: Morphemes are the smallest units of language that carry meaning. A simple word is a morpheme (for example, 'book'), but when we talk about 'grammatical morphemes' we are usually referring to smaller units that are added to words to alter their meaning (for example, the -*s* in 'books' indicates plural) or function words (for example, *the*) which are ordinarily attached to another word.

grammaticality judgement: A test or task in which participants are asked to make a decision about whether a sentence is grammatically correct or not.

hypothesis (plural: hypotheses): A statement of a possible fact that can be tested through research. Most empirical research starts from one or more hypotheses and involves the design of a study that can either show support for the hypothesis or disprove it.

immersion programme: An educational programme in which a second language is taught via content-based instruction. That is, students study subjects such as mathematics and social studies in their second language. Typically, students in immersion programmes share the same first language and teachers adjust their instructional language and materials to meet the needs of second language learners.

information processing: A psychological theory based on the idea that learners' cognitive resources are limited and they can't pay attention to everything at the same time. But with repeated experience and practice, things which at first required attention become automatic, leaving more attention available for focus on something else.

innatist: In language acquisition research, this is the theoretical perspective based on the hypothesis that human beings are born with mental structures that are designed specifically for the acquisition of language.

input: The language that the learner is exposed to (either written or spoken) in the environment.

input flood: A technique for providing a large number of examples of a particular language feature in the input to learners. It has been used in research projects to explore questions related to whether comprehensible input is sufficient for language acquisition.

instrumental motivation: Motivation that is essentially practical, such as the need to learn the language in order to get a better job.

integrative motivation: Motivation for second language learning that is based on a desire to know more about the culture and community of the target language group and even a desire to be more like members of that group.

intensive ESL: In this book, 'intensive' ESL is used to refer to an instructional approach in Quebec where 10–12-year-old French-speaking students learn English as a second language. Most Quebec students in this age group have only an hour or two of ESL instruction each week. 'Intensive ESL' classes provide much more time. Most of the classes observed in intensive ESL research set aside one five-month block of time in one school year and devote full days to ESL instruction during that period. The pedagogical approach observed in these classes is predominantly communicative language teaching. In contrast to immersion programmes, intensive ESL classes do not usually include content-based language teaching.

interaction hypothesis: The hypothesis that language acquisition is based both on learners' innate abilities and on opportunities to engage in conversations, often those in which other speakers modify their speech and their interaction patterns to match the learners' communication requirements. The innate abilities are not seen as being specific to language or language acquisition.

interlanguage: A learner's developing second language knowledge. It may have characteristics of the learner's first language, characteristics of the second language, and some characteristics that seem to be very general and tend to occur in all or most interlanguage systems. Interlanguages are systematic, but they are also dynamic. They change as learners receive more input and revise their hypotheses about the second language.

interlocutor: A participant in a conversation.

language acquisition/language learning: In this book, these two terms are most often used interchangeably. However, for some researchers, most notably Stephen Krashen *acquisition* represents 'unconscious' *internalization of language knowledge*, which takes place when attention is focused on meaning rather than language form, and *learning* is described as a 'conscious' process that occurs when the learner's objective is to learn about the language itself, rather than to understand messages conveyed through the language.

language-related episodes (LREs): Parts of conversational interactions in which language learners talk about the language forms they are using and engage in self- and peer-correction.

longitudinal study: A study in which the same learners are studied over a period of time. This contrasts with a cross-sectional study.

meaning-based instruction: See communicative language teaching.

meta-analysis (plural: meta-analyses): A statistical procedure that allows researchers to combine the findings from a large number of quantitative studies in order to assess the overall patterns of findings on a similar topic.

metalinguistic awareness: The ability to treat language as an object, for example, being able to define a word, or to say what sounds make up that word.

mitigation: In pragmatics, a phrase or tone of voice used to reduce or soften the possible negative impact of what is said.

modified input: Adapted speech that adults use to address children and native speakers use to address language learners so that they will be able to understand. Examples of modified input include shorter, simpler sentences, and basic vocabulary.

modified interaction: Adapted conversation patterns that proficient speakers use in addressing language learners so that the learner will be able to understand. Examples of interactional modifications include comprehension checks, clarification requests, and self-repetitions.

morpheme: See grammatical morphemes.

native-like: The ability to comprehend and produce a second language at a level of performance that is indistinguishable from that of a native speaker.

native speaker: A person who has learned a language from an early age and who is deemed to be fully proficient in that language. Native speakers differ in terms of vocabulary and stylistic aspects of language use, but they tend to agree on the basic grammar of the language. The notion 'native speaker' must always be understood within a specific geographic region or socioeconomic group because there is wide variation among 'native speakers' of most languages.

natural order: See developmental sequence.

negotiation of form: An interaction in which language learners work toward the correct form in a context where meaning is understood. If a teacher is involved in the interaction, he or she seeks to guide students to find the right form instead of providing it for them.

negotiation for meaning: Interaction between speakers who make adjustments to their speech and use other techniques to repair a breakdown in communication. See also modified interaction.

noticing hypothesis: The hypothesis, proposed by Richard Schmidt, that language learners learn only that which they have first 'noticed' or become aware of in the input.

obligatory contexts: Places in a sentence where a particular grammatical form is required if the sentence is to be correct. For example, in the sentence 'Last week, my brother rent a car', the speaker has created an obligatory context for the past tense by the use of 'Last week', but has not used the required form of the verb in that context.

order of acquisition: See developmental sequence.

overgeneralization: This type of error is the result of trying to use a rule or pattern in a context where it does not belong, for example, putting a regular -*ed* ending on an irregular verb, as in 'buyed' instead of 'bought'.

pattern practice drill: A teaching technique in which learners are asked to practise sentences chosen to represent particular linguistic forms. Typical of the audiolingual approach.

performance: The way we use language in listening, speaking, reading, writing. Performance is usually contrasted with competence, which is the knowledge that underlies our ability to use language. Performance is subject to variations due to inattention or fatigue whereas competence, at least for the mature native speaker, is more stable.

phonemic: Small differences in language sounds that can change meaning within a particular language. For example, the consonants *p* and *b* are phonemic in English, but not in Arabic.

pragmatics: Aspects of language use that go beyond vocabulary and grammar to include rules of how to use language appropriately in different contexts and with different speakers. It also includes an understanding of the implied as well as the explicit meaning of language.

private speech: The language we use when we are talking to ourselves, not expecting anyone to hear or respond.

procedural knowledge: Knowledge that underlies fluent or automatic performance. It is contrasted with declarative knowledge.

processability theory: Manfred Pienemann's theory of learners' developing ability to process linguistic elements in different sentence positions.

processing instruction: An approach to instruction in which learners are given explicit information about the language feature to be learned and their practice activities involve the comprehension (not production) of sentences or texts that cannot be understood without a focus on the language itself. The approach was developed by Bill VanPatten.

qualitative research: An approach that uses detailed descriptions of the phenomena being studied rather than counting or measuring the exact amount of some specific variable or variables. Qualitative research requires extensive observation and insightful interpretation.

quantitative research: An approach that requires precise counts or numeric measurements of variables. In a quantitative study, both the variable that is believed to affect learning and the learning itself are measured or 'quantified'. Quantitative research requires careful selection of the measurements that will be used to represent the variables being studied.

rate of learning: The speed with which learners progress in their language development.

recast: To repeat a learner's incorrect utterance, making changes that convert it to a correct phrase or sentence. 'Recast' is also used as a noun, that is, a recast is the interlocutor's modified/corrected form of the learner's utterance.

register: A style or way of using language that is typical of or appropriate for a particular setting. For example, speaking and writing usually require different registers; the register used in writing a research report is different from that used in writing a letter to a friend.

restructuring: Cognitive activity that is seen as causing changes in the way information is organized in the brain, even though no new information has been learned.

scaffolding: The language that an interlocutor uses to support the communicative success of another speaker. It may include the provision of missing vocabulary or the expansion of the speaker's incomplete sentence.

second language (L2): In this book, the term refers to any language other than the first language learned. Thus, it may actually refer to the third or fourth language.

segmental: The individual sounds of a language. Contrasted with 'suprasegmentals', which are patterns of intonation.

significant difference: This is a technical term that refers to differences between groups which, according to a variety of statistical tests, are unlikely to have happened by chance. Such differences can be small or large. Their 'significance' is due to the consistency of the differences as well as their size.

simplification: Leaving out elements of a sentence, for example, using the same form of a verb regardless of person, number, tense ('I go today. He go yesterday').

sociocultural theory: An explanation for knowledge and learning that is based on the assumption that all learning is first social then individual. Learning is viewed as a process that is socially mediated, that is, it is dependent on dialogue in face-to-face interaction. The claim is that during communication, learners jointly construct knowledge which is internalized by the individual.

standard variety: The variety of a given language that is typically used in formal writing and formal public speaking (including broadcasting). The standard variety of widely spoken languages may be different in different places. For example, American English, British English, Canadian English, and Indian English each has its own standard variety, as well as numerous ethnic, regional, and socioeconomic varieties.

structural grading: A technique for organizing or sequencing material in a textbook or lessons. The basis for the organization is a gradual increase in complexity of grammatical features.

subtractive bilingualism: Partially or completely losing the first language as a second language is acquired.

suprasegmentals: The sounds of a language that involve the melody and rhythm of the language (e.g. stress and intonation), rather than the pronunciation of individual sounds.

target language: The language being learned, whether it is the first language or a second (or third or fourth) language.

task-based language teaching (TBLT): Instruction in which classroom activities are 'tasks' similar to those learners might engage in outside the second or foreign language classroom. Tasks may be complex, for example, creating a school newspaper, or more limited, for example, making a phone call to reserve a train ticket.

teacher talk: See modified input and foreigner talk.

transfer: The influence of a learner's first language knowledge in the second language. Also called 'interference'. The term 'cross-linguistic influence' is now preferred by many researchers. It better reflects the complex ways in which knowledge of the first language may affect learners' knowledge and use of another.

transfer-appropriate processing (TAP): Cognitive psychologists have observed that when we learn something new, we also internalize some aspects of the circumstances and thinking processes that were present when we learned it. The TAP hypothesis is that knowledge is easier to retrieve if we are returned to or can recreate those circumstances and thinking processes.

universal grammar (UG): Innate linguistic knowledge which, it is hypothesized, consists of a set of principles common to all languages. This term is associated with Chomsky's theory of language acquisition.

uptake: This term is sometimes used in a general sense to refer to what a learner notices and/or retains in second language input or instruction. Lyster and Ranta's (1997) definition refers to a learner's observable immediate response to corrective feedback on his/her utterances.

variable: An element or characteristic that can be measured or defined. Variables can differ in different groups or change over time within a group or individual. Some examples of variables that are commonly examined in language acquisition research include the amount of time a person has been learning the language, scores on aptitude tests, and performance on measures of language knowledge.

variational features: In contrast to the developmental features in the framework developed by Pienemann and his colleagues, variational features (for example, vocabulary, some grammatical morphemes) can be learned at any point in the learner's development.

variety: A way of speaking and using language that is typical of a particular regional, socioeconomic, or ethnic group. The term 'dialect' is sometimes used. Some language varieties are stigmatized as 'uneducated' but each language variety has its own rules and patterns that are as complex and systematic as those of the so-called 'standard' language. Among the most studied non-standard varieties of English are British Cockney and African-American Vernacular English.

willingness to communicate (WTC): The predisposition of learners toward or away from communicating in a second/foreign language. Several factors contribute to WTC including social, individual, situational, and motivational.

working memory (WM): The cognitive 'space' in which we actively process new information or information that is currently in focus. Also called 'short-term memory'.

zone of proximal development (ZPD): The metaphorical 'place' in which a learner is capable of a higher level of performance because there is support from interaction with an interlocutor. In Vygotsky's theory, learning takes place through and during interaction in the learner's ZPD.

BIBLIOGRAPHY

This list brings together all the works cited in the text as well as those that have been suggested for further reading.

Altenberg, E. P. 2005. 'The judgment, perception, and production of consonant clusters in a second language.' *International Review of Applied Linguistics* 43/1: 53–80.

Ammar, A. and **P. M. Lightbown.** 2005. 'Teaching marked linguistic structures—more about the acquisition of relative clauses by Arab learners of English' in A. Housen and M. Pierrard (eds.): *Investigations in Instructed Second Language Acquisition.* Amsterdam: Mouton de Gruyter. pp. 167–98.

Anderson, J. R. 1995. *Learning and Memory: An Integrated Approach.* New York: Wiley.

August, D. and **T. Shanahan** (eds.). 2008. *Developing Reading and Writing in Second-Language Learners.* New York: Routledge.

Bardovi-Harlig, K. 1999. 'Exploring the interlanguage of interlanguage pragmatics: A research agenda for acquisitional pragmatics.' *Language Learning* 49/4: 677–713.

Bardovi-Harlig, K. 2000. *Tense and Aspect in Second Language Acquisition: Form, Meaning, and Use.* Oxford: Blackwell.

Bardovi-Harlig, K. and **B. S. Hartford.** 1993. 'Learning the rules of academic talk: A longitudinal study of pragmatic development. *Studies in Second Language Acquisition* 15/3: 279–304.

Barlow, M. 2005. 'Computer-based analyses of learner language' in R. Ellis and G. Barkhuizen (eds.). *Analysing Learner Language.* Oxford: Oxford University Press. pp. 335–57.

Bates, E. A. and **B. MacWhinney.** 1981. 'Second-language acquisition from a functionalist perspective: Pragmatic, semantic, and perceptual strategies' in H. Winitz (ed.): *Native Language and Foreign Language Acquisition. Annals of the New York Academy of Science.* New York: New York Academy of Science, Vol. 379: 190–214.

Bennet, G. R. 2010. *Using Corpora in the Language Learning Classroom: Corpus Linguistics for Teachers.* Ann Arbor, MI: University of Michigan Press.

Beretta, A. 2011. 'The language learning brain' in M. Long and C. Doughty (eds.): *The Handbook of Language Teaching.* Oxford: Wiley-Blackwell. pp. 65–80.

Berko, J. 1958. 'The child's learning of English morphology.' *Word* 14, 150–77.

Berko Gleason, J. and **N. Bernstein-Ratner** (eds.). 2009. *The Development of Language* 7th edn. New York: Allyn and Bacon.

Bialystok, E. 2001. *Bilingualism in Development: Language, Literacy, and Cognition.* Cambridge: Cambridge University Press.

Bialystok E. 2009. 'Effects of bilingualism on cognitive and linguistic performance across the lifespan' in I. Gogolin and U. Neumann (eds.): *Streitfall Zweisprachigkeit—The Bilingualism Controversy.* Wiesbaden, Germany: VS Verlag fur Sozialwissenschaften. pp. 53–68.

Bley-Vroman, R. 1990. 'The logical problem of foreign language learning.' *Linguistic Analysis* 20/1–2: 3–47.

Bloom, L. 1991. *Language Development from Two to Three.* Cambridge: Cambridge University Press.

Bloom, L. and **M. Lahey.** 1978. *Language Development and Language Disorders.* New York: John Wiley.

Bongaerts, T. 1999. 'Ultimate attainment in L2 pronunciation: The case of very advanced late L2 learners' in D. Birdsong (ed.): *Second Language Acquisition and the Critical Period Hypothesis.* Mahwah, NJ: Lawrence Erlbaum and Associates. pp. 133–59.

Brooks, N. 1960. *Language and Language Learning.* New York: Harcourt Brace.

Brown, R. 1973. *A First Language: The Early Stages.* Cambridge, MA: Harvard University Press.

Burns, A. 2010. *Doing Action Research in English Language Teaching: A Guide for Practitioners.* New York: Routledge.

Burstall, C. 1975. 'French in the primary school: The British experiment.' *Canadian Modern Language Review* 31/5: 388–402.

Carroll, J. 1991. 'Cognitive abilities in foreign language aptitude: Then and now' in T. Parry and C. Stansfield (eds.): *Language Aptitude Reconsidered.* Englewood Cliffs, NJ: Prentice hall.

Carroll, J. and **S. Sapon.** 1959. *The Modern Languages Aptitude Test.* San Antonio, TX: Psychological Corporation.

Celce-Murcia, M., D. M., Brinton, and **J. M. Goodwin.** 1996. *Teaching Pronunciation: A Reference for Teachers of English to Speakers of Other Languages.* Cambridge: Cambridge University Press.

Chomsky, N. 1959. 'Review of "Verbal Behavior" by B. F. Skinner.' *Language* 35/1: 26–58.

Clément, R., S. C. Baker, and **P. D. MacIntyre.** 2003. 'Willingness to communicate in a second language: The effects of context, norms, and vitality.' *Journal of Language and Social Psychology* 22/2: 190–209.

Collier, V. P. 1989. 'How long? A synthesis of research on academic achievement in a second language.' *TESOL Quarterly* 23/3: 509–31.

Collins Cobuild Concordance and Collocation Sampler http://www.collins.co.uk/corpus/Corpus.Search.aspx

Collins, L. 2002. 'The roles of L1 influence and lexical aspect in the acquisition of temporal morphology.' *Language Learning* 52/1: 43–94.

Collins, L. and **J. White.** 2011. 'An intensive look at intensity and language learning.' *TESOL Quarterly* 45/1: 106–33.

Collins, L., R. H. Halter, P. M. Lightbown, and **N. Spada.** 1999. 'Time and the distribution of time in L2 instruction.' *TESOL Quarterly* 33/4: 655–80.

Conboy, B. D. and **P. K. Kuhl.** 2011. 'Impact of second-language experience in infancy: brain measures of first- and second-language speech perception.' *Developmental Science*, 14/2: 242–48.

Cook, V. 2003. 'The poverty-of-the-stimulus argument and structure-dependency in L2 users of English.' *International Review of Applied Linguistics* 41/3: 201–21.

Cook, V. 2008. *Second Language Learning and Language Teaching* 4th edn. London: Hodder Education.

Corder, S. P. 1967. 'The significance of learners' errors.' *International Review of Applied Linguistics* 5/2–3: 161–69.

Crago, M. 1992. 'Communicative interaction and second language acquisition: An Inuit example.' *TESOL Quarterly* 26/3: 487–505.

Cummins, J. 1984. *Bilingualism and Special Education: Issues in Assessment and Pedagogy.* Clevedon: Multilingual Matters.

Cummins, J. 2000. *Language, Power and Pedagogy: Bilingual Children in the Crossfire.* Clevedon: Multilingual Matters.

Curtiss, S. 1977. *Genie: A Psycholinguistic Study of a Modern-Day Wild Child.* New York: Academic Press.

Dalton-Puffer, C. 2006. 'Questions in CLIL classrooms: Strategic questioning to encourage speaking' in A. Martinez-Flor and E. Uso (eds.): *New Perspectives on Teaching the Language Processing Skills.* Amsterdam: Mouton de Gruyter. pp. 187–213.

Day, R., J. Bassett, B. Bowler, S. Parminter, N. Bullard, N. Prentice, M. Furr, M. Mahmood, D. Stewart, and **T. Robb.** 2011. *Bringing Extensive Reading into the Classroom.* Oxford: Oxford University Press.

DeKeyser, R. M. 1998. 'Beyond focus on form: Cognitive perspectives on learning and practicing second language grammar' in C. J. Doughty and J. Williams (eds.): *Focus on Form in Classroom Second Language Acquisition.* Cambridge: Cambridge University Press. pp. 42–63.

DeKeyser, R. M. 2000. 'The robustness of critical period effects in second language acquisition.' *Studies in Second Language Acquisition* 22/4: 493–533.

DeKeyser, R. M. 2001. 'Automaticity and automatization' in P. Robinson (ed.): *Cognition and Second Language Instruction.* Cambridge: Cambridge University Press. pp. 125–51.

DeKeyser, R. M. 2007. 'Introduction: Situating the concept of practice' in R. DeKeyser (ed.): *Practice in a Second Language: Perspectives from Applied Linguistics and Cognitive Psychology.* Cambridge: Cambridge University Press. pp. 1–18.

de Villiers, J. G. and **P. A. de Villiers.** 1973. 'A cross-sectional study of the acquisition of grammatical morphemes.' *Journal of Psycholinguistic Research* 2/3: 267–78.

Derwing, T. M. and **M. J. Munro.** 2009. 'Putting accent in its place: Rethinking obstacles to communication.' *Language Teaching* 42/4: 476–90.

Derwing, T. M. and **M. Rossiter.** 2003. 'The effects of pronunciation instruction on the accuracy, fluency, and complexity of L2 accented speech.' *Applied Language Learning* 13/1: 1–17.

Donato, R. 1994. 'Collective scaffolding in second language learning' in J. Lantolf and G. Appel (eds.): *Vygotskian Approaches to Second Language Research.* Norwood, NJ: Ablex. pp. 33–56.

Dörnyei, Z. 2001a. *Motivational Strategies in the Language Classroom.* Cambridge: Cambridge University Press.

Dörnyei, Z. 2001b. *Teaching and Researching Motivation.* Harlow: Longman.

Dörnyei, Z. 2005. *The Psychology of the Language Learner: Individual Differences in Second Language Acquisition.* Mahwah, NJ: Lawrence Erlbaum and Associates.

Dörnyei, Z. 2009. *The Psychology of Second Language Acquisition.* Oxford: Oxford University Press.

Dörnyei, Z. and **P. Skehan.** 2003. 'Individual differences in second language learning' in C. J. Doughty and M. H. Long (eds.): *The Handbook of Second Language Acquisition.* Oxford: Blackwell. pp. 589–630.

Doughty, C. 1991. 'Second language instruction does make a difference: Evidence from an empirical study of SL relativization.' *Studies in Second Language Acquisition* 13/4: 431–69.

Doughty, C. and **E. Varela.** 1998. 'Communicative focus on form' in C. Doughty and J. Williams (eds.): *Focus on Form in Classroom SLA.* Cambridge: Cambridge University Press. pp. 114–38.

Duff, P. 1995. 'An ethnography of communication in immersion classrooms in Hungary.' *TESOL Quarterly* 29/3: 505–37.

Dunn, W. E. and **J. P. Lantolf.** 1998. 'Vygotsky's Zone of Proximal Development and Krashen's i+1: Incommensurable constructs; incommensurable theories.' *Language Learning* 48/3: 411–42.

Echevarria, J., M. Vogt, and **D. J. Short.** 2004. *Making Content Comprehensible for English Language Learners: The SIOP Model.* Boston: Pearson.

Eckman, F., L. Bell, and **D. Nelson.** 1988. 'On the generalization of relative clause instruction in the acquisition of English as a second language.' *Applied Linguistics* 9/1: 1–20.

Ellis, N. C. 2001. 'Memory for language' in P. Robinson (ed.): *Cognition and Second Language Instruction.* Cambridge: Cambridge University Press. pp. 33–68.

Ellis, N. C. 2002. 'Frequency effects in language acquisition: A review with implications for theories of implicit and explicit language acquisition.' *Studies in Second Language Acquisition* 24/2: 143–188.

Ellis, N. C. 2003. 'Constructions, chunking, and connectionism: The emergence of second language structure' in C. J. Doughty and M. H. Long (eds.): *The Handbook of Second Language Acquisition.* Oxford: Blackwell. pp. 63–103.

Ellis, N. C. 2005. 'At the interface: Dynamic interactions of explicit and implicit language knowledge.' *Studies in Second Language Acquisition* 27/2: 305–52.

Ellis, N. C. 2009. 'Optimizing the input: Frequency and sampling in usage-based and form-focused learning' in M. H. Long and C. J. Doughty (eds.): *The Handbook of Language Teaching.* Malden, MA: Wiley-Blackwell. pp. 139–158.

Ellis, N. C., R. Simpson-Vlach, and **C. Maynard.** 2008. 'Formulaic language in native and second language speakers: Psycholinguistics, corpus linguistics, and TESOL.' *TESOL Quarterly* 42/3: 375–96.

Ellis, R. 2012. *Language Teaching Research and Language Pedagogy.* Malden, MA: Wiley-Blackwell.

Ellis, R. and **G. Barkhuizen.** 2005. *Analysing Learner Language.* Oxford: Oxford University Press.

Ellis, R., S. Loewen, C. Elder, R. Erlam, J. Philp, and **H. Reinders.** 2009. *Implicit and Explicit Knowledge in Second Language Learning: Testing and Teaching.* Bristol, UK: Multilingual Matters.

Erard, M. 2012. *Babel No More: The Search for the World's Most Extraordinary Language Learners.* New York: Free Press.

Erlam, R. 2005. 'Language aptitude and its relationship to instructional effectiveness in second language acquisition.' *Language Teaching Research* 9/2: 147–171.

Ganschow, L. and **R. L. Sparks.** 2001. 'Learning difficulties and foreign language learning: A review of research and instruction.' *Language Teaching* 34/2:79–98.

Gardner, D. 2004. 'Vocabulary input through extensive reading: A comparison of words found in children's narrative and expository reading materials.' *Applied Linguistics* 25/1: 1–37.

Gardner, H. 1993. *Multiple Intelligences: The Theory in Practice.* New York: Basic Books.

Gardner, R. C. and **W. E. Lambert.** 1972. *Attitudes and Motivation in Second Language Learning.* Rowley, MA: Newbury House.

Gass, S. M. 1982. 'From theory to practice' in M. Hines and W. Rutherford (eds.): *On TESOL '81.* Washington, DC: TESOL. pp. 129–139.

Gass, S. M. 1988. 'Integrating research areas: A framework for second language studies.' *Applied Linguistics* 9/2: 198–217.

Gass, S. M. 1997. *Input, Interaction, and the Second Language Learner.* Mahwah, NJ: Lawrence Erlbaum and Associates.

Gatbonton, E. and **N. Segalowitz.** 1988. 'Creative automatization: Principles for promoting fluency within a communicative framework.' *TESOL Quarterly* 22/3: 473–92.

Gatbonton, E. and **N. Segalowitz.** 2005. 'Rethinking communicative language teaching: A focus on access to fluency.' *Canadian Modern Language Review* 61/3: 325–53.

Gatbonton, E., P. Trofimovich, and **M. Magid.** 2005. 'Learners' ethnic group affiliation and L2 pronunciation accuracy: A sociolinguistic investigation.' *TESOL Quarterly* 39/3: 489–511.

Genesee, F. 1976. 'The role of intelligence in second language learning.' *Language Learning* 26/2: 267–80.

Genesee, F. 1987. *Learning through Two Languages.* New York: Newbury House.

Genesee, F., K. Lindholm-Leary, W. M. Saunders, and **D. Christian** (eds.). 2006. *Educating English Language Learners: A Synthesis of Research Evidence.* Cambridge: Cambridge University Press.

Goldschneider, J. M. and **R. M. DeKeyser.** 2001. 'Explaining the natural order of L2 morpheme acquisition in English: A meta-analysis of multiple determinants.' *Language Learning* 51/1: 1–50.

Greer, D. L. 2000. 'The eyes of hito: A Japanese cultural monitor of behavior in the communicative language classroom.' *JALT Journal* 22/1: 183–95.

Guilloteaux, M. J. and **Z. Dörnyei.** 2008. 'Motivating language learners: A classroom-oriented investigation of the effects of motivational strategies on student motivation.' *TESOL Quarterly* 42/1: 55–77.

Guiora, A., B. Beit-Hallahami, R. Brannon, C. Dull, and **T. Scovel.** 1972. 'The effects of experimentally induced changes in ego states on pronunciation ability in a second language: An exploratory study.' *Comprehensive Psychiatry* 13/5: 421–8.

Hahn, L. D. 2004. 'Primary stress and intelligibility: Research to motivate the teaching of suprasegmentals.' *TESOL Quarterly* 38/2: 201–23.

Hahne, A. 2001. 'What's different in second-language processing? Evidence from event-related brain potentials.' *Journal of Psycholinguistic Research* 30/3: 251–66.

Hamilton, R. 1994. 'Is implicational generalization unidirectional and maximal? Evidence from relativization instruction in a second language.' *Language Learning* 44/1: 123–57.

Harley, B. 1998. 'The role of focus-on-form tasks in promoting child L2 acquisition' in C. Doughty and J. Williams (eds.): *Focus on Form in Classroom Second Language Acquisition.* Cambridge: Cambridge University Press. pp. 156–74.

Harley, B. and **M. Swain.** 1984. 'The interlanguage of immersion students and its implications for second language teaching' in A. Davies, C. Criper, and A. Howatt (eds.): *Interlanguage.* Edinburgh: Edinburgh University Press. pp. 291–311.

Hatch, E. 1978. 'Discourse analysis and second language acquisition' in E. Hatch (ed.): *Second Language Acquisition: A Book of Readings*. Rowley, MA: Newbury. pp. 401–35.

Heath, S. B. 1983. *Ways with Words*. Cambridge: Cambridge University Press.

Hedge, T. 2000. *Teaching and Learning in the Language Classroom*. Oxford: Oxford University Press.

Hoare, P. and **S. Kong.** 2008. 'Late immersion in Hong Kong: Still stressed but making progress?' in T. W. Fortune and D. J. Tedick (eds.): *Pathways to Multilingualism: Emerging Perspectives on Immersion Education*. Clevedon: Multilingual Matters. pp. 242–66.

Horst, M. 2005. 'Learning L2 vocabulary through extensive reading: A measurement study.' *Canadian Modern Language Review* 61/3: 355–82.

Horwitz, E. K., **M. B. Horwitz**, and **J. Cope.** 1986. 'Foreign language classroom anxiety.' *Modern Language Journal* 70/2: 125–32.

Howard, E. R., J. Sugarman, D. Christian, K. Lindholm-Leary, and **D. Rogers.** 2007. *Guiding Principles for Dual Language Education* 2nd edn. Washington, DC: Center for Applied Linguistics. http://www.cal.org/twi/guidingprinciples.htm

Hu, M. and **I. S. P. Nation.** 2000. 'Unknown vocabulary density and reading comprehension.' *Reading in a Foreign Language* 13/1: 403–30.

Hulstijn, J. and **B. Laufer.** 2001. 'Some empirical evidence for the involvement load hypothesis in vocabulary acquisition.' *Language Learning* 51/3: 539–58.

Hunter, J. 2012. 'Small talk: developing fluency, accuracy, and complexity in speaking.' *ELT Journal* 66/1: 30–41.

Itard, J.-M.-G. 1962. *The Wild Boy of Aveyron (L'enfant sauvage)*. New York: Meredith.

Jarvis, S. and **A. Pavlenko.** 2008. *Crosslinguistic Influence in Language and Cognition*. New York: Routledge.

Johnson, J. and **E. Newport.** 1989. 'Critical period effects in second language learning: The influence of maturational state on the acquisition of English as a Second Language.' *Cognitive Psychology* 21/1: 60–99.

Johnson, R. K. 1997. 'The Hong Kong education system: Late immersion under stress' in R. K. Johnson and M. Swain (eds.): *Immersion Education: International Perspectives*. Cambridge: Cambridge University Press. pp. 171–89.

Kasper, G. and **K. R. Rose.** 2002. 'Pragmatic Development in a Second Language.' *Language Learning* 52/Supplement 1.

Keenan, E. and **B. Comrie.** 1977. 'Noun phrase accessibility and Universal Grammar.' *Linguistic Inquiry* 8/1: 63–99.

Kellerman, E. 1986. 'An eye for an eye: Crosslinguistic constraints on the development of the L2 lexicon' in E. Kellerman and M. Sharwood Smith (eds.): *Crosslinguistic Influence in Second Language Acquisition.* New York: Pergamon. pp. 35–48.

Klein, W. and **C. Perdue.** 1993. *Utterance Structure.* Amsterdam: John Benjamins. http://www.mpi.nl/world/tg/lapp/esf/esf.html

Kojic-Sabo, I. and **P. M. Lightbown.** 1999. 'Students' approaches to vocabulary learning and their relationship to success.' *Modern Language Journal* 83/2: 176–92.

Krashen, S. 1982. *Principles and Practice in Second Language Acquisition.* Oxford: Pergamon.

Krashen, S. 1985. *The Input Hypothesis: Issues and Implications.* London: Longman.

Krashen, S. 1989. 'We acquire vocabulary and spelling by reading: Additional evidence for the input hypothesis.' *Modern Language Journal* 73/4: 440–64.

Lado, R. 1964. *Language Teaching: A Scientific Approach.* New York: McGraw-Hill.

Lambert, W. E. 1987. 'The effects of bilingual and bicultural experiences on children's attitudes and social perspectives' in P. Homel, M. Palij, and D. Aaronson (eds.): *Childhood Bilingualism: Aspects of Linguistic, Cognitive, and Social Development.* Mahwah, NJ: Lawrence Erlbaum and Associates. pp. 197–221.

Lambert, W. E. and **G. R. Tucker.** 1972. *Bilingual Education of Children: The St. Lambert Experiment.* Rowley, MA: Newbury.

Lantolf, J. P. (ed.). 2000. *Sociocultural Theory and Second Language Learning.* Oxford: Oxford University Press.

Lapkin, S., D. Hart, and **B. Harley.** 1998. 'Case study of compact Core French models: Attitudes and achievement' in S. Lapkin (ed.): *French Second Language Education in Canada: Empirical Studies.* Toronto, Canada: University of Toronto Press. pp. 3–30.

Leow, R. P. 1997. 'Attention, awareness, and foreign language behavior.' *Language Learning* 47/3: 467–505.

Li, S. 2010. 'The effectiveness of corrective feedback in SLA: A meta-analysis.' *Language Learning* 60/2: 309–365.

Lieven, E. and **M. Tomasello.** 2008. 'Children's first language from a usage perspective' in P. Robinson and N. C. Ellis (eds.): *Handbook of Cognitive Linguistics and Second Language Acquisition.* New York: Routledge. pp. 168–96.

Lightbown, P. M. 1983a. 'Acquiring English L2 in Quebec classrooms' in S. Felix and H. Wode (eds.): *Language Development at the Crossroads.* Tübingen: Gunter Narr. pp. 151–75.

Lightbown, P. M. 1983b. 'Exploring relationships between developmental and instructional sequences in L2 acquisition' in H. W. Seliger and M. H. Long (eds.): *Classroom-Oriented Research in Second Language Acquisition.* Rowley, MA: Newbury House. pp. 217–45.

Lightbown, P. M. 1998. 'The importance of timing in focus on form' in C. Doughty and J. Williams (eds.): *Focus on Form in Classroom Second Language Acquisition.* Cambridge: Cambridge University Press. pp. 177–96.

Lightbown, P. M. 2007. 'Fair trade: Two-way bilingual education.' *Estudios de Lingüística Inglesa Aplicada* 7: 9–34.

Lightbown, P. M. 2008a. 'Easy as pie? Children learning languages.' *Concordia Working Papers in Applied Linguistics* 1:1–25. http://doe.concordia.ca/copal/index.php/copal/volumes.html

Lightbown, P. M. 2008b. 'Transfer appropriate processing as a model for classroom second language acquisition' in Z. Han (ed.): *Understanding Second Language Process.* Clevedon, UK: Multilingual Matters. pp. 27–44.

Lightbown, P. M. 2012. 'Intensive L2 instruction in Canada: Why not immersion?' in C. Muñoz (ed.): *Intensive Exposure Experiences in Second Language Learning.* Bristol, UK: Multilingual Matters. pp. 25–44.

Lightbown, P. M. and **N. Spada.** 1990. 'Focus on form and corrective feedback in communicative language teaching: Effects on second language learning.' *Studies in Second Language Acquisition* 12/4: 429–48.

Lightbown, P. M. and **N. Spada.** 1994. 'An innovative program for primary ESL in Quebec.' *TESOL Quarterly* 28/3: 563–79.

Lightbown, P. M., R. Halter, J. L. White, and **M. Horst.** 2002. 'Comprehension-based learning: The limits of "do it yourself".' *Canadian Modern Language Review* 58/3: 427–64.

Lindholm-Leary, K. 2001. *Dual Language Education.* Clevedon, UK: Multilingual Matters.

Loewen, S. and **J. Philp.** 2006. 'Recasts in the adult English L2 class: characteristics, explicitness, and effectiveness.' *Modern Language Journal* 90/4: 536–56.

Loewen, S., S. Li, F. Fei, A. Thompson, K. Nakatsukasa, S. Ahn, and **X. Chen.** 2009. 'Second language learners' beliefs about grammar instruction and error correction.' *Modern Language Journal* 93/1: 91–104.

Long, M. H. 1983. 'Native speaker/non-native speaker conversation and the negotiation of comprehensible input.' *Applied Linguistics* 4/2: 126–41.

Long, M. 1996. 'The role of the linguistic environment in second language acquisition' in W. Ritchie and T. Bhatia (eds.): *Handbook of Second Language Acquisition.* New York: Academic Press. pp. 413–68.

Long, M. H. and **P. Porter.** 1985. 'Group work, interlanguage talk, and second language acquisition.' *TESOL Quarterly* 19/2: 207–28.

Long, M. and **C. Sato.** 1983. 'Classroom foreigner talk discourse: Forms and functions of teachers' questions' in H. W. Seliger and M. H. Long (eds.): *Classroom-Oriented Research in Second Language Acquisition.* Rowley, MA: Newbury House. pp. 268–85.

Long, J., C. Brock, G. Crookes, C. Deicke, L. Potter, and **S. Zhang.** 1985. 'The effect of teachers' questioning patterns and wait time on pupil participation in public high school classes in Hawaii for students of limited English proficiency.' *TESOL Quarterly* 19/3: 605–07.

Lyster, R. 1994. 'The effect of functional–analytic teaching on aspects of French immersion students' sociolinguistic competence.' *Applied Linguistics* 15/3: 263–87.

Lyster, R. 1998. 'Recasts, repetition and ambiguity in L2 classroom discourse.' *Studies in Second Language Acquisition* 20/1: 51–81.

Lyster, R. 2004. 'Differential effects of prompts and recasts in form-focused instruction.' *Studies in Second Language Acquisition* 26/3: 399–432.

Lyster, R. 2007. *Learning and Teaching Language through Content: A Counterbalanced Approach.* Amsterdam: John Benjamins.

Lyster, R. and **H. Mori.** 2006. 'Interactional feedback and instructional counterbalance.' *Studies in Second Language Acquisition* 28/2: 269–300.

Lyster, R. and **L. Ranta.** 1997. 'Corrective feedback and learner uptake: Negotiation of form in communicative classrooms.' *Studies in Second Language Acquisition* 19/1: 37–61.

Lyster, R. and **K. Saito.** 2010. 'Oral feedback in classroom SLA: A meta-analysis.' *Studies in Second Language Acquisition* 32/2: 265–302.

MacIntyre, P. 1995. 'How does anxiety affect second language learning? A reply to Sparks and Ganschow.' *Modern Language Journal* 79/1: 90–9.

Mackey, A. 1999. 'Input, interaction and second language development: An empirical study of question formation in ESL.' *Studies in Second Language Acquisition* 21/4: 557–87.

Mackey, A. and **J. Goo.** 2007. 'Interaction research in SLA: A meta-analysis and research synthesis.' in A. Mackey (ed.): *Conversational Interaction in Second Language Acquisition: A Series of Empirical Studies.* Oxford: Oxford University Press. pp. 407–452.

Mackey, A. and **J. Philp.** 1998. 'Conversational interaction and second language development: Recasts, responses and red herrings.' *Modern Language Journal* 82/3: 338–56.

Mackey, A., S. M. Gass, and **K. McDonough.** 2000. 'How do learners perceive interactional feedback?' *Studies in Second Language Acquisition* 22/4: 471–497.

MacWhinney, B. 1997. 'Second language acquisition and the competition model' in A. M. B. de Groot and J. F. Kroll (eds.): *Tutorials in Bilingualism: Psycholinguistic Perspectives.* Mahwah, NJ: Lawrence Erlbaum and Associates. pp. 113–44.

MacWhinney, B. 2000. *The CHILDES Project: Tools for Analyzing Talk* (2 volumes). Mahwah, NJ: Lawrence Erlbaum and Associates. http://childes.psy.cmu.edu/

Masgoret, A. M. and **R. C. Gardner.** 2003. 'Attitudes, motivation, and second language learning: A meta-analysis of studies conducted by Gardner and associates.' *Language Learning* 53/1: 123–63.

McCormick, D. E. and **R. Donato.** 2000. 'Teacher questions as scaffolded assistance in an ESL classroom' in J. K. Hall and L. Verplaetse (eds.): *Second and Foreign Language Learning through Classroom Interaction.* Mahwah, NJ: Lawrence Erlbaum and Associates. pp. 183–201.

McDonough, K. 2004. 'Learner–learner interaction during pair and small group activities in a Thai EFL context.' *System* 32: 207–24.

McLaughlin, B. 1987. *Theories of Second Language Learning.* London: Edward Arnold.

McLaughlin, B. 1990. 'Restructuring.' *Applied Linguistics* 11/1: 113–28.

Meara, P. M. 1980. 'Vocabulary acquisition: A neglected aspect of language learning.' *Language Teaching and Linguistics Abstracts* 13: 221–46.

Meara, P. M. 2005. 'Designing vocabulary tests for English, Spanish and other languages' in C. Butler, M. dos Angeles Gómez-Gonzales, and

S. Doval-Suárez (eds.): *The Dynamics of Language Use: Functional and Dynamic Perspectives*. Amsterdam: John Benjamins. http://www.lognostics.co.uk/tools/ pp. 269–83.

Meisel, J. M. 1987. 'Reference to past events and actions in the development of natural second language acquisition' in C. Pfaff (ed.): *First and Second Language Acquisition Processes*. Cambridge, MA: Newbury House.

Meisel, J. M., H. Clahsen, and **M. Pienemann.** 1981. 'On determining developmental stages in natural second language acquisition.' *Studies in Second Language Acquisition* 3/2: 109–35.

Muñoz, C. 2006. 'The effects of age on foreign language learning: The BAF project' in C. Muñoz (ed.): *Age and the Rate of Foreign Language Learning*. Clevedon, UK: Multilingual Matters. pp. 1–40.

Munro, M. J. and **T. M. Derwing.** 2011. 'The foundations of accent and intelligibility in pronunciation research.' *Language Teaching* 44/3: 316–27.

Nagy, W. E., P. A. Herman, and **R. Anderson.** 1985. 'Learning words from context.' *Reading Research Quarterly* 20/2: 233–53.

Nation, I. S. P. 2001. *Learning Vocabulary in Another Language*. Cambridge: Cambridge University Press.

Nation, I. S. P. 2007. 'The four strands.' *Innovation in Language Learning and Teaching* 1/1: 1–12.

Nation, I. S. P. and **J. Macalister.** 2010. *Language Curriculum Design*. New York: Routledge.

Netten, J. and **C. Germain** (eds.). 2004. 'Intensive French in Canada.' *Canadian Modern Language Review* 60/3: pp. 249–435.

Newport, E. 1990. 'Maturational constraints on language learning.' *Cognitive Science* 14/1: 11–28.

Nicholas, H., P. M. Lightbown, and **N. Spada.** 2001. 'Recasts as feedback to language learners.' *Language Learning* 51/4: 719–58.

Norris, J. M. and **L. Ortega.** 2000. 'Effectiveness of L2 instruction: A research synthesis and quantitative meta-analysis.' *Language Learning* 50/3: 417–528.

Norton Peirce, B. 1995. 'Social identity, investment, and language learning. *TESOL Quarterly* 29/1: 9–31.

Norton, B. and **K. Toohey.** 2001. 'Changing perspectives on good language learners.' *TESOL Quarterly* 35/2: 307–22.

Obler, L. 1989. 'Exceptional second language learners' in S. Gass, C. Madden, D. Preston, and L. Selinker (eds.): *Variation in Second*

Language Acquisition, Vol. II: Psycholinguistic Issues. Clevedon: Multilingual Matters. pp. 141–59.

Odlin, T. 2003. 'Cross-linguistic influence' in C. J. Doughty and M. H. Long (eds.): *The Handbook of Second Language Acquisition.* Oxford: Blackwell. pp. 436–86.

Ohta, A. 2000. 'Rethinking recasts: A learner-centered examination of corrective feedback in the Japanese classroom' in J. K. Hall and L. Verplaetse (eds.): *Second and Foreign Language Learning through Classroom Interaction.* Mahwah, NJ: Lawrence Erlbaum and Associates. pp. 47–71.

Oliver, R. and **A. Mackey.** 2003. 'Interactional context and feedback in child ESL classrooms.' *Modern Language Journal* 87/4: 519–33.

Ortega, L. 2007. 'Meaningful L2 practice in foreign language classrooms: A cognitive-interactionist SLA perspective' in R. DeKeyser (ed.): *Practice in a Second Language: Perspectives from Applied Linguistics and Cognitive Psychology.* Cambridge: Cambridge University Press. pp. 180–207.

Paradis, J., F. Genesee, and **M. B. Crago.** 2011. *Dual Language Development and Disorders: A Handbook on Bilingualism and Second Language Learning* 2nd edn. Baltimore: Paul H. Brookes.

Patkowski, M. 1980. 'The sensitive period for the acquisition of syntax in a second language.' *Language Learning* 30/2: 449–72.

Pearson, B. Z. 2008. *Raising a Bilingual Child: A Step-by-Step Guide for Parents.* New York: Living Language (Random House).

Piaget, J. 1951. *Play Dreams, and Imitation in Childhood.* New York: Norton. (Originally published as *La formation du symbole chez l'enfant.* Neuchâtel: Delchaux et Niestlé.)

Pica, T. 1983. 'Methods of morpheme quantification: Their effect on the interpretation of second language data.' *Studies in Second Language Acquisition* 6/1: 69–78.

Pica, T. 1994. 'Research on negotiation: What does it reveal about second language acquisition? Conditions, processes, and outcomes' *Language Learning* 44/3: 493–527.

Pienemann, M. 1988. 'Determining the influence of instruction on L2 speech processing.' *AILA Review* 5/1: 40–72.

Pienemann, M. 1999. *Language Processing and Second Language Development: Processability Theory.* Amsterdam: John Benjamins.

Pienemann, M. 2003. 'Language processing capacity' in C. J. Doughty and M. H. Long (eds.): *The Handbook of Second Language Acquisition.* Oxford: Blackwell. pp. 679–714.

Pienemann, M., M. Johnston, and **G. Brindley.** 1988. 'Constructing an acquisition-based procedure for second language assessment.' *Studies in Second Language Acquisition* 10/2: 217–43.

Pimsleur, P. 1966. *The Pimsleur Language Aptitude Battery.* New York: Harcourt, Brace, Jovanovic.

Piper, T. 2006. *Language and Learning: The Home and School Years* 4th edn. Upper Saddle River, NJ: Merrill/Prentice-Hall.

Piske, T. 2007. 'Implications of James E. Flege's research for the foreign language classroom' in O. Bohn and M. Munro (eds.): *Language Experience in Second Language Speech Learning.* Amsterdam: John Benjamins. pp. 301–314.

Piske, T., I. R. A. MacKay, and **J. E. Flege.** 2001. 'Factors affecting degree of foreign accent in an L2: A review.' *Journal of Phonetics* 29/3: 191–215.

Ranta, L. 2002. 'The role of learners' language analytic ability in the communicative classroom' in P. Robinson (ed.): *Individual Differences and Instructed Language Learning.* Amsterdam: John Benjamins. pp. 159–80.

Reid, J. (ed.). 1995. *Learning Styles in the ESL/EFL Classroom.* New York: Heinle and Heinle.

Richards, J. 1974. 'A non-contrastive approach to error analysis' in J. Richards (ed.). *Error analysis.* London: Longman. pp. 172–88.

Ringbom, H. 1986. 'Crosslinguistic influence and the foreign language learning process' in E. Kellerman and M. Sharwood Smith (eds.): *Crosslinguistic Influence in Second Language Acquisition.* New York: Pergamon Press. pp. 150–72.

Robinson, P. (ed.). 2002. *Individual Differences and Instructed Language Learning.* Amsterdam: John Benjamins.

Robinson, P. and **N. C. Ellis.** 2008. 'Conclusion: Cognitive linguistics, second language acquisition, and L2 instruction—issues for research' in P. Robinson and N. C. Ellis (eds.): *Handbook of Cognitive Linguistics and Second Language Acquisition.* New York: Routledge. pp. 489–545.

Roy, D. 2009. 'New horizons in the study of child language acquisition.' *INTERSPEECH–2009,* Brighton, UK.

Sachs, J., B. Bard, and **M. Johnson.** 1981. 'Language learning with restricted input: Case studies of two hearing children of deaf parents.' *Applied Psycholinguistics* 2/1: 33–54.

Samuda, V. 2001. 'Guiding relationships between form and meaning during task performance: The role of the teacher' in M. Bygate, P. Skehan, and M. Swain (eds.): *Researching Pedagogic Tasks: Second Language Learning, Teaching, and Testing.* London: Longman. pp. 119–40.

Savignon, S. 1972. *Communicative Competence: An Experiment in Foreign-language Teaching.* Philadelphia, PA: Center for Curriculum Development.

Schachter, J. 1974. 'An error in error analysis.' *Language Learning* 24/2: 205–14.

Schachter, J. 1990. 'On the issue of completeness in second language acquisition.' *Second Language Research* 6/1: 93–124.

Schieffelin, B. 1990. *The Give and Take of Everyday Life: Language Socialization of Kaluli Children.* Cambridge: Cambridge University Press.

Schleppegrell, M. 2004. *The Language of Schooling.* Mahwah, NJ: Lawrence Erlbaum Associates.

Schmidt, R. 1990. 'The role of consciousness in second language learning.' *Applied Linguistics* 11/1: 17–46.

Schmidt, R. 2001. 'Attention' in P. Robinson (ed.): *Cognition and Second Language Instruction.* Cambridge: Cambridge University Press. pp. 3–32.

Schulz, R. A. 2001. 'Cultural differences in student and teacher perceptions concerning the role of grammar teaching and corrective feedback: USA–Colombia.' *Modern Language Journal* 85/2: 244–58.

Schumann, J. 1979. 'The acquisition of English negation by speakers of Spanish: a review of the literature' in R. W. Andersen (ed.): *The Acquisition and Use of Spanish and English as First and Second Languages.* Washington, DC: TESOL.

Schwartz, B. 1993. 'On explicit and negative data effecting and affecting competence and linguistic behavior.' *Studies in Second Language Acquisition* 15/2: 147–163.

Segalowitz, N. 2010. *Cognitive Bases of Second Language Fluency.* New York: Routledge.

Seidlhofer, B. 2011. *Understanding English as a Lingua Franca.* Oxford: Oxford University Press.

Selinker, L. 1972. 'Interlanguage.' *International Review of Applied Linguistics* 10/2: 209–31.

Setter, J. and **J. Jenkins.** 2005. 'Pronunciation.' *Language Teaching* 38/1: 1–17.

Sharwood Smith, M. 1993. 'Input enhancement in instructed SLA: Theoretical bases.' *Studies in Second Language Acquisition* 15/2: 165–79.

Sheen, Y. 2006. 'Corrective feedback and learner uptake in communicative classrooms across instructional settings.' *Second Language Teaching Research* 8/3: 263–300.

Sheen, Y. 2010. 'Differential effects of oral and written corrective feedback in the ESL classroom.' *Language Teaching Research* 32/2: 203–34.

Simpson, R. C., S. L. Briggs, J. Ovens, and **J. M. Swales.** 1999. *The Michigan Corpus of Academic Spoken English* (MICASE). Ann Arbor, MI: The Regents of the University of Michigan. http://micase.elicorpora.info.

Sinclair, J. M. (ed.). 2004. *How to Use Corpora in Language Teaching.* Philadelphia, PA: John Benjamins.

Skehan, P. 1989. *Individual Differences in Second Language Learning.* London: Edward Arnold.

Skinner, B. F. 1957. *Verbal Behavior.* New York: Appleton–Century-Crofts.

Slobin, D. I. 1973. 'Cognitive prerequisites for the development of grammar' in C. A. Ferguson and D. I. Slobin (eds.): *Studies of Child Language Development.* New York: Holt, Rinehart, and Winston. pp. 175–208.

Slobin, D. I. 1985–1997. *The Crosslinguistic Study of Language.* Vols 1–5. Mahwah, NJ: Lawrence Erlbaum and Associates.

Smith, N. and **I. M. Tsimpli.** 1995. *The Mind of a Savant: Language Learning and Modularity.* Oxford: Blackwell.

Snow, C. 1995. 'Issues in the study of input: Fine-tuning, universality, individual and developmental differences, and necessary causes' in P. Fletcher and B. MacWhinney (eds.): *The Handbook of Child Language.* Oxford: Blackwell. pp. 180–93.

Snow, C. and **M. Hoefnagel-Höhle.** 1978. 'The critical period for language acquisition: Evidence from second language learning.' *Child Development* 49/4: 1114–28.

Spada, N. 2011. 'Beyond form-focused instruction: Reflections on past, present and future research.' *Language Teaching* 44/2: 225–36.

Spada, N. and **M. Fröhlich.** 1995. *The Communicative Orientation of Language Teaching Observation Scheme: Coding Conventions and Applications.* Sydney: Macmillan.

Spada, N. and **P. M. Lightbown.** 1993. 'Instruction and the development of questions in L2 classrooms.' *Studies in Second Language Acquisition* 15/2: 205–24.

Spada, N. and **P. M. Lightbown.** 1999. 'Instruction, L1 influence and developmental readiness in second language acquisition.' *Modern Language Journal* 83/1: 1–22.

Spada, N. and **P. M. Lightbown.** 2002. 'L1 and L2 in the education of Inuit children in northern Quebec: Abilities and perceptions.' *Language and Education* 16/3: 212–40.

Spada, N. and **Y. Tomita.** 2010. 'Interactions between type of instruction and type of language feature: A meta-analysis.' *Language Learning* 60/2: 1–46.

Spada, N., P. M. Lightbown, and **J. L. White.** 2005. 'The importance of form/meaning mappings in explicit form-focussed instruction' in A. Housen and M. Pierrard (eds.): *Investigations in Instructed Second Language Acquisition.* Amsterdam: Mouton de Gruyter. pp. 199–234.

Spada, N. and M. Santos Lima. 2010. 'EFL and ESL teacher and learner views about integrated and isolated form-focused instruction.' Proceedings of the IX International Conference of the Brazilian Association of Canadian Studies: Porto Alegre, Brazil.

Spada, N., K. Barkaoui, C. Peters, M. So, and **A. Valeo.** 2009. 'Developing a questionnaire to measure learners' preferences for isolated and integrated form-focused instruction.' *System*, 37/1: 70–81.

Spada, N., L. Jessop, W. Suzuki, Y. Tomita, and **A. Valeo.** 2009. The Contributions of Isolated and Integrated Form-Focused Instruction on Different Aspects of L2 Knowledge and Use. Paper presented at the American Association for Applied Linguistics: Denver, CO.

Spielmann, G. and **M. J. Radnofsky.** 2001. 'Learning language under tension: New directions from a qualitative study.' *Modern Language Journal* 85/2: 259–78.

Storch, N. 2002. 'Patterns of interaction in ESL pair work.' *Language Learning* 52/1: 119–58.

Swain, M. 1985. 'Communicative competence: Some roles of comprehensible input and comprehensible output in its development' in S. Gass and C. Madden (eds.): *Input in Second Language Acquisition.* Rowley, MA: Newbury House. pp. 235–53.

Swain, M. 1988. 'Manipulating and complementing content teaching to maximize second language learning.' *TESL Canada Journal* 6/1: 68–83.

Swain, M. 2000. 'The output hypothesis and beyond: Mediating acquisition through collaborative dialogue' in J. P. Lantolf (ed.): *Sociocultural Theory and Second Language Learning.* Oxford: Oxford University Press. pp. 94–114.

Swain, M. and **S. Lapkin.** 1998. 'Interaction and second language learning: Two adolescent French immersion students working together.' *Modern Language Journal* 82/3: 338–56.

Swain, M. and **S. Lapkin.** 2002. 'Talking it through: Two French immersion learners' response to reformulation.' *International Journal of Educational Research* 37/3–4: 285–304.

Swain, M., P. Kinnear, and **L. Steinman.** 2010. *Sociocultural Theory and Second Language Education: An Introduction through Narratives.* Bristol: Multilingual Matters.

Tarone, E. and **M. Swain.** 1995. 'A sociolinguistic perspective on second-language use in immersion classrooms.' *Modern Language Journal* 79/2: 166–178.

Tarone, E. and **B. Swierzbin.** 2009. *Exploring Learner Language.* Oxford: Oxford University Press.

Taylor, D., M. Caron, and **L. McAlpine.** 2000. 'Patterns of perceived language ability and use in Arctic Quebec.' *Bilingual Education and Bilingualism* 3/4: 283–96.

Tomita, Y. 2011. The Role of Form-Focused Instruction: Learner Investment in L2 Communication. Unpublished thesis. University of Toronto. https://tspace.library.utoronto.ca/bitstream/1807/29892/1/Tomita_Yasuyo_201106_PhD_thesis.pdf

Toohey, K. 2000. *Learning English at School: Identity, Social Relations and Classroom Practice.* Clevedon: Multilingual Matters.

Trahey, M. and **L. White.** 1993. 'Positive evidence and preemption in the second language classroom.' *Studies in Second Language Acquisition* 15/2: 181–204.

Trofimovich, P. 2005. 'Spoken-word processing in native and second languages: An investigation of auditory word priming.' *Applied Psycholinguistics* 26/4: 479–504.

Trofimovich, P., P. M. Lightbown, R. H. Halter, and **H. Song.** 2009. 'Comprehension-based practice: The development of L2 pronunciation in a listening and reading program.' *Studies in Second Language Acquisition* 31/4: 609–39.

VanPatten, B. 2004. 'Input processing in SLA' in B. VanPatten (ed.): *Processing Instruction: Theory, Research, and Commentary.* Mahwah, NJ: Lawrence Erlbaum and Associates. pp. 5–31.

VanPatten, B. and **T. Cadierno.** 1993. 'Explicit instruction and input processing.' *Studies in Second Language Acquisition* 15/2: 225–41.

VanPatten, B. and **J. Williams** (eds.). 2007. *Theories in Second Language Acquisition: An Introduction.* Mahwah, NJ: Lawrence Erlbaum and Associates.

Vygotsky, L. S. 1978. *Mind in Society.* Cambridge, MA: Harvard University Press.

Wajnryb, R. 1992. *Classroom Observation Tasks: A Resource Book for Language Teachers and Trainers.* Cambridge: Cambridge University Press.

Walker, R. 2010. *Teaching the Pronunciation of English as a Lingua Franca.* Oxford: Oxford University Press.

Watson-Gegeo, K. A. 1992. 'Thick explanation in the ethnographic study of child socialization: A longitudinal study of the problem of schooling for Kwara'ae (Solomon Islands) children' in W. A. Corsaro and P. J. Miller (eds.): *Interpretive Approaches to Children's Socialization. Special issue of New Directions for Child Development* 58: 51–66.

Werker, J. F., W. M. Weikum, and **K. A. Yoshida.** 2006. 'Bilingual speech processing in infants and adults' in P. McCardle and E. Hoff (eds.): *Childhood Bilingualism: Research on Infancy through School Age.* Clevedon: Multilingual Matters. pp.1–18.

Wesche, M. B. 1981. 'Language aptitude measures in streaming, matching students with methods, and diagnosis of learning problems' in K. Diller (ed.): *Individual Differences and Universals in Language Learning Aptitude.* Rowley, MA: Newbury House. pp. 119–39.

White, J. 1998. 'Getting the learners' attention: A typographical input enhancement study' in C. Doughty and J. Williams (eds.): *Focus on Form in Classroom SLA.* Cambridge: Cambridge University Press. pp. 85–113.

White, J. 2008. 'Speeding up acquisition of *his/her*: Explicit L1/L2 contrasts help' in J. Philp, R. Oliver, and A. Mackey (eds.): *Second Language Acquisition and the Younger Learner: Child's Play?* Amsterdam: John Benjamins. pp. 193–228.

White, J. and **P. M. Lightbown.** 1984. 'Asking and answering in ESL classes.' *Canadian Modern Language Review* 40/2: 228–44.

White, L. 1987. 'Against comprehensible input: the input hypothesis and the development of L2 competence.' *Applied Linguistics* 8: 95–110.

White L. 1989. *Universal Grammar and Second Language Acquisition.* Amsterdam: John Benjamins.

White, L. 1991. 'Adverb placement in second language acquisition: Some effects of positive and negative evidence in the classroom.' *Second Language Research* 7/2: 133–61.

White, L. 2003. *Second Language Acquisition and Universal Grammar.* Cambridge: Cambridge University Press.

White, L., N. Spada, P. M. Lightbown, and **L. Ranta.** 1991. 'Input enhancement and syntactic accuracy in L2 acquisition.' *Applied Linguistics* 12/4: 416–32.

Wode, H. 1978. 'Developmental sequences in naturalistic L2 acquisition' in E. M. Hatch (ed.): *Second Language Acquisition: A Book of Readings.* Rowley, MA: Newbury House. pp. 101–17.

Wode, H. 1981. 'Language acquisitional universals: A unified view of language acquisition' in H. Winitz (ed.): *Native Language and Foreign Language Acquisition.* New York: *Annals of the New York Academy of Sciences* 379. pp. 218–34.

Wong Fillmore, L. 1979. 'Individual differences in second language acquisition' in C. J. Fillmore, W.-S. Y. Wang, and D. Kempler (eds.): *Individual Differences in Language Ability and Language Behavior.* New York: Academic Press. pp. 203–28.

Wong Fillmore, L. 2000. 'Loss of family languages: Should educators be concerned?' *Theory into Practice* 39/4: 203–10.

Yule, G. and **D. Macdonald.** 1990. 'Resolving referential conflicts in L2 interaction: The effect of proficiency and interactive role.' *Language Learning* 40/4: 539–56.

Zimmerman, C. B. 2009. *Word Knowledge: A Vocabulary Teacher's Handbook.* Oxford: Oxford University Press.

Zobl, H. 1980. 'The formal and developmental selectivity of L1 influence on L2 acquisition.' *Language Learning* 30/1: 43–57.

Zobl, H. 1984. 'The wave model of linguistic change and interlanguage systems.' *Studies in Second Language Acquisition* 6/2: 160–85.

INDEX

Glossary entries are shown by 'g' after the page number.